"Pixar is a creative company that has made it a priority to constantly re-examine itself, but even in a company like ours, certain leadership impediments can become impossible to see, and detrimental calcification can set in. As a consultant to me, Bill Adams has been an astonishingly quick study who was able to identify leadership issues and put me on a constructive path to remedy them. Bill's ability to see complex problems and help me generate gettable, actionable solutions has been both remarkable and pivotal in allowing us to bring a fresh leadership reset to a company in its 30th year. Bill and his partner Bob have captured the essence of the wisdom and the tools they bring to helping leaders in *Scaling Leadership*. I cannot recommend the book strongly enough—especially if you think you don't need it!"

Jim Morris, President, Pixar Animation Studios

"The Leadership Circle lens is a gift that keeps on giving! Its enormous database has long provided unrivaled *quantitative* power. Now, in *Scaling Leadership*, Anderson and Adams open up the corresponding *qualitative* treasure-trove to further illuminate the paths to truly transformative leadership. A must-read for all leaders, and those who help them!"

Robert Kegan and Lisa Lahey, Harvard University faculty and
co-authors of *Immunity to Change*, and *An Everyone Culture*

"The future of capitalism is conscious capitalism. A conscious business can only emerge through conscious leadership at scale. Anderson and Adam, in *Scaling Leadership*, clearly and practically show you how to become a more conscious and effective leader, how to replicate that in your teams, and how to scale conscious leadership throughout the organization. Read this book and put it into practice!"

John Mackey, Co-founder and CEO, Whole Foods Market,
Co-founder, Conscious Capitalism Inc.

"*Scaling Leadership* and the Full Circle Group approach is a powerful path to step changing leaders' capabilities individually and as a team to drive positive change and deliver outstanding results. As an organization, it moves you from reactive, defensive and excuse making to creative, purposeful and outcome focused. I highly recommend the book and the approach to CEOs and their teams."

Erik Fyrwald Chief Executive Officer and President at
Syngenta International AG and Director Eli Lilly and Company

"*Scaling Leadership* is an excellent read—really on the mark. I am enthused to endorse. It hits any number of themes that are essential to leading well. I will call out two that resonate strongly with my experience. First, we lead people, not balance sheets or machines. In the end, our ability to call forth discretionary energy is what distinguishes us as leaders, and that the ability to do that is learnable. This book will challenge you to do just that and will show you how. Second, as I transitioned into the president and later the CEO role, I needed to rethink my role and understand where my leverage came from. The migration was from what had gotten me there—business/financial acumen, strategic skill, problem-solving, focus, etc.—to a far greater focus on understanding how to create a highly engaged culture tied to purpose/aspiration and cultivate leaders who could do the same. The prior skills are really important (I still use them routinely) but would have been limiting if I hadn't augmented them with new skills. The emphasis this book places on these themes—and the way the authors develop the case—makes great sense. I strongly recommend this book to anyone in (or aspiring to) a senior position of leadership."

Gerry Anderson, Chairman and CEO, DTE Energy

"To scale-up your business you must scale exceptional leadership. Anderson and Adams have written a definitive work on *Scaling Leadership*—the kind of leadership that is built for scale and multiplies effective leadership throughout the organization. Do not miss this book. In this well-researched book, senior leaders describe, in their own words, the kind of leadership that scales, and the kind that fails to scale. This book will challenge you to step up your game, it will confront you and inspire you. More importantly, it will show you what you need to do to scale your leadership."

Verne Harnish, Founder Entrepreneurs' Organization (EO)
and author of *Scaling Up* (Rockefeller Habits 2.0)

"Wow! What a book! Anderson and Adams have mined their rich set of data on what makes leaders truly excellent, and they have struck gold. By helping us understand the way that some core leadership strengths actually become liabilities at scale, they solve one of the most important leadership mysteries. Now we understand what the true leadership superpowers are—and we can see how to cultivate them. *Scaling Leadership* is fascinating, bold, and brave. It will help you shift from the patterns that have helped you in the past to those that will create a better future. I am very excited this book is in the world."

Dr. Jennifer Garvey Berger, author *Simple Habits for Complex Times* and *Changing on the Job*.

"If it is your aspiration to improve your leadership performance and that of your team… read this book! *Scaling Leadership* is a natural sequel to Adam's and Anderson's earlier book, *Mastering Leadership*. It introduces a model that produces a .93 correlation between 18 creative competencies and leadership effectiveness. Working from a four-quadrant model based on input from thousands of leaders around the world, the authors lay out a developmental path opens to all. The book is rich with real-life examples, case studies, and supporting metrics. Each chapter ends with a homework assignment that takes the reader on their own personal journey. A powerful examination of the human side of enterprise, the book invites the reader to access the unlimited bank of feedback available to each of us that can inform his/her leadership performance. It is not an easy journey. The first 12 chapters outline the actions and attitudes required for true development. The last chapter presents a compelling assessment of why we need to take the trip!"

Stephen Ewing: Chairman of the Board of AAA Michigan
and ACG, Retired President and CEO of MCN Energy
Group Inc., Retired Vice-Chair DTE Energy.

"'Leaders bring the weather.' What a great description of the importance of senior leadership and the reason why we so often focus on trying to change leadership behavior. In my experience, the Leadership Circle Profile described in *Scaling Leadership* is unparalleled in terms of the leadership mindset (and subsequent behavior) change that it triggers. It isn't an approach that leaves leaders feeling inadequate, but instead empowers leaders to focus their time and energy on those things that really matter, and it helps them avoid those behaviors that cancel out all of the good things that they do. And when applied at scale, it can not only change the lives of individual leaders, but it can transform the organizations they lead."

Tammy Lowry, Global Head of Talent Innovation, F. Hoffmann-La Roche Ltd

"Brave, bold, effective leaders will be inspired by Anderson and Adams new book, *Scaling Leadership*. This brilliant work combines their deep experience and rich database working with world-class leaders, with keen insights for individual growth, and more importantly, how to nourish and grow your future leaders. Any person in a leadership role, interested in their own growth and the growth and success of their organizations through exemplary leadership should get this book now."

Val DiFebo, CEO, Deutsch NY

"There are healthy and unhealthy ways to scale businesses. We can no longer afford an unhealthy approach to growth—the toll on people and the planet is too high. This book is an indispensable guide to healthy growth, written by two true masters of the art of leadership."

Raj Sisodia, FW Olin Distinguished Professor of Global Business, Babson College, Co-founder and co-chairman, Conscious Capitalism International

"*Scaling Leadership* and *Mastering Leadership* are fundamental to our leadership development program, succession planning, and our ability to break through inflection points in our business. They have had an immediate impact on our performance, and more importantly, in our relationships inside and outside the organization."

Pierre Trapanese, CEO, Northland Controls

"Looking back on my thirty plus years in business, Bill Adams has been the single most important positive influence on my development as a leader. His coaching opened my eyes to understand who I was as a leader, who I wanted to be, and how to get there. Equally important, Bill's work doesn't stop with a single person but is always done in the context of team leadership, team effectiveness, and the ways in which individuals bring a greater awareness of themselves and others can leverage that knowledge to drive concrete business results. Through *Scaling Leadership*, Bill's, and his partner Bob's, insights are available to everyone who wants a chance to expand beyond their Peter Principle—and their organization."

Robert Fugate, President, RFA Management, LLC

"The conversation on leadership has never been so important to the future of our society, our planet and humankind. This book is an invitation to re-think what true leadership is. Anderson and Adams, using hard data, challenge at the core our acquired views on leadership and show us how leadership is first and foremost a transformational journey that has the power to change our lives, our workplaces and make us better human beings. I will add it to the recommended reading list for my teams!"

—Paolo De Martin, CEO, SCOR Global Life

"As I wrote in *What Got You Here Won't Get You There*, leaders must grow and develop if they hope to grow their organizations. In *Scaling Leadership*, Anderson and Adams reveal their research and life experiences that show how effective leaders evolve in order to scale and expand their influence exponentially. So, if you ever hope to 'get there,' start here with this book."

Marshall Goldsmith, Best-selling author and speaker

"This book is stunning! *Scaling Leadership* is a natural and robust sister-book to *Mastering Leadership*. Clearly concerned about the future of leadership, the authors take a strong stand, based on extensive research, for the necessity of transforming leaders to be equipped to be responsive, thoughtful, aware, real, and visionary in the face of what seems to be an immense and unrelenting challenge. It's not easy to be a leader today. This book contains layers of meaning, and will be more than motivating for leaders, coaches, and organization development practitioners—this is deeply exciting work. And true development of leaders depends on it. *Scaling Leadership* is a call to development, as well as a call to courage and grace, and it is a practical approach to being a leader in today's pressured and often chaotic world."

Christine M. Wahl, M.A.Ed., MCC, Creator of the Leadership Coaching Program at Georgetown University, Winner of the Art Shirk Legacy Award for Outstanding Contribution to Leadership of the Planet.

"*Scaling Leadership* offers a very useful, practical and well-researched way for each of us to assess the quality of our leadership in work and life. It presents a strong business case for self-awareness. The call is to deepen our humanity, our capacity for spiritual consciousness, and our ability to think differently about the complexity around us. These are much-needed qualities in a reductionist world that too often promises a false certainty, an attraction to dominance and an either/or way of thinking."

> Peter Block, Partner, Designed Learning and author of *Flawless Consulting: A Guide to Getting Your Expertise Used* and *An Other Kingdom.*

"To thrive in the future, leaders will need to learn how to scale their own leadership. In a world where anything that can be distributed will be distributed, leaders will need to be both very clear about where they want to go and very flexible about how they will get there. The future will reward clarity, but punish certainty. Clarity will scale, but certainty will not. *Scaling Leadership* shows you how to scale your leadership in a way that is both caring and precise."

> Bob Johansen, Distinguished Fellow, Institute for the Future and author of *The New Leadership Literacies*

"Bill Adams and Bob Anderson's extensive data and relentless analytical rigor compel us to consider that vertical development does determine how far we can scale our individual and collective leadership to meet the scope and complexity of the challenges we face at every level."

> Zafer Achi, Director Emeritus, McKinsey & Company

"It is rare to find literature on leadership characteristics and the distinguishing markers of excellence that are so thoroughly based on statistical analysis. Anderson and Adams offer some startling new evidence that the conventional view on what makes for great leadership may not be the whole story. Read, be surprised and get clarity in which way both strengths and vulnerabilities can add to effectiveness."

> Dr. Susanne Cook-Greuter, Research director, Vertical Development Academy (VeDA)

"Ever wonder what senior leaders have to say about leadership, what works and what doesn't? Well, here it is. *Scaling Leadership*—drawing on science, experience and story—has answers. This book will show you how to amplify your leadership and multiply leadership throughout the organization. Anderson and Adam's first book, *Mastering Leadership*, is a classic. *Scaling Leadership* will join it."

> Michael Bungay Stanier, author of the WSJ-bestseller *The Coaching Habit*

"This is an amazing book! *Scaling Leadership* takes what is elusive about leadership and puts it in plain sight. The authors expertly unpack how to scale leadership with such clarity that you and your team can apply it day-to-day in operations. If you want to lead your organization to create what matters, then you need to know how to scale leadership, individually and collectively. If you don't want to be derailed by a rate-limiting leadership bottleneck, at a time when your organization can least afford it, then apply what is in this book.

There is so much unique about *Scaling Leadership*, especially how it incisively differentiates between the strengths that the best leaders use to get results a very different pattern of behavior ineffective leaders use to cancels out their leadership. The insights and tools that Anderson and Adams so carefully and clearly reveal are simply brilliant and practical.

What is even more extraordinary, however, is the view you get on the journey through this book. *Scaling Leadership* gives direction and sets you on the path of developing the highest and best in yourself and those you lead. It shows you how to do the most difficult and yet, the highest leverage thing you can do as a leader—let go so you can scale.

They say that 'leaders bring the weather,' following the path laid out here will lead to weather that is, in a word, beautiful."

Gary Colpaert, Vice President Clinical & Support Services, Froedtert Hospital

"In their new book, *Scaling Leadership*, Bob Anderson and Bill Adams artfully remind us that in business and in life, we either progress (scale) or regress (fail). They teach us why and how we can lead people and enterprises with a proactive, creative style. 'Be Proactive' is still the first basic habit of highly effective leaders."

Stephen M.R. Covey, CEO, CoveyLink and co-author of *Speed of Trust*

"Leaders either continue to develop their leadership skills and scale their organizations or risk becoming obsolete. This smart book reveals the direct link between your own development and the organization's growth potential. If you want to learn how to help your business thrive, read this book!"

Steve Arneson, Ph.D., President, Arneson Leadership Consulting

"As we transition from hierarchy to networks, emerging and seasoned leaders must develop and deploy new competencies daily in order to scale their organizations. I appreciate the authors' authenticity, as they confess that this book comes in part from their own pain and mistakes and from their research, their many conversations with colleagues, and from their work with leaders who have 'been there and done that.' They openly share their insights, experiences, and lessons about how best to engage, develop and retain talent."

Dr. Beverly Kaye, co-author of *Love 'Em or Lose 'Em, Up Is Not the Only Way*, and *Help Them Grow or Watch Them Go*

"*Scaling Leadership* offers leaders across the globe a profound, challenging, and deeply empowering roadmap to scale leadership within their organizations. Being leaders of an organization deeply committed to scaling its impact in the world, we could not put the book down. The stories, distinctions and practices shared by Bob and Bill throughout the book are both accessible and transformative. For those of us who realize the crucial role leadership plays in the stewarding of our organizations and our shared world, there are no excuses. This book shows you exactly what defines great leadership, why it is of the utmost importance to develop it, and how you can do just that. Enjoy!"

Laurens van Aarle and Joel Monk, Founders of Coaches Rising (or www.coachesrising.com)

"The world urgently needs more conscious leaders. Without them, we will not overcome our tremendous challenges and create a world that truly works. Nobody understands this better and has studied the phenomenon of conscious leadership more deeply than Bob and Bill. In their seminal work, *Mastering Leadership,* they taught us what conscious leadership looks like. In this marvelous book, we learn how to scale conscious leadership in organizations and maximize its impact. If you aspire to create a better world through the people you lead, you must read this book."

Sebastian Ross, Chief People Officer Telemedicine Clinic and President Conscious Capitalism Spain

"*Scaling Leadership* delivers the most street-savvy, evidence-based and conscious leadership approach on the planet. If you want to future-proof your organization, thrive in the face of rip-roaring change, and cultivate a flourishing world, then drink deep from the wisdom of these pages and then share it with every leader you know."

Barrett C. Brown, PhD, Global leadership expert and author of *The Future of Leadership for Conscious Capitalism*

"In their groundbreaking book, *Scaling Leadership*, organizational experts Bob Anderson and Bill Adams have once again raised the bar for leaders in any business in any industry. In these fast-changing and disruptive times, great leadership is needed more than ever before—we can no longer afford to take it for granted. With this book in hand, you'll have a clear path to raising your own performance as a leader, while raising the performance of your teams."

Barry O'Reilly, Founder, ExecCamp, Business Advisor and author of *Unlearn* and *Lean Enterprise*.

"I first met Bob Anderson in February 1992 when I attended a workshop on empowerment. It was clear even then that he was going to make great contributions to help us all become better leaders. Now twenty-seven years later, we have his latest contribution. In *Scaling Leadership*, he and Bill Adams have continued the journey they started in *Mastering Leadership*. It is true that there is a lot of research that is foundational for the theories they propose. For those who are looking for evidence, this will be comforting. For me, it is the translation of all this research into principles that are the core to all successful leaders. I give only two, of the many insights, that were meaningful to me.

'The moment we start to work on our effectiveness as leaders, we begin to improve our effectiveness as human beings. Because our humanity is ultimately the foundation of our leadership, these paths are inseparable.'

And if you are looking for a reason to read this book you only have to look at their definition of leadership. 'Again, we define leadership as scaling the capacity and capability for the organization to create what matters most.'"

Bain J Farris, President and CEO Farris Advisors

"*Scaling Leadership* redefines the Peter Principle in a way I thought was truly compelling. People are promoted to their highest level of development. Read this book if you are interested in pushing past your comfort zone to enhance your leadership skills and scale these skills up into your organization."

Jennifer Mueller, author, *Creative Change: Why we resist it, how we can embrace it.*

"*Scaling Leadership* gracefully articulates the gaps between ineffective and effective leaders. Anderson and Adams show us how to lead confidently, authentically and effectively. Their simple and practical approach can benefit leaders at all levels."

Amanda Setili, author of *Fearless Growth: The New Rules to Stay Competitive, Foster Innovation, and Dominate Your Markets*

"Comprehensive, well-researched and actionable, Anderson and Adams have created a book that will give you that next inch forward on your leadership journey. A must have for anyone with a leadership library."

Adam Kreek, Management Consultant, Executive Coach, Olympic Gold Medalist

# *Scaling* LEADERSHIP

*Building Organizational
Capability and Capacity to Create
Outcomes that Matter Most*

ROBERT J. ANDERSON
WILLIAM A. ADAMS

Foreword by Ed Catmull, Co-founder, Pixar Animation Studios,
President, Pixar Animation and Disney Animation,
Author of *Creativity, Inc.*

WILEY

Published by John Wiley & Sons, Inc., Hoboken, New Jersey.

Published simultaneously in Canada.

*Library of Congress Cataloging-in-Publication Data:*

Names: Anderson, Robert J., author. | Adams, W. A. (Bill), author.
Title: Scaling leadership : building organizational capability and capacity
  to create outcomes that matter most / Robert J. Anderson, William A. Adams.
Description: Hoboken, New Jersey : John Wiley & Sons, Inc., [2019] | Includes
  bibliographical references and index. |
Identifiers: LCCN 2018051019 (print) | LCCN 2018051758 (ebook) | ISBN
  9781119538301 (ePub) | ISBN 9781119538271 (Adobe PDF) | ISBN 9781119538257
  (hardcover)
Subjects: LCSH: Leadership.
Classification: LCC HD57.7 (ebook) | LCC HD57.7 .A5293 2019 (print) | DDC
  658.4/092--dc23
LC record available at https://lccn.loc.gov/2018051019

Printed in the United States of America

V10007171_122718

# Contents

# Foreword

So much disruption; so little time. Not only are organizations expected to provide great products and services, but to do so while the landscape is shifting and quaking. For those of us leading, it's both scary and thrilling. It is our job to lead our teams into these great challenges. I don't know about you, but I'm in over my head, and I need help.

Transforming any group's performance is hard and certainly takes longer than we expect. The most difficult step is the first—transforming ourselves. *Scaling Leadership* is about transforming ourselves with a conscious desire to transform our organizations. It is about becoming creative both as leaders and as problem solvers.

But creative leadership means more than being creative as a leader— it means the that the entire organization becomes creative. The potential of the people and leaders around us is enormous. We may not see it directly, but our leadership greatly determines whether or not that potential is realized.

It never ceases to amaze me that the personality traits of great leaders are so diverse. It is also a source of bafflement as to why so many leaders fail to recognize when they are holding back their organization. There are reasons for this of course. As we rise in an organization, it becomes increasingly difficult to stay connected with the realities on the ground. Too often this happens without our being aware of it. Many leaders don't believe they are leading unless they are confident, decisive and in full command. Asking for help is a sign of weakness. Some feel the responsibility of delivering results so strongly that they rely on their skills and experience to tell others what to do. In doing so, they impede the learning and development of the talented people around them and limit scale.

These beliefs are illusions, a great handicap made even more serious by increasing complexity. They lead to leaders being reactive, inadvertently holding back their creativity, as well as that of their team.

Our actions set the tone. We can either create a safe or an unsafe environment. While we set the tone, we are the ones least likely to see it. However, everyone else feels, sees, and reacts to it. The environment might feel safe to senior leaders, but if it is tailored to them, they can be blind to the effects. The tone leaders set defines whether people feel safe, able to disagree, take risks, or whether they are cautious and very careful—not wanting to look bad or put their careers at risk.

People usually will not say what they feel if the environment is unsafe, so introspection is exceptionally important. How do we see through our own delusions? Self-assessment should not be a solo activity. We can be stuck in the bubble of our own limited views and illusions. Given that we will never experience what other's experience, how do we open ourselves to other perspectives?

In *Scaling Leadership*, Bill and Bob provide a guide for those of us who are open to growth—to methodically examine how we are perceived, to the effect our leadership has on the people we lead, to move away from reactivity to creativity, to move toward integration, to develop the potential of each person in the organization, and to recognize the emotional and human element of everyone around us.

In many ways, our workplace is our family and community. We want the health that comes from a balance between our work community and our home life. We want purposefulness, openness, and safety at every level of the organization. This is the organization of our aspirations and one that scales to meet the opportunities and threats we face.

Ed Catmull
Co-founder, Pixar Animation Studios, President,
Pixar Animation and Disney Animation
Author of *Creativity Inc.*

# Acknowledgments

We would like to acknowledge four people who played a huge part in the development of this book. First, Lani Van Dusen, the Executive Director of the Worldwide Institute for Research and Evaluation (WIRE). Lani and her team conducted all the research behind this book. Her professional competence and high ethical research standards have greatly contributed to this book. Second, Peter Economy worked with us to author this book. Peter's writing and editing helped this book immensely. It is a far more focused and readable book because of Peter. Third, our graphic designer, Zoie Young, who artistically created the cover and all the figures throughout this book. And finally, Scott Anderson, who provided all the project management support for the book. He kept us on track (no small task) and managed all the details that it takes to pull a book like this together. We are grateful to all of you for your professionalism and passion.

We want to thank the partners at TLC and FCG: David Spach, Dave Schrader, Steve Athey, Nate Delahunty, Adelle Richards, Roma Gaster, Padraig O'Sullivan and Cindy Adams. Your friendship, love, and partnership have made all the difference. We also want to thank Betsy Leatherman and Paul Byrne, whose leadership has greatly helped us grow the business and expand our impact. We also acknowledge our worldwide staff and international Licensees. Your passion and dedication to our work has made is inspiring. You each bring such commitment and integrity to the organization every single day. We are the organization we are because of you. Without you being who you are and doing what you do, we could not be having the impact that we are. Thank you.

We also acknowledge all of the thought leaders mentioned in this book and in the bibliography. We all stand on the shoulders of giants, and you all have made important contributions to the field that have greatly informed this book. In particular, we want to thank Bob Kegan and Lisa Lahey. Bob and Lisa's seminal work on Stages of Adult Development, Immunity to Change, and Deliberately Developmental Organizations have deeply informed our lives and our work. We could not be more grateful for their contribution, support, and friendship.

**Bob:** I first acknowledge and thank my wife Kim. Kim is the love of my life. Her constant and unwavering love and generosity of spirit supports me in all I do and most definitely in writing this book. I am a better man because of you, Kim. I am grateful beyond words.

Thanks to my partner and co-author, Bill. Bill is one of the best men I know. He is also my best friend. He is as good a consultant as there is. More than any other person, Bill understood what I was up to with my life's work and has applied it in ways that are well beyond where I could have taken it. Bill is a true master. His contribution to this book is huge. It is a far better book because of Bill's co-authorship. Bill's CEO leadership of our organizations has been amazing. On top of all that, Bill is an example for me of a loving husband, father, and grandfather. Even though the demands of the business on him are intense, he is all about his beautiful family.

Finally, I want to thank my children, Katherine, Rob, and Scott. You know how much I love you. I have had the great privilege of being your father and of traveling around the world with each of you. Our times together are the best of my life.

**Bill:** I want to acknowledge my Savior, Jesus Christ. I stand all amazed at the grace that He offers me.

I want to acknowledge my partner in this world and beyond, Cynthia Adams. From the bottom of my heart, thank you. Every moment of my life is enriched because of you, and has been from the beginning. You are my best friend, faith partner, greatest support, business partner and greatest teacher. You are my one and only. No matter what is required and where it has taken us, we have traveled it as partners. I am a better man, father, husband, and person because of you. My gratitude and love for you are endless.

I want to say thank you to the countless clients and dedicated leaders all over the world who are committed to doing their work to be better human beings and more effective leaders. After 35 years in this business, they number in the thousands. Thank you for jumping in and playing life full out.

Thanks to my co-author and partner, Bob Anderson. You are brilliant and an amazing leader who is actively stewarding the planet. Because of your work, thousands of leadership consultants worldwide are having an impact on helping the leaders of the world be more effective. I am honored and privileged to be your partner and friend. I want to acknowledge you for your dedication and contribution to making the world a better place. I admire the father, husband, son, and brother that you choose to be.

# Introduction

Life scales, or it dies. Growth is built into all living organisms. I (Bob) stepped outside my front door one morning to find the sidewalk carpeted with a thick layer of tiny seeds from a massive locust tree. Each one of these seeds is capable of scaling into a massive tree that will one day produce millions of seeds every season. In that sense, each seed has within it the potential to become a forest.

Businesses are not that different from the trees in our yards. They seek to grow, and they either achieve growth or they die. So, in a sense, scale is life. And yet, we are living in a time when unrestricted growth threatens our planet. We must scale much more than the *size* of our organizations. We must scale new and innovative solutions to complex business, organizational, and global problems. And we must do so in a world that's becoming increasingly complex, uncertain, and volatile. This capability is now both a business and global imperative. The key is leadership.

Leaders must learn to scale themselves by scaling leadership. But not just any kind of leadership will do. We need leaders who are both effective and conscious—capable of scaling innovation, adaptability, sustainability, agility, and engagement as the organization's growth strategy. Furthermore, we need leaders capable of growing organizations in such a way that all stakeholders thrive. Ownership, and its return, is but one of the stakeholders. Employees want a workplace where people thrive.

Customers want to buy from a great company that serves them exquisitely and to which they are wildly committed. Suppliers want win-win, long-term relationships. Communities deserve to be uplifted in our places of business. The planet and its ecosystem must be tended, sustained, and enriched. Great businesses scale on all these fronts and optimize the interdependent welfare of all their stakeholders.

The only way for this to happen is for *conscious leaders to scale conscious leadership*. This is the future of leadership.

*Scaling Leadership* is about how senior leaders develop conscious leadership at scale in their organization. It is about *you* becoming that leader and how *we*, collectively, become leaders who rapidly develop the leadership that is required to grow the organization in our increasingly complex and disrupted world.

So, how do we do this? Where does the time, bandwidth, and attention come from in a world that's already full 24/7? If you're like most of the leaders with whom we work, you're extremely busy. Most of us are underwater, over our heads. We have no more time to give, yet the organization *wants* to grow, *pushes* us to grow, *pulls* us internationally. It wants to double or triple revenue over the next five years. Suddenly, you have 20 business leaders reporting to you and none of them are in the same country. You are good at what you do, but you are promoted to a level of scale and complexity for which you feel unprepared. If this sounds familiar, you are not alone. You are likely reaching the limits to scale in your own leadership, individually and collectively.

We see this happening everywhere we go and we, the authors, are in it with you. It is ironic to be writing a book about scale when we are profoundly challenged with scaling our own business. Rapid growth solves a lot of problems and brings with it a whole lot more. Suddenly, the systems, technologies, and processes we developed and implemented over years are inadequate for the volume and complexity required. They must be redesigned. Leadership that worked well (or at least we thought so) when we were smaller, no longer serves the organization. We are challenged to reinvent ourselves. When we did an organizational culture survey during all this, we realized we needed to take our own medicine. Our leadership was neither scaling, nor was it creating the kind of thriving culture we promote through our work.

So, we wrote *Scaling Leadership* right through the middle of meeting the limits of scale in our own leadership. It has not been easy. This book, if you let it, will confront you. It did us. It will challenge you to evolve your leadership. It will point out the ways you lead that are working for you. And it will show you how you are getting in your own way. As such, this book is a double-edged sword.

All we can say is that we are in it with you. We do not write this book from a place of being above it all or on the other side of the steep learning curve we face as leaders. Rather, we write from a place of compassion and humility in our shared humanity. We are learning together how to lead effectively in a world that is faster paced, more volatile, more ambiguous, more complex, and in more peril than we ever imagined possible.

The only way out is *through*. This book will point the way through, but it will not be us doing the pointing. Our peers in leadership will do the pointing. This book is unique. In it, we turn to leaders like you to teach all of us.

This book is light on theory, and we hope, pontification. It is about what leaders have to say about leadership. How do leaders talk to other leaders about leadership? To learn about that, we turned to the written comments within our huge 360-degree assessment database. We sorted it, and we studied what's in it. We wanted to learn how senior leaders talk to other senior leaders about leadership. We let leaders teach us, and in this book, we pass along what we have gleaned from them about the kind of leadership that is capable of scale—and the kind that is not.

This is *not* another book about business growth strategies (e.g., how to grow your business within your industry). It *is* about how we increase the multiple on our leadership and scale it. How? By becoming the kind of leader who is more and more capable of leading growth and continuing to lead effectively with the complexity that comes with growth, especially rapid growth. In short, we scale the organization by scaling leadership—by being the kind of leader who develops other leaders.

*Scaling Leadership* is about how leaders successfully transform themselves and then scale that as they transform their organizations. In the first half, we describe the core findings from our study of leaders' written comments. We discuss what we learned by "listening in" on these feedback conversations. We explore what leaders are telling us about what works, what does not, and how all that relates to the kind of leadership that can scale leadership as a strategy to transform the organization. Finally, if the arguments we make are compelling, and you want to scale leadership and transform your organization, we end the first half of this book (Chapter 8) with how to do exactly that.

Because *Scaling Leadership* is about taking your leadership to the next level of effectiveness, the second half of this book goes deep into the individual journeys required of us to transform ourselves. While development theory and research are greatly helpful, our chapters are intentionally light on theory because we are most interested in how leaders describe, in their own words, what happens to our leadership as it matures. As it turns out, leaders are quite precise about this.

To help you scale your leadership, we have two companion products. We offer a Leadership Circle Profile (LCP) Self-Assessment and a Leadership Development Plan (LDP). Both are free with your purchase of this book and can be found at www.leadershipcircle.com. Simply click on the link for the Self-Assessment and, after you complete it, we will send you the results and a Leadership Development Plan that follows along with action steps we suggest throughout this book. Let this book guide you through a series of powerful activities that, if you take them seriously, will transform your leadership.

It is our hope that *Scaling Leadership* can help you become a more effective leader. More than that, we hope it helps you continue to harvest your extraordinary, radically human exquisiteness of being and use it in service of others, the organization, and our shared world.

Enjoy the read.

Bob and Bill

# Chapter 1
# Exposed at Scale
*Spiritual Boot Camp for Leaders*

Most of us believe that what separates the poor or average leader from one who is truly great is unknown and mysterious—giving rise to the popular misconception that leadership is one of the most studied and least understood subjects. This is not the case. Not anymore.

There has been a great deal of research on leadership over the past 70 years, and we are now standing at a new threshold. We know very well what works, what makes a difference. In our book *Mastering Leadership*, we describe this new threshold. We take the best of the field and integrate it into a model of leadership that reveals something universal about human nature, about leadership, and therefore how to develop it in practical ways. In *Scaling Leadership*, we take the mystery out of leadership by exploring how senior leaders, in their own words, are crystal clear about what works, what does not, and what to do about it. It is about what we already, most clearly and deeply, know about great leadership.

A critical prerequisite to effective organizational leadership is leadership of self. We define self-leadership as *creating outcomes that matter most*. Optimal self-leadership is the wherewithal to show up in our lives in ways that best serve our desired outcomes—loving families, strong relationships and friendships, work that matters, and futures worthy of our life's commitment. Self-leadership is the lifelong stance of continually focusing on a desired future and—in the midst of the current realities of our lives and organizations—taking action (individually and with others) to bring that vision into being. This stance is foundational to leadership.

Organizational leadership is *scaling the capacity and capability in the organization to create outcomes that matter most*—to create its desired, optimal, and viable future. Leadership scales capacity and capability in others, through teams, and in the organization. Leadership also scales the capability in an organization to perform and thrive by constantly, and agilely, reinventing itself in the midst of volatile, ever-changing conditions.

## LEADERSHIP AT SCALE

As businesses grow, their long-term, sustainable success depends on more than developing great products and services, securing necessary financing, or hiring and retaining talented people. It also depends on scaling leadership.

Scott (name changed to protect identity), the president of a very successful high-profile corporation in the entertainment industry and one of our clients, made this candid observation: "Our leadership was exposed at scale." He told us as they attempted to meet the doubling of their business and expand internationally, the capacity and capability of their leadership was exposed.

We started working with Scott in 2016, which gave us a chance to get up close to his leadership. Scott is incredibly intelligent, as smart as they come, and a highly committed leader. Scott and his organization operate from a higher purpose.

Scott shared with us this explanation:

> We have impact on the lives of people around the world for the better. I want to unleash the power of the organization to continue to succeed in this purpose. This requires that we, as a team of leaders, learn how to better lead the organization and increase the likelihood of obtaining success year in and year out. I also believe that as leaders, if we can do this here, it will

spill out in other areas of our lives, making a positive difference in many ways. Not to sound corny, but this is not about the burden of legacy; it is about the joy of it. It is about the joy of quiet and influential leadership inspiring people around the world while succeeding as a business by creating great entertainment with a powerful message.

It is not surprising that, under Scott's leadership, the company has enjoyed great success with a string of impactful offerings into the market. Not only did they grow rapidly, but almost overnight, they significantly increased their business in China. This, along with other factors, stress-tested the organization. As Scott told us, "When our business grew, our leadership and what made us effective and ineffective was 100 percent exposed." He knew that leadership and the growth of an organization go hand in hand. At a certain point, the effectiveness or ineffectiveness of leaders determines whether or not an organization can grow. A business can't outgrow the effectiveness of its leadership!

To scale effectively, Scott and his leadership team had to rethink in detail the design of their organizational structure and leadership system. They needed to learn how to stretch their current creative talent across a much broader portfolio. They changed who would report to whom and in what ways, and they took on the development of leaders, at all levels. Scott said he saw his job as a leader is to develop other leaders, and do it well. Most of their creative talent had never considered themselves to be leaders, but because they were thrust into leadership positions, they had to learn to lead.

Fortunately for the organization, Scott saw the need to create the right conditions for scaling leadership across the organization. And that's what he did, leading the organization to tremendous growth as well as creative and financial success.

Ineffective leadership caps the ability of an organization to grow, and this liability is exposed the minute you start to scale. Leadership that works at one level of scale is likely to run into serious limitations at the next level. The men and women who may be well-suited to lead a 100-person business unit with $30 million in annual revenue may be unable to lead a 250-person business unit with $100 million in annual revenue. As an organization becomes larger and more complex, the number of people being led is larger, and the issues and opportunities requiring a leader's attention are more numerous, more frequent, and more consequential than ever.

Is your leadership built for scale, or are you already beyond the level of scale and complexity for which your leadership is optimized? If so, you are likely feeling over your head. You may be getting great results but at a higher energetic cost—that is, diminishing returns on ever-higher expenditures of time and effort. You may have a gnawing sense that working more hours is not the solution (and you would be right). The harder you go, the more you get in your own way. If you're trying to scale or grow the business through your own capability alone and not through the capability of other leaders and teams, then you won't scale successfully.

If these kinds of outcomes feel familiar to you, chances are you are facing a significant development gap. And if that's the case, then you're in good company. Let's take a moment to explore this development gap and understand why you should be concerned about it.

## THE DEVELOPMENT GAP

We all know the feeling of leading in a world that is moving fast and is more chaotic and disrupted, and less predictable than ever. It's not your imagination—these conditions have been well documented. In his 2008 book *Leaders Make the Future*, Bob Johansen, a foremost futurist, wrote: "In my 40 years of forecasting the future, the direst forecasts yet are in this book." Johansen claimed that we had entered a "VUCA" business environment of constantly escalating *volatility, uncertainty, complexity*, and *ambiguity*.

**Volatility:** Challenges can appear overnight and be of unknown duration and intensity. Disruption on multiple fronts is accelerating.

**Uncertainty:** We are required to operate with incomplete information in unpredictable environments.

**Complexity:** Challenges are highly interdependent and difficult to map; there are unknown unknowns.

**Ambiguity:** Causal relationships are difficult to see and it's hard to agree about what something means.

Over the past decade, the term VUCA has become part of the business lexicon as executives, managers, and others grapple with its effects.[1]

We recently met with Bob and asked: "Do you believe the VUCA environment will subside anytime soon?"

His response was rather alarming and exciting: "We haven't seen anything yet!" In his recent book, *The New Leadership Literacies: Thriving in a Future of Extreme Disruption and Distributed Everything,* Bob describes the future as a *scramble.*[2] He says, "VUCA has never before been so global, so interconnected, and so scalable. Local VUCA is not new, the VUCA *world* is unprecedented."

The level of disruptive change coming at us is unprecedented, and we can only expect it to increase. As leaders, we must learn to navigate the permanent whitewater in which our organizations operate. It is not enough to cope with the volatility and unpredictability in our markets; we must develop a new level of leadership literacy, mastery, and agility. We either rise to meet the challenge or get swamped. This is the new normal.

Is your leadership built for scale in this environment? Will you rise to meet the challenge, or will you fall behind the market leaders? Will you watch from the sidelines as established companies learn to adapt and startups constantly disrupt those who do not? Think about Snapchat, Airbnb, Lyft, WeWork, and many other market leaders that didn't exist 10 years ago.

We recently met with a successful senior leader, Gerard, who works for a large multinational organization and debriefed his Leadership Circle Profile 360 assessment (LCP). The LCP provides feedback on a leader's effectiveness and the Creative and Reactive elements in the person's leadership style. Gerard walked into the meeting and stated: "You're not going to turn me into one of those touchy-feely leaders— somebody who has his emotions out front. I'm not going to be giving you or anybody else a hug!"

Gerard had been recently promoted to president, making him responsible for 75 percent of the business's revenue and resources. The company serves hundreds of thousands of customers around the globe. When we first met Gerard, he was in over his head—far beyond the edge of his own effectiveness as a leader. He had tried to overcome this challenge by working longer and harder. Seemingly, Gerard had unlimited work capacity. However, personally working longer and harder would not solve his challenge. He needed to build the capacity of his team to lead.

The company's CEO could see that there was a problem. He knew that Gerard was one of his most impactful leaders, passionate about the organization, and committed to contribute all he could to its mission and growth. But, he also knew that if Gerard couldn't expand his leadership, the company couldn't grow and succeed over time. This meant he would not last long as president.

One example illustrates how Gerard struggled. He is very loyal to his people—even when they're not performing. As a result, he doesn't have direct conversations with his people in a courageous, authentic way. So as business performance issues mounted, he reacted. He fired one of his key managers without warning—a person to whom he had always given stellar performance reviews. The employee said, "I don't understand. You told me over and over again how well I'm performing. You never mentioned any significant issues. This action is coming out of left field."

Gerard's action sent a loud and clear message to everyone in the organization: *your heads will be on a platter if you don't perform, and you may not see it coming.* As a result of this and other moves, many people who reported to him shut down, which had exactly the opposite effect from what was desired.

As you might expect, Gerard's Leadership Circle Profile was very Reactive. We suggested that, despite all his past success, his leadership had reached its upper limits of scale. He did not understand. We pointed out his low *Balance* score (a measure of work-life balance) and asked, "How long are you working each day?" He worked almost constantly, and his work defined him. He based his sense of value and self-worth on his reputation for getting results. After communicating the results of the Leadership Circle Profile with Gerard—explaining his obvious strengths as a leader and the Reactive tendencies that were getting in his way—he realized that working longer and harder was not scaling for him. The way he had achieved his success in the past had become suboptimal. Gerard was standing in his own way and canceling himself out. His inability to scale his leadership was constraining his tremendous talent.

Gerard was being challenged by his past success, by the organization's push for rapid growth, and by the complexity of the business environment to develop a more complex and sophisticated way of knowing and leading. Complexity of mind is not a more complicated, convoluted mind; rather, it is the elegant mind of mastery. Gerard needed to find a way to scale his genius as well as his influence as a leader.

*Scale can only be achieved by developing capacity and capability in others.* Effective leaders develop other leaders. Gerard must face his development gap and the challenge to grow beyond it.

To be clear, Gerard is not a problem to be solved. There is nothing inherently wrong with him or his leadership capability. But he is facing the inevitable: the organization's need for scale and the escalating complexity of his context have put him in over his head.

Each of us faces development gaps in our leadership. They are not problems with us, and there is no shame in having them. Rather, they are the inevitable consequence of leading successfully in an increasingly complex world. They are challenges that can be met and overcome if we evolve as leaders and see our leadership as a kind of spiritual pressure cooker. The very pressure that success, scale, and complexity bring is a force for our own evolution and transformation.

Steve Athey, one of our partners, brilliantly synthesized what we mean by a development gap (Figure 1.1). We often ask leaders where they would rank the business reality they face on a scale from high VUCA to high SCSC (stability, certainty, simplicity, clarity). Regardless of the industry or company size or location, leaders always choose high VUCA. This has become our leadership context. We all know it, and we all know it will only accelerate.

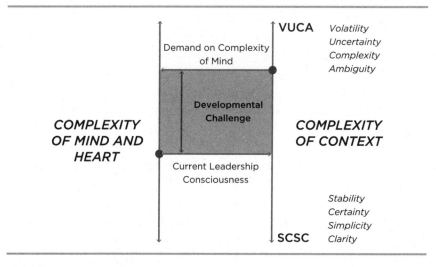

**FIGURE 1.1**    The Development Gap

The complexity of the context we face as leaders makes a demand on our consciousness—our complexity of mind and heart, our inner game, and our Internal Operating System. It requires that the complexity of mind and heart of our leadership, individually and collectively, be more than a match for the complexity we face. Otherwise, we get in the way of the very things we are trying to accomplish. For most of us, our inner game (the complexity and structure of our internal meaning-making system, our decision-making system, our level of self-awareness and emotional intelligence, our mental models, and the inner beliefs and assumptions by which we define and deploy ourselves moment to moment) lacks the capacity and maturity to thrive amid all the complexity.

Hence, most of us are in way over our heads. We are running an internal operating system that is not complex enough for the complexity we face. This is our development gap.

Since the context in which we lead will continue to challenge us, the rate of our leadership development, individually and collectively, must at least keep pace with the rate of change and escalating complexity, if not close the gap. If we do not develop and stay ahead of all of this change, we—and our organizations, products, and services—will become increasingly less relevant. This is an outcome that no leader can allow to happen on his or her watch. *It is a business imperative today that we transcend our current level of leadership.*

In *Mastering Leadership*, we describe three progressively developing levels of leadership—Reactive, Creative, and Integral. Creative leadership is more effective at leading in complex environments than is Reactive, and Integral is even more so. Each level of leadership is powered (like Intel inside) by a different (also progressively maturing) internal landscape or Internal Operating System that governs how we deploy ourselves moment to moment. Rather than explain this here, we will let the leaders in our written comment study describe the fundamental difference between Reactive leadership, and the kind that shows up at Creative and Integral.

For now, it is enough to say that Gerard is challenged to grow beyond his Reactive way of leading, harvest its strengths, and reconfigure it at the Creative level. Creative leadership is far more capable of scaling amid complexity as both his responsibilities and the organization grow. As Gerard makes this transition, he will forego running all the key decisions and creative innovations through his position. Instead, he will find enjoyment in developing that capacity in others. He will become a guide, mentor, and developer of others, helping to bring out *their* best. Developing leaders will require Gerard to not always be the center of the show nor to make every decision nor be credited with every innovation. He will foster an organization that has this capability. In that way, he will scale his leadership.

If Gerard continues to lean into his development gaps, he may eventually face the limits of—and be challenged to grow beyond—Creative leadership. Harvesting all the strengths of the Creative leader, he may transform Creative into Integral leadership, the next level of leadership maturity. If so, he will evolve even greater capacity to lead amid complexity.

Inherently, leadership becomes a kind of spiritual boot camp. The very pressure that success, scale, and complexity bring is a force for our own transformation and evolution. It's essentially a spiritual process.

## THE SPIRITUAL JOURNEY OF LEADERSHIP

When we step into a position of leadership, we step into a transformative crucible. The *crucible* metaphor comes from alchemy. It is the container in which enough heat and pressure build up to catalyze a transformation—for example, transforming lead into gold.

Leadership is a crucible. Along with being a spouse or parent, teacher, or coach, we can think of no better crucible for transformation than leadership. By its nature, leadership will push us to our limits—and maybe beyond them. It will call on the highest and best of who we are and what we offer to meet the daily challenges we face.

This is what we mean by leadership as a spiritual boot camp. The moment we start to work on our effectiveness as leaders, we begin to improve our effectiveness as a *human being*. Because our humanity is ultimately the foundation of our leadership, these paths are inseparable. This puts us right in the middle of a spiritual path.

By *spiritual*, we don't mean *religious*, except that the essence of all religions is radical (at the root) transformation. This choice calls on the highest and deepest within us. We are challenged to become higher versions of ourselves—to mine our true human greatness and put it in service of others. We are challenged to become spiritually intelligent—literate in the pathways of transformation. This is the spiritual path we take as leaders.

The choice to be a more effective leader means facing our development gaps. Amid the current complexity, we cannot *not* be in over our heads. Welcome to the club. Escalating complexity is a benevolent force on every leader, relentlessly pressing us with our need to develop. Like a drill sergeant in our spiritual boot camp, it aims to evolve us.

There is no shame in having development gaps. We all have them. Welcome to the human race and to leadership. We can and must extend compassion for ourselves and others while facing the steepness of our learning curve, both individually and collectively. If we risk being *radically human* and lead by *learning out loud* with our colleagues, there is plenty of grace, forgiveness, and compassion in the system—and support from those around us.

At its essence, leadership is a calling to serve. In a world increasingly at risk, leadership is a vocation that can link diverse people from all walks of life to create remarkable achievements. As such, leaders play a key role in designing a thriving future for all who inhabit this beautiful planet.

Leadership—the kind that multiplies capacity and capability in and through others—fundamentally requires that we become more fully human, well-rounded, integrated human beings. At its heart, great leadership is *radically human*—that is, showing up in more transparent, authentic, vulnerable, empathetic, passionate, and compassionate ways, and even loving one another (characteristics that separate us from machines). We bring that humanity into every meeting room. We make humility and humanness our foundation. We continuously evolve our leadership so we can become a leader who gives back to the planet, makes a difference, and enables those in our charge to collectively create results that are innovative, durable, and congruent with what the world needs most.

Leadership is the deployment of *self* into circumstances. As a leader, *you* are your primary asset. How you show up moment to moment is your *leadership impact*. In this book, we ask these key questions: *When you lead, who shows up? Which self do you deploy?*

**REFLECTION**

This book will be far more effective for you if you apply its ideas. Take time to reflect on these questions:

- Are you successfully scaling effective leadership in your organization? Why or why not?

- How is the current VUCA business environment affecting your organization? Your team? You?

- Do you have a development gap in your leadership? How does this impact your effectiveness as a leader?

# Chapter 2
# Profiles in Leadership
*Every Leader Has One*

Jim Geiger, the CEO of LiquidWeb and a long-term client of ours, offered this brilliant insight regarding leaders: "Leaders bring the weather." That is, when a great leader walks into the room, everyone is on notice and everyone notices—the energy is palpable.

The tone, mood, presence, focus, and behavior of the leader *is* the weather in any organization—a force of nature. And everyone who works there can feel it, see it, experience it, and describe how it impacts them and those around them. They know if this weather either supports what they are trying to create or destroys it. They can describe if the weather brings out the best in individual employees and teams, or if it lowers their performance. They know if they should relax, contribute, and take risks, or remain cautious, reserved, and careful.

Leaders bring the weather, and they define to a large degree what can and can't happen in their organizations.

So, what is this *weather*—this powerful leadership presence that leaders bring with them wherever they go? In effect, the *weather* is the leader's *profile in action*. Each of us has a leadership profile. It's the way we show up to our people, how we tend to respond to certain situations or crises, what is and is not permissible to discuss, and much more.

Since those who work directly for the leader experience the weather firsthand, they are often more aware and capable of describing it than the leader. This is why feedback is so valuable, and leaders need people around them to provide it.

Think about your own leadership. What kind of weather do *you* bring? Are you aware of it? Do you know how it impacts others in ways you intend or don't intend? Think about how leaders affect *you* in your own job. Does the effect that leaders have on you make you feel good, bad, or somewhere in between? Why? What do these leaders do that makes you feel that way?

When we work with leadership teams, we often ask this simple but powerful question: "Do you agree that leadership matters and that, all other things being equal, effective leadership outperforms ineffective leadership?"

There is nearly universal agreement that *leadership matters*—to results, performance, culture, engagement, agility, adaptability, sustainability, job satisfaction, and more. We also agree that individual and collective leadership effectiveness *is a primary driver of performance*. Furthermore, *there is a strong consensus on what great leadership looks like*. "We know it when we see it." And we can describe what leaders do that works and what does not.

We all want to work for great leaders who inspire us to give our best.

As a result, when we go into an organization, we often ask: "Of all the leaders here, if you were to pick two or three whom you most admire, respect, and appreciate, who would they be? What made them that way, and why did you choose them?" When we ask those questions, 80 percent of the people name the same two or three leaders—men and women who stand out among all the rest.

As we continue to ask these questions, we get a clear picture or profile of effective leaders, their qualities and characteristics. Employees know who they are; we know what makes great leaders great—it's not a mystery. Hence, we approached the research for this book with this clear hypothesis: When leaders provide feedback to each other, they describe—with remarkable accuracy—what *effective leadership* is and is not, and what it looks like in real life and in real organizations. We wanted to learn about effective leadership, as experienced and described by *other* leaders. What is leadership *unplugged* or *unvarnished*—stripped of all the models, theories, frameworks, and pontifications? How do real leaders describe leadership when they provide feedback about the kind of weather the leader brings? What works and what does not? What is the optimal profile?

## OPTIMAL LEADERSHIP CIRCLE PROFILE

Since our research is conducted through the Leadership Circle Profile (LCP), we offer a brief overview of the Profile and the Universal Model of Leadership on which the LCP is based (*Mastering Leadership* develops this in far greater depth). Our goal is to provide just enough context for you to understand the new results presented here.

Since every leader has a profile and we all can describe our view of effective leadership, then we should be able to measure (quantitatively and qualitatively) what great leadership looks like. Through the lens of the LCP, the Optimal Leadership Circle Profile looks like the one displayed in Figure 2.1.

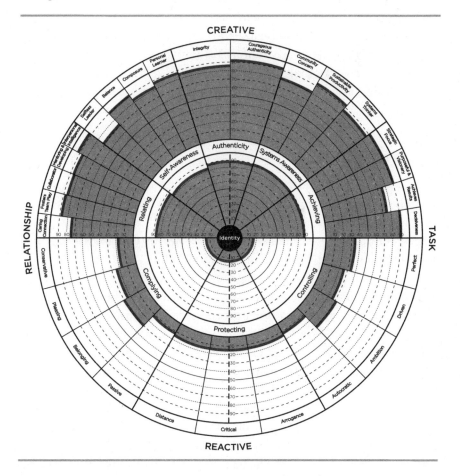

**FIGURE 2.1**   Optimal Leadership Circle Profile

We arrived at the Optimal LCP by asking 50,000 leaders and employees worldwide to describe ideal leadership: *What kind of leadership, if it existed, would enable the organization to thrive in its current market-place and into the future?* Consistently, people give us this Optimal Profile in every kind of business, all around the world.[1] Keep in mind that this in no way represents the goal for any individual leader, as we must each leverage our unique set of gifts and strengths. It does, however, express an important consensus view of what great leadership looks like.

Since you may not know anything about the LCP and how extraordinary this optimal picture is, we will start with the basics and then gradually explain the more complex aspects of the LCP throughout the book.

As you can see, we display a leader's 360-degree feedback results in the form of a circle. We do this for many reasons, the primary one being that the circle represents *wholeness*. No matter what an individual leadership Profile may be, each of us is a whole, complete human being. In measuring a leader's strengths and liabilities, it is easy to lose track of our extraordinary wholeness. You're reminded of this by presenting the LCP in the form of a circle.

### Creative Leadership

The Leadership Circle Profile is divided into two hemispheres, upper and lower. The upper half, labeled *Creative*, represents the kind of leadership that emerges as leaders mature into Creative leadership.

In the outer Creative half of the circle, we display the 18 Creative Competencies that tend to arise naturally as we move into the Creative level of leadership. (See Appendix A for definitions of all dimensions on the LCP.) These competencies are well researched and strongly correlated to measures of leadership effectiveness and business performance. Figure 2.2 shows our research on the relationship between the average rater score on all 18 Creative Competencies correlated with a measure of Leadership Effectiveness on the LCP. The items that make up the Leadership Effectiveness scale are shown in Table 2.1.

The correlation between the average rater score on all 18 Creative Competencies and Leadership Effectiveness is 0.93. It is based on more than one million rater surveys from around the world. This remarkably strong correlation shows that as *you improve your scores in the Creative half of the circle, you will likely be experienced as a more effective leader.*

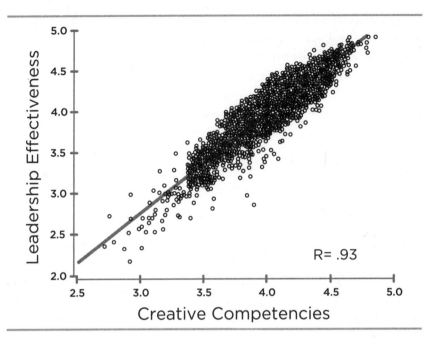

**FIGURE 2.2**   Leadership Effectiveness and Creative Competencies

**Creative Leadership and Business Performance**

In *Mastering Leadership*, we provide evidence for how Reactive and Creative leadership relate to organizational performance. We created an Index of Business Performance and asked managers to evaluate the performance of the business with respect to market share, profitability, return on assets, quality of products and services, and other metrics. We then correlated the resulting Index of Business Performance with the *Leadership*

**Table 2.1**   Leadership Effectiveness Scale

☑  I am satisfied with the quality of leadership that he/she provides.

☑  He/she is the kind of leader that others should aspire to become.

☑  He/she is an example of an ideal leader.

☑  His/her leadership helps this organization to thrive.

☑  Overall, he/she provides very effective leadership.

*Effectiveness* measure on the LCP and confirmed a strong correlation between *Leadership Effectiveness* and *Business Performance* (0.61 for 2,000 organizations and 250,000 surveys). As expected, since Creative Competencies are so highly correlated to Leadership Effectiveness, we found that they were also positively and solidly correlated to Business Performance. (See Appendix B for a full description of the findings.)

### Reactive Leadership

The Reactive half of the circle in the LCP is comprised of 11 Reactive Tendencies. (See Appendix A for definitions.) Imbedded in each Reactive tendency is a strength, but it is a strength being run reactively. In effect, these are default behaviors. They are go-to strengths on which we habitually rely when we feel under pressure or at risk.

When we run our strengths reactively, we often create unintended consequences that limit our effectiveness. When we deploy a strength reactively, we often cancel out that strength and introduce liabilities in its place. Consequently, *Reactive Tendencies are inversely correlated to Leadership Effectiveness*. Figure 2.3 shows the correlation between Leadership Effectiveness and the average rater score on the 11 Reactive Tendencies.

The correlation between Reactive Tendencies and Leadership Effectiveness is –0.68. This solid inverse relationship shows that the more we lead reactively, the less likely we will be experienced as an effective leader over time.

Yes, Reactive leaders can and do get results—sometimes extraordinary results. They may sell more, innovate more, and deliver more than anyone else in the organization. But, they often leave behind them a trail of broken, disenchanted, and disengaged employees, peers, and other stakeholders who invariably feel pushed, coerced, pressured, or let down. Hence, the performance that results from the Reactive approach to leadership is often at the expense of those who report to and work with Reactive leaders. They feel at risk, vulnerable, unsafe.

Reactive Leaders create an unhealthy "or-else" ultimatum culture that brings burnout and diminishing returns over time. How do *you* respond when your leader puts you in an "or-else" situation, when you're told to "do it my way, *or else*"? Is it a positive or a negative for your engagement and ultimately your performance on the job?

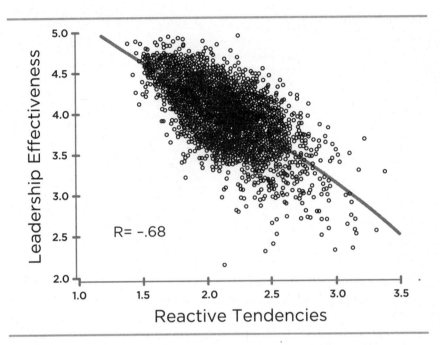

**FIGURE 2.3**   Leadership Effectiveness and Reactive Leadership

People who work for Reactive leaders often despair that anything will ever change. Sadly, as long as those Reactive leaders retain their positions, their employees are probably right. We know immediately when we walk into an organization led by a Reactive leader. Employees tell us, "I know why you're here, and it's not going to help." These unfortunate souls have already been through multiple rounds of performance improvement—the management's flavor of the month—and real change never occurs. Until a fundamental shift occurs—from Reactive to Creative leadership—meaningful change will never take place.

**Push-Pull of Leadership Effectiveness**

Our research also reveals that when Reactive Tendencies increase, Creative Competencies tend to decrease. Figure 2.4 shows this relationship.

As Reactive scores increase, Creative scores decrease. (The correlation is inverse and strong at −0.76.) Reactive leadership can severely limit the full deployment of Creative Competencies. The minimum system requirement for a leader to have consistent access to these

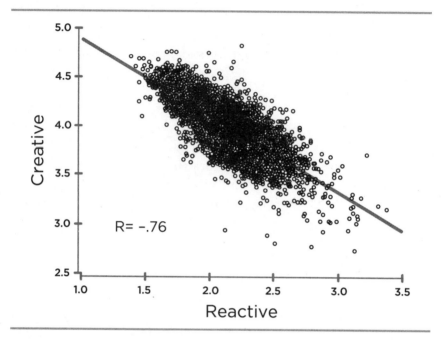

**FIGURE 2.4**   Creative Competencies and Reactive Tendencies

competencies is Creative leadership. Reactive Tendencies interrupt Creative Competencies, resulting in reduced Leadership Effectiveness.

In the LCP, as scores get higher, they radiate farther from the center of the circle. Thus, the Optimal Profile looks like a mushroom (see Figure 2.1) with high scores in the top half of the circle and low scores in the bottom half. This is all you need to know about the LCP to understand the research and results presented in this book.

### A Tale of Two Leaders

Let's contrast two actual leaders, one Reactive and the other Creative. We once worked with a business whose CEO scheduled an all-hands meeting with hundreds of employees. The business had new ownership, and performance needed to be turned around quickly. This meant cost-cutting and downsizing. During the all-hands meeting, a female employee stood up and asked the CEO this question: "When are you going to answer some of the questions that have been submitted anonymously—the questions that people are afraid to bring up in front of the leadership team and their coworkers?"

Not happy with this pointed question, the CEO said: "I don't appreciate your question. Asking questions anonymously was not *my* idea, and in my experience, it isn't very useful."

Keep in mind that this CEO is a great guy and a talented leader. But by displaying Reactive behavior to his employees, he created a moment that might have defined his leadership for a long time at the company. In fact, it took him months to recover from the strong negative impression he set in motion during that one-minute interaction.

Contrast that with Peter Harmer, managing director and CEO of Insurance Australia Group (IAG), a large general insurance company headquartered in Sydney. A day or so after the monthly senior executive meeting, we hold a WebEx call with all leaders across the company where they can listen and ask questions. If there isn't time to answer all the questions during the meeting, they are all answered on the company's social media platform connecting more than 10,000 employees to one another. IAG's leadership team is completely transparent, and employees are encouraged to take part in the company's business. Many do.

Reactive leadership shuts down the valuable insights and contributions of employees while diminishing organizational capacity and capability. Creative leadership, on the other hand, opens up employee contributions, thus increasing the organization's capacity and capability.

How do *you* lead? How do leaders in your organization lead, Reactively or Creatively?

## CONDITIONS FOR SCALE

The Leadership Circle Profile is designed to measure all the leadership conditions necessary and sufficient for scaling leadership. The *right conditions* must be present for leadership at scale to occur. It is very similar to how a lump of coal is transformed, under the right conditions, into a beautiful diamond. You might have some of the elements required to create one—a source of carbon, tremendous pressure and heat, and millions of years buried under the earth's surface—but if the exact conditions required to create a diamond are not in place, then it just won't happen. Likewise, if the conditions for scaling your leadership are not right, it won't happen.

The Inner Circle of the Creative half of the LCP represents *a complete set of conditions necessary for leadership to scale* (see Figure 2.5). Each condition is interdependent with all the others—that is, each requires and is required by the others. The 18 dimensions in the outer circle are the competencies required to put those conditions in place.

Six conditions are required for scale: Creative Leadership, Deep Relationship, Radically Human, Systems Awareness, Purposeful Achievement, and Generative Tension.

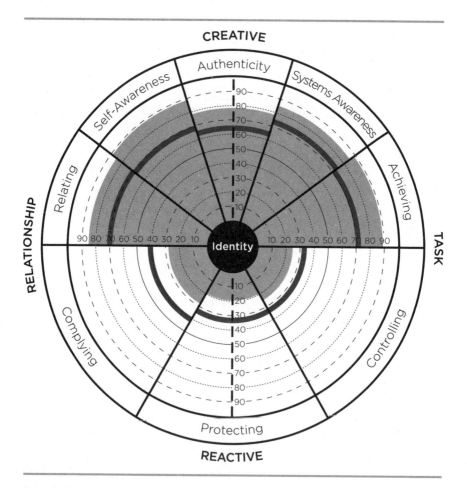

**FIGURE 2.5**   The Inner Circle

## Condition 1: Creative Leadership

The most effective response to escalating complexity is to create a more agile, innovative, adaptive, engaging, high-performance, and high-fulfillment culture and organizational structure. This kind of organization simply cannot arise from Reactive leadership; Creative leadership is required. So, the first condition for scale is to adopt an evolutionary posture toward your leadership—upgrade leadership, individually and collectively, from Reactive to Creative (and eventually Integral leadership). This is an overarching condition. All other conditions depend on and support this move.

In the LCP, this condition is represented by a move from the Reactive half of the circle to the Creative half.

Reactive leadership limits scale while Creative leadership scales in multiples. Creative leaders raise the game of everyone around them. They act as proficiently in one-on-one interactions as they do in team and organizational settings. They know when to be a member of the team, when to participate, when to open the door for others, and when to lead by providing direction. And they accomplish all this (and more) in an easy manner that invites and inspires others to perform at their best and play full out.

Creative leaders create commitment and loyalty to the organization and its mission. They also create an open, honest, authentic, optimistic, generative, and innovative culture where the best ideas can emerge, be implemented, and where everyone is encouraged to develop.

## Condition 2: Deep Relationship

Leadership is scaling the capacity and capability of others and the organization to create outcomes that matter most. Scale is achieved by multiplying our talent through and with others, which only happens in deep relationship. Great leaders foster deep relationship.

Deep relationship is represented in the LCP as *Relating*.

Deep relationship is more than a means to scale, yet scale depends on it. A worthy end in itself, it means great leaders genuinely love and care about the people they work with and who work for them. Members of great teams—the highest performing ones—love each other. Work becomes joyful when we persevere together in relationships that nurture and challenge us.

The best leaders get things done through the relationships they develop at every level inside and outside the organization (one on one, one on team, team on organization). The deeper those relationships, the more solid are the foundations for scale. When the people we lead and with whom we work know we care—know we have their best interests at heart—they are willing to give their discretionary energy to creating what matters. Scale requires being in deep relationship based on the firm foundation of trust, transparency, and honesty. It is foundational to the courageous truth-telling required to be collectively intelligent, getting our best thinking on the table, and innovating creative solutions to vexing problems.

Deep relationship *unlocks human imagination.* An expanded imagination (versus constricted) is an essential condition for the organization, and its leadership, to scale. It also requires learning to be very relationally and interpersonally skillful, developing the abilities to mentor and develop those around us and to foster the high levels of teamwork and collaboration.

Deep relationship allows leadership teams to *persevere together.* This is a crucial differentiating capability for leadership today—to hang in with each other over the long haul, to build through experience an unassailable trust that can survive the vicissitudes of a VUCA world. This creates a *durable agility* in the organization that allows for strategic pivoting when the VUCA world comes knocking.

### Condition 3: Radically Human

Taking an evolutionary posture toward our leadership and leading the organization's ongoing evolution is a radically human requirement. It demands the vulnerability to learn "out loud" in deep relationship with those around us with an unusual degree of humility, self-awareness, courage, and integrity.

This radically human condition is represented in the LCP by the dimensions of *Self-Awareness* and *Authenticity.*

Typically, leaders see the changes needed in the organization as outside themselves. That means we try to change *it* and not *us.* Although our development gaps are on full display, we prefer the insulating delusion that *others* need to do most of the changing. Leading ongoing, even disruptive change requires letting ourselves be disrupted. It means starting with yourself as both the problem and the solution, and doing so openly with those you lead. This encourages your people to do the same. It's a highly vulnerable act. And it's the most powerful thing a leader can do to hold the organization accountable to evolve.

Some think we need to know all the answers and exert control over the people who work for and with us. But these false beliefs—the illusion of knowing and the illusion of control—prevent us from evolving. We need to shift from *knowing* to *learning* and from *controlling* to *empowering*. Leaders who scale leadership start with themselves by letting go and then learn out loud (publicly), and embracing the vulnerability of not knowing. You drop your defenses and transparently lead the transformation as the one who does the most changing. You ask for feedback, listen for learning, and seek first to understand. You own your mistakes (knowing everyone makes them) and apologize. You have nothing to lose except your ego.

All of this requires more than learning new skills. It requires maturing the inner game of leadership. The inner game runs the outer game, and the kind of leadership that scales rises on a highly mature inner game. This is a profound shift of mind and heart (about which we have more to say as this book unfolds).

To go higher, you must go deeper, becoming literate in the pathways of transformation and getting in leadership shape.

When we choose to be more radically human with one another (beautifully incomplete, imperfect, and vulnerable in our evolving), we begin to create this condition for scale. We do so with *fierce humility and vulnerability to be a learner on a journey with other learners*. We are humbled by the magnitude of our mission. We understand we are tiny compared to the waters in which we navigate. Yet, we can lead into the magnificence of what is emerging through deep relationship with each other and with all our stakeholders.

### Condition 4: Systems Awareness

Highly Creative leaders think "big picture;" they see and design systems for higher, more durable, and more agile performance in a VUCA world.

Design is the primary determinate of performance. Thus, you and your organization are perfectly designed for the performance you are getting. Organizations need to be *designed* for engagement, adaptability, innovation, agility, and scaling leadership. Typically, they are not. Therefore, leaders capable of scaling organizations that are fit for a VUCA reality must develop the capacity (individually and especially collectively) to think systemically and design an organization capable of thriving into the future.

This condition is represented on the LCP by the dimension of *Systems Awareness*.

Scaling leadership throughout the organization requires leaders to be designed for development. In *Mastering Leadership*, we describe how we work with our clients to take a systemic approach to scaling leadership. This book builds on that. Fredric Laloux's book, *Reinventing Organizations,* provides multiple case studies of leaders successfully scaling their organizations with new and innovative designs. Robert Kegan and Lisa Lahey, in their book *An Everyone Culture*, describe Deliberately Developmental Organizations, how they are designed, and the kinds of structures and processes used to create a culture where everyone grows.

These organizations are designed to harvest the *feedback-rich environment* all around us. We've heard that we need to get more feedback from the people who work with us and for us, as well as from our customers, our suppliers, our communities, and on and on. Most organizations are a wasteland of feedback and support, yet every one of us is constantly swimming in a feedback-rich environment. What's often missing is that leaders don't harvest this feedback and act on it.

In most leadership systems, feedback is energy in the system that is typically ignored, wasted, or discarded versus being valued, respected, and leveraged. How do we treat feedback in the organization as free solar, wind, or geothermal energy for the system? When we think of feedback as free energy, we design systems and practices that enable us to harvest the feedback around us to use effectively and efficiently. We can't scale leadership without institutionalizing supportive, challenging feedback systems for development.

### Condition 5: Purposeful Achievement

Great leaders call us, individually and collectively, to a higher purpose. They inspire us to give our discretionary energy to a cause greater than ourselves. Being driven by purpose, they turn that purpose into a clear, lofty, strategic vision that translates into strategy and execution.

This condition is represented by the dimension of *Achieving* on the LCP.

Great leaders catalyze alignment by channeling the aspirations and dreams of those who work *for* and *with* them. They coauthor a vision and direction with their people by engaging in dialogue that aligns everyone in the organization. They clearly see that their personal values and purposes can be fulfilled by working toward these purposes. With an abiding focus on mission and vision, organizations naturally fall into high alignment. People can disagree strongly—and they often do—but they do so in trust, knowing all are committed to the same things.

The condition of purposefulness is required by every one of the other conditions. It is the beating heart of Creative leadership, the motivation to develop oneself, authentically, vulnerably, radically. It is the glue of alignment and the durable agility need to persevere together.

In the presence of powerful purpose and compelling vision, people and systems evolve. It is a condition for leadership at scale.

### Condition 6: Generative Tension

Tension is a component in each of the conditions. There is a *Generative Tension* in the gap between our aspirations and our current reality. Victor Frankl called it *Noö-Dynamics*. Robert Fritz called it *Structural Tension*. Peter Senge called it *Creative Tension*. Gary Hamel and C. K. Prahalad called it *Strategic Intent*.

Great leaders cultivate this tension at every level. They establish it by committing to what matters most, and by fiercely and compassionately telling the truth about current situations. At the personal level, leaders cultivate it by facing their development gaps. At the organizational level, they orchestrate the dialog that establishes organizational identity (mission, vision, values), an honest SWOT analysis, and the rigors of transformational redesign.

Leadership that scales requires holding everyone—ourselves, our team, and the organization—in a development gap. Thus, as leaders, we become the Chief Development Officer of our organizations. We adopt and take responsibility for an aggressive *Development Agenda*—one on self, one on other, one on team, and team on organization. We commit to building the capacity and capability of leaders in teams and throughout the company.

## BRIDGING THE DEVELOPMENT GAP

The LCP is designed to drive, individual and collective, leadership development. It provides direct feedback to leaders on how they are showing up, both Reactively and Creatively, helping leaders make the shift into Creative leadership and more effectively lead in today's VUCA environment. (See Figure 2.6.)

Every leader has a profile, and every leadership team and Extended Leadership Team has a collective leadership profile that reflects how team members show up together to lead the organization. That profile is either cancelling out the conditions for leadership at scale or putting the conditions in place and getting a multiple on leadership. Again, we ask, which self are you deploying?

The investment needed to upgrade our individual and collective leadership so we can thrive in a VUCA environment is now, more than ever, a business imperative.

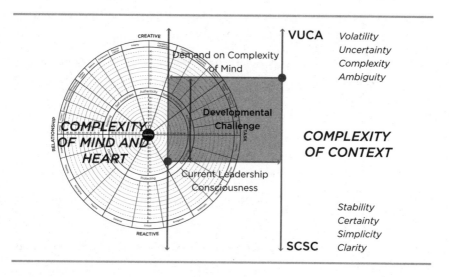

**FIGURE 2.6** The Development Gap

## HOMEWORK

Reflecting on your LCP results and completing a development plan as you read further will greatly enhance your leadership. Here's your homework:

Take 20 minutes to fill out the free Leadership Circle Self-Assessment that comes with this book. You can find a link to it at www.leadershipcircle.com.

After you complete the assessment, we will email you your results, an interpretation guide, and a leadership development plan to be used with this book.

# Chapter 3
# Getting a Street View on Leadership

*How Senior Leaders Describe Other Senior Leaders*

As a leader, you have likely spent considerable time thinking about the strengths that would make you, and the leaders on your team, more effective. We all want to know what works and what does not. We want our leadership to give us a competitive advantage in the marketplace.

These questions are not new, but they are rarely addressed in a new way—from a *street view* of leadership—not what leadership pundits say, not more theory. Rather, it's how leaders describe, in their own words, the differences between *effective* and *ineffective* leadership. When asked to provide feedback on our leadership strengths and weaknesses, how would they describe you or me?

To answer these questions, we did something we have not seen done before (not that it hasn't been done, but we have not seen it). We turned to the written comments in our LCP database—the open-ended comments provided at the end of each survey in response to questions about our greatest leadership strengths and challenges. We hypothesized that this could be a gold mine—that is, if we sifted our database and studied the feedback leaders provide to each other, we would learn a lot about how effectively Creative and Reactive leaders lead.

So, we analyzed our database of written comments gathered from more than 150,000 leaders around the world. Since most 360 surveys have more than 10 raters, in effect, we were able to draw from more than 1.5 million surveys. We sorted and sampled this data and then performed a Matrix Content Analysis on the written comments. (See Appendix C for a description of the study methodology.)

We focused our study on senior leadership (levels 1 through 3 or 4 in large organizations). The following list shows the selection criteria applied to leaders in the study.

- Executive leadership
- Large organizations
- At least five direct reports
- No more than two leaders from the same organization
- English speaking
- Australia, New Zealand, the United States, United Kingdom, and Canada

The LCP database was rank-ordered (see Appendix C for this methodology), and four samples were taken. On one end of the database, we sampled from the most highly Creative and least Reactive leaders; on the other end, we sampled the most highly Reactive and least Creative leaders. These two groups represent 56 percent of our database (28 percent in each group). We also sampled the middle two groups (Mid-Creative and Mid-Reactive) to represent the full spectrum of leadership found in our data (see Figure 3.1).

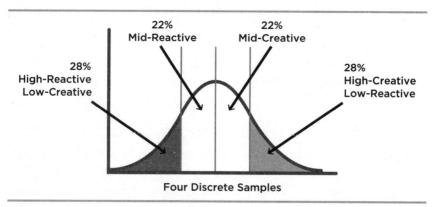

**Four Discrete Samples**

**FIGURE 3.1** Four Discrete Samples

**Table 3.1**    Composition of Leaders in the Comment Study Sample

- 237 companies
- 29 industries
- 6 countries
- 4113 raters

- Executive Leaders
- 100 highly Reactive leaders
- 100 highly Creative leaders
- 50 in each of the middle groups

- 186 males (62%)
- 114 females (38%)
- 22% of the highly Reactive group were female
- 54% of the highly Creative group were female
- These differences are reflective of the overall database

## SAMPLE DEMOGRAPHICS

The large sample used in our research (see Table 3.1) includes 300 senior leaders from 237 companies in 29 industries and 6 countries, along with 4,113 raters (mostly senior and upper-middle managers—board members through level 4 leaders), who provided both quantitative and written feedback to the 300 leaders.

## HOW DIFFERENT ARE THESE GROUPS?

While we sampled the leaders in our study and sorted them into four groups (see Figure 3.1), we start our review of the results of this study by focusing on the differences between the High-Creative and the High-Reactive leaders.

Given the way we sampled the database, we expected to see big differences between these two groups, and we did. Figure 3.2 shows the aggregate leadership Profile of High-Creative (and Low-Reactive) leaders. Scores in the top (Creative) half of the Profile for this group of 100 leaders are quite high, while Reactive scores in the bottom half are quite low.

For the 100 leaders in the High-Reactive group, the picture is reversed; these Profiles are very different, as expected (see Figure 3.3). The Profiles in Figures 3.2 and 3.3 show just how differently these two groups of leaders are being experienced by those around them.

These two groups represent 56 percent of the Extended Leadership Teams of large Western organizations. Both groups are highly talented and capable, but they are completely different in terms of how they show up as leaders.

Figure 3.4 summarizes the average Creative and Reactive score for the two groups' Profiles. The average score for all 18 key Creative

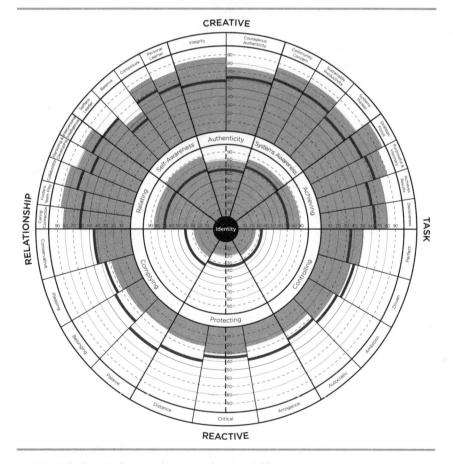

**FIGURE 3.2** High-Creative Leaders' Profile

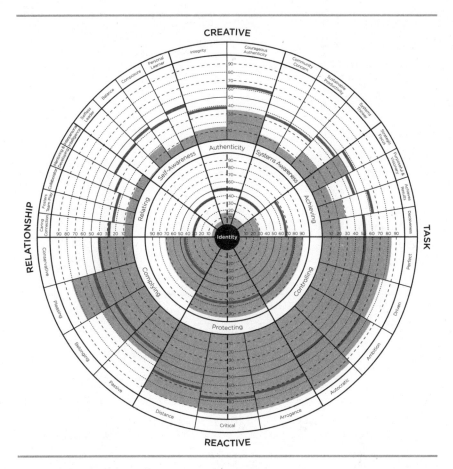

**FIGURE 3.3**   High-Reactive Leaders' Profile

Competencies in the top half of the circle for the *High-Creative* leaders is at the 87th percentile (higher than 87 percent of leaders in our norm base). The *Reactive* scores for this group average at the 9th percentile (lower than 91 percent of leaders in the norm base). In contrast, the key Creative Competency scores of the High-Reactive leaders averaged at the 14th percentile with the Reactive scores averaging at the 94th percentile.

Every leader has a profile, and the Profile of these two groups of leaders shows large measured differences. But, would these differences show up in the workplace? Statisticians use a metric called *Effect Size* to measure if such a difference would be experienced in day-to-day work environments. An effect size score of less than 0.3 is not meaningful, but at 0.3 and beyond, statisticians expect to see noticeable differences in the

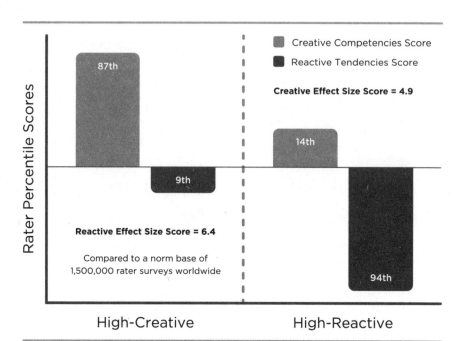

**FIGURE 3.4** Average Creative and Reactive Scores for the Two Profiles

impact of these two groups of leaders on the organizations and people they lead. Effect sizes beyond 0.8 suggest large, practical, and meaningful differences in the way these leaders lead. The effect size between the Creative scores of these two groups is 4.9, and the effect size between their Reactive scores is 6.4. Clearly the difference between these two groups is *huge*!

The same is true of the Leadership Effectiveness scores for these two groups. The previous chapter introduced the five-question Leadership Effectiveness scale that measures the degree to which a leader is perceived by others as being effective (see Table 2.1). We also showed that this result correlates highly (0.93) to the average key Creative Competency score in the top half of the circle, while the average Reactive score is strongly but inversely correlated (–0.68). Given these correlations, we would expect to see different Leadership Effectiveness scores between these two groups (see Figure 3.5). The Leadership Effectiveness of High-Creative leaders averaged at the 87th percentile verses the 10th percentile for High-Reactive leaders. The effect size here between our scores was very high at 4.37.

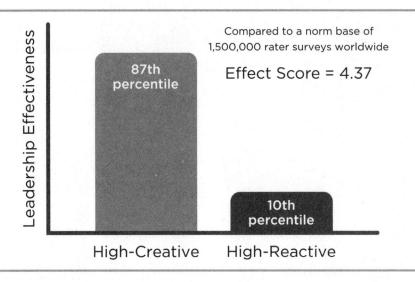

**FIGURE 3.5**   Leadership Effectiveness of High-Creative and High-Reactive Leaders

Not only are the percentile scores dramatically different, but the effect size scores are huge. *These groups could not be more different in the way they show up as leaders!*

### SO WHAT?

Let's be clear who we are learning from and about. This study is focused on the membership of the Extended Leadership Teams (ELT) of large organizations (including the CEO and his or her direct reports, their direct reports, and perhaps Level 4 managers—see Figure 3.6).

The ELT of most organizations is comprised of leaders across the entire spectrum of leadership—from highly Creative and effective to highly Reactive and ineffective. This begs the question about your ELT: "How collectively effective is *your* team of leaders?"

When a wide distribution of Creative and Reactive leaders is on the ELT, our experience suggests there is much wasted energy. The collective intelligence of most ELTs is often below the average intelligence of team members because the high performers and the low performers cancel out each other. The most highly effective leaders are counterbalanced by the least effective—their efforts are negated for the most part. This is not a

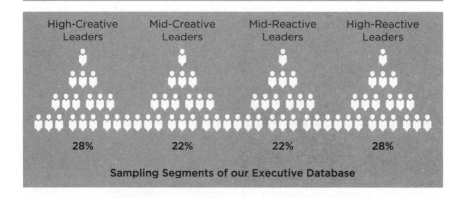

**FIGURE 3.6**   Representative Sample of the Extended Leadership Team

picture of competitive advantage. Rather, it is a picture of the development gap seen in most organizations.

*The organization cannot perform at a level higher than the collective effectiveness of the top leadership group.* When high-performing standouts are dragged down by poor performers, frustrating the high performers and stifling the performance of business that employs them, the leadership team is not optimized to operate effectively in a VUCA business environment.

In the next few chapters, we'll look at how leaders describe in writing the differences between these two groups of leaders—what makes Creative leadership so effective and Reactive leadership so ineffective. These differences show up in the written comments.

---

**REFLECTION**

Take time to reflect on and answer these questions:

- How do you show up as a leader? Creative? Reactive?
- How does the way you show up impact your direct reports, your teams, and your organization?
- Do you believe you are as effective as you can be as a leader? As a leadership team? If not, what needs to change? How will you change it?

# Chapter 4
# High-Creative Leadership Strengths

*What Differentiates the Most Effective Leaders*

All leaders have strengths. All leaders have weaknesses, even the best leaders. In this chapter we ask: "How do leaders describe the very best leaders?" You will see that what they say differentiates the most effective leaders from the least effective, focusing on the strengths of the most effective, High-Creative leaders.

We analyzed 1,350 pages of written comments around these two questions:

1. What is this person's greatest leadership strength, asset, skill, or talent?
2. What is this person's greatest leadership challenge or area for development?

We engaged an independent research firm to perform a Matrix Content Analysis on these written comments. The researchers sorted the data into 77 categories of the most commonly mentioned themes comprised of 40 leadership strengths and 37 leadership liabilities. (See Appendix D for a description of the research firm, the research methodology, and definitions of all 77 categories of strengths and weaknesses.) After sorting the data into categories/themes, the researchers calculated endorsement scores for each—that is, how often these strengths or liabilities were mentioned.

Here's an example of how they kept score: If a group of us was rating Nadia and only one of us endorses her for *courage*, her endorsement score is a one-half (.5) point. If three or more of us endorse Nadia for that same quality, her score is one (1) point. This is the maximum score allowed on a given strength or liability. Therefore, if Nadia has 20 raters and all endorse her for courage, it would still count as one (1) point.

So, the maximum score any leader can get on a given theme is 1. And with 100 leaders in each group (High-Creative and High-Reactive), the maximum score for any theme for the entire group would be 100 (not likely, but theoretically possible).

## STRENGTHS OF HIGH-CREATIVE LEADERS

Here are a few quotes from leader-raters[1] describing different High-Creative leaders in their written comments:

> She has a deep and broad knowledge of the business, and she relates well to people. Her naturally collaborative and engaging style enables her to build teams and challenge people constructively. She engenders respect, trust, and a willingness in people to stretch themselves and work together.

> He is the kind of leader who challenges and motivates you to do your best. You feel comfortable stretching because you know he won't second-guess a judgment call. If he disagrees after the fact, he will turn the situation into a learning opportunity rather than offer unproductive criticism.

> I have always found her leadership style compelling because she does a great job of communicating. She is able to convey reality in a meaningful, tangible way by using stories, examples, and analogies that paint the picture for people. So, her greatest strength is her ability to connect people to the mission in a way they understand.

| CREATIVE | THEMATIC STRENGTHS | REACTIVE |
|---|---|---|
| 79 | Strong People Skills | 28 |
| 76 | Visionary | 54 |
| 61 | Team Builder | 18 |
| 53 | Personable/Approachable | 20 |
| 49 | Leads by Example | 7 |
| 49 | Passion & Drive | 61 |
| 46 | Good Listener | 3 |
| 46 | Develops People | 11 |
| 43 | Empowers People | 18 |
| AVG 54.4    42 | Positive Attitude | 20    AVG 24.0 |

Creative leaders endorsed **2.3 times** more often than Reactive leaders

**FIGURE 4.1**   Top 10 Most-Endorsed Strengths for High-Creative Leaders

We are impressed by how caring, precise, and well-written most comments are. In our years of experience, we find that raters genuinely care about the person for whom they are providing feedback, and their comments reflect this. They consistently assume that if the leaders receiving the feedback would take it in and act on it, they could take their leadership to the next level.

On the *left side* of Figure 4.1 are the endorsement scores for the top 10 strengths of the 100 leaders in the High-Creative leader group, in rank order from highest to lowest. (Each score has a bar graph extending from the middle to provide a visual representation of the relative strength of these scores.) On the *right side* are the scores on these same thematic strengths for the High-Reactive group of leaders.

At a glance, you can compare and see the difference between how High-Creative and High-Reactive leaders are described. Each thematic strength in the figure is presented using descriptors commonly used by raters in this study.

## TOP 10 SKILLS FOR HIGH-CREATIVE LEADERS

Descriptions of the 10 most strongly endorsed strengths of High-Creative leaders, in language commonly found in the written comments, are listed below:

1. **Strong People Skills:** Has a high level of interpersonal capability. Is caring, compassionate, big-hearted, and respectful. Connects well with others and makes them feel valuable.
2. **Visionary:** Communicates a compelling vision of the future that fosters alignment. Knows and sets strategic direction and business plans that allow teams/organizations to thrive.
3. **Team Builder:** Unites, engages, and supports the team's efforts. Gives support to team members and advocates for initiatives.
4. **Personable/Approachable:** Is friendly, likable, and has a good sense of humor. Maintains an open-door policy. Is accessible and available.
5. **Leads by Example:** Good role model. "Walks the talk."
6. **Passion and Drive:** Enthusiastic, driven, and strongly committed to the success of the organization and self.
7. **Good Listener:** Attentive and present when people are presenting their views.
8. **Develops People:** Shares experience and provides mentoring, coaching, career planning, and development experience to ensure growth and development.
9. **Empowers People:** Shares leadership and encourages people to take ownership, find their own solutions, make their own decisions, and learn from mistakes. Trusts people's ability and their willingness to follow directions.
10. **Positive Attitude:** Optimistic and upbeat with a can-do attitude.

*Strong People Skills* is number one on the list. Look at the huge difference in the scores for High-Creative and High-Reactive leaders on this strength: 79 for High-Creative leaders and only 28 for High-Reactive leaders. This means that, with a high score of 79, a very high percentage of High-Creative leaders were endorsed for their strong people skills. By comparison, with a score of 28, a relatively low number of High-Reactive leaders were endorsed for people skills.

Both High-Creative and High-Reactive leaders are described as having considerable visionary and strategic strengths. High-Creative leaders are much stronger in this category with a score of 76 compared to 54. Think about combining clear, compelling, strategic vision with strong people skills. *This is a powerful combination.* And while High-Reactive leaders have considerable visionary strength, they do not multiply that strength through people. Their people strengths are described as quite low by comparison.

High-Creative leaders were strongly endorsed on *passion and drive* with a score of 49; however, High-Reactive were even more strongly endorsed at 61. This is curious. Is it possible that High-Reactive leaders over-drive and/or might they be driven differently in a way that limits their effectiveness? Our researchers point out that High-Reactive leaders were described as more *driven*, while High-Creative were more *passionate.*[2] The distinction here is that *passion* has more to do with creating something larger than oneself—mission, impact, the organization's contribution, and so on—while *driven* is more about an individual's ambition to succeed. Our research suggests that there is a difference in how these two groups of leaders are motivated and motivate others. (We will say more about this distinction as we go along.)

As we scan the list and compare scores, you can see these additional large differences between High-Creative and High-Reactive leaders:

- Team builder: 61 to 18
- Leads by example: 49 to 7
- Good listener: 46 to 3
- Develops people: 46 to 11

These are big differences. In fact, as we average the scores for both lists, we see that these top 10 strengths are mentioned *2.3 times more often for High-Creative leaders than for High-Reactive leaders.*

### BIGGEST STRENGTH GAPS

Figure 4.2 shows the biggest strength gaps between High-Creative and High-Reactive leaders.

The biggest gaps between High-Reactive and High-Creative leaders are in the areas of *people skills, listening, team building,* and *leading by example.* The gaps are a little smaller but still substantial in *calm presence, empowering people, acting with integrity,* and *leading with vision.*

The gaps are big because these two groups of leaders are experienced in very different ways. Recall that the High-Creative group had an average Leadership Effectiveness score at the 87th percentile while the High-Reactive leaders were ranked at the 10th percentile on Effectiveness. If you want to know what kind of leadership scales, just look at the top 10 list for High-Creative leaders and the biggest gaps list! This is what leaders say works most powerfully.

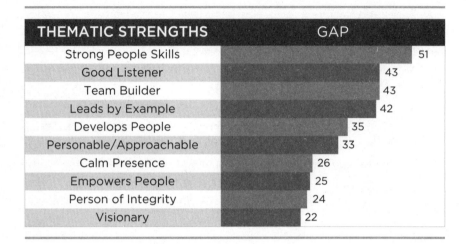

| THEMATIC STRENGTHS | GAP |
|---|---|
| Strong People Skills | 51 |
| Good Listener | 43 |
| Team Builder | 43 |
| Leads by Example | 42 |
| Develops People | 35 |
| Personable/Approachable | 33 |
| Calm Presence | 26 |
| Empowers People | 25 |
| Person of Integrity | 24 |
| Visionary | 22 |

**FIGURE 4.2**   Biggest Gaps between High-Creative and High-Reactive Leader Strengths

## WHAT SURPRISED US?

We were surprised—in fact, blown away—by the predominance of relationship strengths embodied in High-Creative leaders. Then we asked ourselves why we were so surprised. As we reflected on this, we realized we have been looking at leadership effectiveness through a *quantitative* lens more than a *qualitative* lens. Quantitative and qualitative measures emphasize two different stories that, when they come together, make a complete story.

If you look closely at the LCP of High-Creative leaders in Chapter 3 (see Figure 3.2), you will notice that the inner-circle Relating Score is at the 85th percentile, while in the High-Reactive Profile (see Figure 3.3), this score is at the 5th percentile—a difference of 80 percentile points. Clearly, High-Creative leaders lead more relationally. Why, then, were we so surprised?

When we look through the *quantitative* lens at our correlation research, we see that *Achieving* (comprised of *Purpose, Vision, Strategy, Results Focus,* and *Decisiveness*) is more positively correlated to Leadership Effectiveness and Business Performance than is *Relating* (comprised of *Caring, Teamwork, Collaboration, Mentoring,* and *Interpersonal Competence*). Both *Achieving* and *Relating* are high, but *Achieving* is higher.

Furthermore, when we put *Relating* and *Achieving* together in a regression equation, *Achieving* takes up more of the explanation of what makes for an effective leader. This has always made sense to us—after all, the LCP is a business survey, not a marriage survey. So naturally, getting results would be most highly correlated and pick up most of the variation in Leadership Effectiveness. Consequently, we expected more of a focus on *Achieving Results* to top the list of High-Creative leaders. This was not the case.

When we look at the written comment data, it's skewed toward relationship, suggesting that effective leadership is about *leading people.* When you combine these people strengths with the other High-Creative endorsed strengths of passion, vision, authenticity, and a calm approachable presence, you have a recipe for *creating the conditions for scaling leadership.*

This research strongly suggests that if you lead, you are in the people business. You still need to have the other leadership skills, qualities, and capabilities to be sure, but *leading in today's VUCA world makes being in relationship at scale non-negotiable.* This may be why, in the latest research, female leaders are found to be higher performing than male leaders; women tend to lead more *relationally* than men.


## CONTRIBUTION OF WOMEN LEADERS

Another important finding in this study has to do with *gender* differences within senior leadership ranks. If you recall the demographics for this study (see Chapter 3, Table 3.1) and look at the number of women in the High-Creative and High-Reactive leader groups, you can get a sense for why women leaders are making a notable contribution to the leadership of their organizations. There are proportionally fewer women overall in this study (62 percent male to 38 percent female, which is consistent with the ratio in our database of women at senior levels), yet there are more women in the High-Creative group (54 percent) and significantly fewer women in the High-Reactive group (22 percent). In other words, women tend to lead more Creatively than men. When we measure this quantitatively, *women leaders are rated 15 to 20 percentile points more Creative and less Reactive than their male counterparts.*

A 2017 study confirms our findings. Nordea—one of Europe's largest banks—conducted a study of almost 11,000 publicly traded companies around the globe. The study showed that, on average, companies led by women CEOs or board chairs performed better than those companies led by men. They delivered an annualized return of 25 percent since 2009, more than twice as much as the 11 percent generated by companies in the MSCI World Index. Unfortunately, only 4 percent of the companies surveyed by Nordea had a woman serving as CEO or board chair. In 96 percent of the companies, men served in those positions.[3]

To summarize, this data suggests that *women lead more effectively than men*. Since we see a strong positive correlation between Leadership Effectiveness and Creative Competency scores, we conclude that women are more effective because they tend to lead more Creatively and less Reactively. Women leaders are more Creative, more effective, and tend to get better results than men. The predominance of relationship strengths in the Top 10 list suggests that *women are more effective because they lead more relationally*. Doing so also requires a high degree of self-awareness and authenticity.

Mary Edwards is a good example.

A few years ago, we debriefed the Leadership Circle Profile with a senior leader at Accenture named Mary Edwards. Mary's results on Leadership Effectiveness put her in the 97th percentile, meaning she scored higher than 97 percent of the leaders in our norm base. Whenever we have a chance to work with a leader that is as exceptional as Mary, we ask, "What have you learned about being a leader that makes you so effective?"

Mary pondered the question, then said it all boiled it down to three things:

> The first thing I learned, over 20 years ago, was how to act confident when I wasn't feeling confident, how to be comfortable being uncomfortable. I had joined a consulting firm and was surrounded by super-smart people. I often had a voice in my head that said, "You're not good enough, you don't know enough, you're not skilled enough, you don't have enough to add." At first, the voice kept me from fully contributing and from feeling powerful. If I was ever going to lead in a direction or to bring value to the organization, I had to speak up with the confidence I sometimes wasn't feeling. I had to enter a room with the confidence I sometimes wasn't feeling. I had to learn to get comfortable taking on uncomfortable things— whether that was new assignments, providing feedback, or

dealing with difficult client situations. If I couldn't do those things, how would my team ever have confidence in me or follow me into uncomfortable situations? I couldn't make myself feel confident or comfortable—but I could act that way. Eventually, I actually became confident and comfortable even in situations that were quite uncomfortable; I gained confidence that I had the ability to figure things out.

Second, I learned that I needed to create an environment around me where people know that I want and need ongoing feedback. I learned that it's hard for a leader in a position of power to create an environment where people will be open, frank, and honest with what they think. People are afraid they will be punished for telling the hard truth when, in fact, the hard truth is what all leaders need to be the best they can be, to manage risk, and to drive to the best outcomes. To counter this tendency, I spend a lot of time reinforcing with my teams that they can tell me anything, including if there is something I am doing that is not good for the team or for the client. I commit to doing the same for them. And then I regularly do that—immediately and often—and ask them to do the same for me. For instance, after a client discussion, I might say, "You handled that really well. I noticed that when the client asked a question, you were unsure in your response, which you signaled by talking more. One thing you might try the next time you are feeling that way is pausing, instead of talking. Give yourself time to think." And then I will always say something like, "Is there anything I could have done better? It's really hard to see yourself in these meetings. I know I interrupted the client once and shouldn't have. Is there anything else you noticed?" In this way, I give and get feedback that helps us do better as individuals and as a team. As a result, I get the very best from my people and together we create the very best from all of us. It's a feedback-rich environment.

Third, I realized that I am very directive by nature. I communicated in a way that made my team believe I had it all figured out and there was no room for discussion. In fact, I wanted the discussion that led to the better idea. So I had to learn to help the team understand that—not just once, but all the time.

I learned that I had to say to people, "I may sound like I have thought through something and come to a conclusion. That's just how I tend to communicate. This is just my thought right now and it may or may not have merit. I want your ideas and together we will figure out what is best."

We also worked with another female leader, an extremely talented executive who rose rapidly through the leadership ranks—five levels in just five years—in one of the largest, most successful food manufacturers in the United States. We asked her what led to her success with this company and she didn't hesitate to answer:

Oh, that's easy. I decided a number of years ago that whenever I was asked a question or to give my opinion or advice in a meeting, I would always tell the truth. I never hold back. So now people just trust me. They trust that whether I'm right or wrong, whether they agree or disagree, I'm going to give them the straight truth every time. That's been so valued in my organization that I've just moved up, up, up.

In a VUCA world in which collective leadership carries the day, relational, emotionally intelligent, and authentic leadership is at a premium. We believe this is exactly what women are bringing into leadership.

*Why, then, do women have such a hard time getting promoted into senior leadership positions?* We believe it is because of systemic bias created and maintained by a male-dominated power structure. This is the downside of a patriarchy. Patriarchy maintains that women have their place (not at the top), and men know best. It does not include honor, or respect women for their contributions. Instead, it discriminates against them.

We men have been doing all we can for centuries to keep women out of leadership. Fortunately, this attitude is changing, but every one of us in a leadership position can and must use our influence to accelerate this change. Making women full and equal partners in leadership is a competitive advantage and, in an increasingly VUCA world, has never been more necessary.

If you're not leading in a way that makes leadership more inclusive and leveraging the full power and potential of female leadership, then you're not doing your job. We men can all learn a great deal from what women are bringing to leadership.

## SCALING LEADERSHIP

To scale our organizations, we must scale leadership. This is an inherently human process. In the combination of the two lists presented in this chapter (the top 10 list of High-Creative leader strength and the biggest strength gap list), we get a street view of the kind of leadership required for scale. Table 4.1 organizes the strengths of the two lists into the Conditions for Scale.

**Table 4.1**   Leadership Strengths That Create the Conditions for Scale

| Creative Leadership | |
| --- | --- |
| **Deep Relationship** | **Radically Human** |
| Strong people skills | Person of integrity |
| Good listener | Leads by example |
| Team builder | Calm presence |
| Develops people | Personable and approachable |
| Empowers people | Positive attitude |
| **Systems Awareness** | **Purposeful Achievement** |
| **Generative Tension** | Visionary |
| | Passion and drive |

This list goes a long way in describing the conditions for scale outlined earlier. Implied in this list is the fundamental shift from Reactive to Creative. The first condition of scale is making this shift individually and collectively. *This is a very big deal.* As this book unfolds, we will see more and more the importance of upgrading from Reactive to Creative leadership.

The condition of *Deep Relationship* (strong people skills, good listener, team builder, develops people, empowers people) is strongly revealed by the strengths that most differentiate High-Creative leaders. The best leaders lead through relationship and in deep relationship. They listen well. They develop other leaders. They do this one on one, in teams, and across the organization.

The condition of *Radically Human* is also evidenced by this list (leads by example, person of integrity, calm demeanor, positive attitude). The best leaders lead by example with the highest integrity, transparency, and vulnerability. They build an on-the-table culture that is feedback-rich, open, easeful, approachable, and positive.

*Purposeful Achievement* (visionary, passionate, and driven) is required for scale. High-Creative leaders lead from purpose and with passion. They translate that into a vision of the future that captures people's imagination and strategically orients the whole organization. When combined with their people, team building, mentoring, and empowering strengths, they create clarity and alignment on vision and strategy. They align the organization around a co-created vision and strategy and empower people in the organization to go after it. This puts the whole organization in *Generative Tension*. Everyone is in a development gap.

If you want to put in place the conditions for scaling your leadership, these lists point you in the right direction. They are the strengths that work. Then you need to embed all this in the design of the organization, which is the condition of *Systems Awareness*.

Earlier, we met Peter Harmer—the CEO at IAG, a large financial services firm based in Australia. Peter has put in place the conditions for scale, and he has done so systemically. He has designed his organization for learning, for relationship at scale, and has created a feedback-rich environment.

After receiving his LCP feedback, Peter started improving his relationships—first with himself and then with his team and organization. Peter noticed that he had been given a high score on *Distance* and he immediately went to his team to learn what this meant. They told Peter they didn't think he cared. When there were big problems to be dealt with, he always remained calm—nonplussed, unemotional, robotic. What Peter thought was a strength—his ability to remain calm on the outside when he was actually concerned, even anxious, on the inside—had become a liability for his leadership. He was overplaying it.

Peter learned that he needed to be more transparent, vulnerable, and let his team know that he was concerned, if not terribly worried. He needed to let go and be more radically human, to step into deeper relationship with his team and to scale that across the organization. And the good news—for Peter, his team, and his organization—is that he did all that and more.

When we asked Peter about how he is scaling leadership and relationship, he said, "We have our executive team meeting once a month, and the next day or so we have a WebEx conference call with any of our leaders who wish to join. We go 20 minutes, then open up the meeting for Q&A. We don't have time to answer all the questions from the 1,500 or so participants, but we make a commitment to getting answers for every question within 36 hours of the meeting. This allows me to be in a direct relationship with all my people. I want them to know that I'm there."

That's a *huge* commitment for a CEO! In Peter, you see a leader putting in place all the conditions, first in himself and then embedding them into the design of the system. Peter is a High-Creative leader. He is scaling leadership to grow his organization.

The next chapter explores the strengths of High-Reactive leaders. Spoiler alert: *Many of these strengths do not differentiate you as a leader.* They are important to develop, but when over-relied upon, they limit the leadership's scalability.

## HOMEWORK

- In their book, *Immunity to Change*, Robert Kegan and Lisa Lahey recommend identifying your One Big Thing.[4] What is the one change you could make in the way you lead that would unlock your leadership and take it to the next level?

- Using your LCP Self-Assessment results and the lists of what works (Figures 4.1 and 4.2), we suggest you clarify one strength you want to develop further—the one that would make the most difference in your effectiveness.

- As you reflect on what your One Big Thing might be, we suggest you also solicit feedback. Simply ask people who know you well and whom you trust to help you answer this question: "What is the one thing, if I improved it, that would take my leadership to a whole new level?"

- A Leadership Development Plan comes with this book. It is designed to be used in conjunction with your LCP Self-Assessment and will be sent to you when you complete your self-assessment. Write down your One Big Thing in your Development Plan. There, you will also find suggestions for how to solicit feedback.

# Chapter 5
# The Strengths of High-Reactive Leaders
## *Non-Differentiating Strengths*

High-Reactive leaders have tremendous strengths, too. Consider this comment about Paul. Would you guess that he is a Reactive leader based on the feedback he received?

> Paul's greatest strength is his keen, absolutely brilliant mind. He has a powerful and unique combination of technical savvy, business acumen, and reptilian charisma.

Paul is extraordinarily talented and brings tremendous strength and drive to the table, but we cannot tell from this statement alone that he is a High-Reactive leader. What we learned from this study is that High-Reactive leaders are most strongly endorsed/acknowledged for a much different set of strengths than are High-Creatives. Looking carefully, we see that Paul's strength is being measured as *technically savvy* and *powerfully smart*. In fact, we guess that he was promoted rapidly because of these core skills and strengths.

## TOP 10 STRENGTHS OF HIGH-REACTIVE LEADERS

Here are the top 10 strengths of High-Reactive leaders, listed in rank order:

1. **Drive and Passion:** Enthusiastic, driven, and strongly committed to the success of the organization and self.
2. **Visionary:** Communicates a compelling vision of the future that fosters alignment. Knows and sets strategic direction and business plans that allow teams and organizations to thrive.
3. **Strong Networker:** Builds partnerships with other business leaders. Is good at bringing diverse groups together and provides a strong customer focus.
4. **Domain/Technical Knowledge:** Excellent knowledge, technical skills, and experience—particularly related to the organizational culture and market.
5. **Results Focused:** Knows what needs to be accomplished and how to get results. Holds people accountable, can be depended on to deliver results. Is reliable and action-oriented.
6. **Intelligent/Brilliant:** Keen mind and sharp thinker.
7. **Strong People Skills:** Has a high level of interpersonal capability. Is caring, compassionate, big-hearted, and respectful. Connects well with others and makes them feel valuable.
8. **Creative/Innovative:** Thinks outside the box and pushes for change.
9. **Personable/Approachable:** Is friendly, likable, and has a good sense of humor. Maintains an open-door policy. Is accessible and available.
10. **Positive attitude:** Optimistic and upbeat with a can-do attitude.

Figure 5.1 presents the strengths of High-Reactive leaders on the *right side* in rank order, from highest to lowest. On the *left side* are the scores for the same strengths for High-Creative leaders. *Passion and drive* top the list of strengths for the High-Reactive leader. These strengths were highly endorsed at 61—even more strongly than High-Creative leaders who scored 49. *Visionary,* at 54, was strongly endorsed but not as strong as High-Creatives at 76. Then come the moderate scores for *domain/technical knowledge, results focused, intelligent/brilliant,* with *strong people skills* down the list and not highly endorsed at 28. *Creative/innovative,*

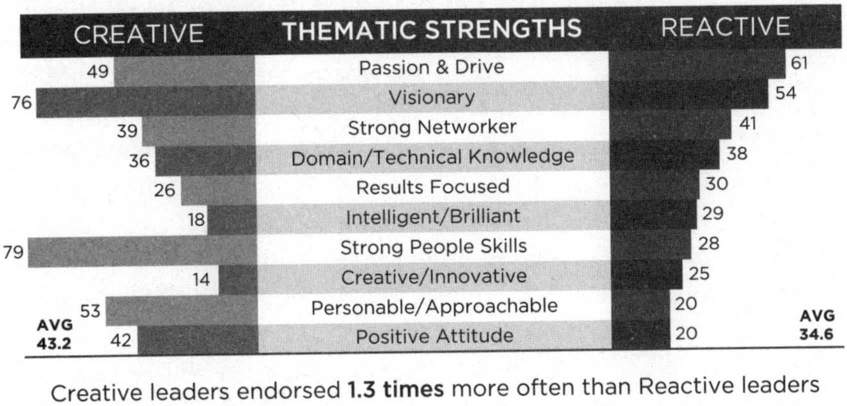

| CREATIVE | THEMATIC STRENGTHS | REACTIVE |
|---|---|---|
| 49 | Passion & Drive | 61 |
| 76 | Visionary | 54 |
| 39 | Strong Networker | 41 |
| 36 | Domain/Technical Knowledge | 38 |
| 26 | Results Focused | 30 |
| 18 | Intelligent/Brilliant | 29 |
| 79 | Strong People Skills | 28 |
| 14 | Creative/Innovative | 25 |
| 53 | Personable/Approachable | 20 |
| AVG 43.2  42 | Positive Attitude | 20  AVG 34.6 |

Creative leaders endorsed **1.3 times** more often than Reactive leaders

**FIGURE 5.1**    Top 10 Most-Endorsed Strengths for High-Reactive Leaders

*personable/approachable,* and *positive attitude* round out the bottom of the top 10 strengths of High-Reactive leaders.

High-Reactive leaders lead with a very different set of strengths than High-Creative leaders. Furthermore, most scores for High-Reactive leaders are moderate to low. Note that *High-Creative leaders are endorsed 1.3 times more often on the strengths for which High-Reactive leaders are most strongly endorsed.* Recall that High-Creative Leaders are endorsed 2.3 times more often for the top 10 High-Creative leader strengths.

Clearly, High-Creative leaders have a tremendous advantage over their High-Reactive counterparts in the kind of strengths they bring to their organizations.

## NON-DIFFERENTIATING STRENGTHS

In Chapter 4, we explored the largest gaps between the strengths of High-Reactive and High-Creative leaders. The three largest gaps were *strong people skills* (51), *good listener* (43), and *team builder* (43). As we discussed the magnitude and import of these gaps, we wondered what we weren't seeing in the data. Like a blinding flash of the obvious, this new question emerged: "What are the *smallest* gaps between these strengths?"

To answer this question, we looked again at the gap list (High-Creative leader scores minus High-Reactive leader scores), but this time we studied the bottom of the list, eager to see what we might learn. Figure 5.2 shows the strengths that had gaps of one point (+ 1) or less than zero. Most of these gaps are negative numbers, meaning High-Reactive leaders are endorsed more often than High-Creative leaders.

High-Reactive leaders are rated 12 points higher on *passion and drive* than High-Creative leaders. In addition, High-Reactive leaders are endorsed more often for being *intelligent, creative/innovative, thorough, hard-working, results focused,* and more.

This led us to another question: "Is it possible to be *too* driven?"

Obviously, the answer is *yes*. We may have worked for or with people whose work-life balance is completely out of whack, who drive themselves and others beyond what is sustainable. And we may ourselves be overdriven from time to time.

High-Reactive leaders are described by other senior leaders as more driven and far less effective than High-Creative leaders. This result is consistent with decades of leadership research showing that *excessive drive* is a big issue with many leaders. We have all heard statements such as, "He's wound too tight," "She is constantly in overdrive," "He is excessively ambitious," and "He is too aggressive for his own good." Such statements indicate that someone is *too driven*—perhaps even dangerously so.

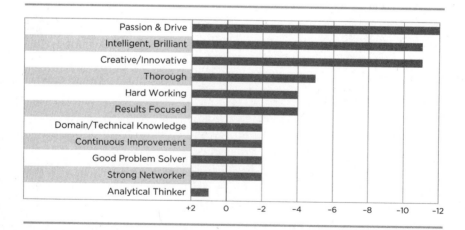

**FIGURE 5.2**    Smallest/Negative Strength Gaps

Almost three decades ago, Robert Kaplan wrote *Beyond Ambition*, which describes what happens to leadership effectiveness when leaders become too driven. Kaplan said: "All expansive [driven] individuals are alike in their highly developed drive to accomplish and to be accomplished. Yet there are important differences in how compulsive that already above-average drive is."[1]

The leader-raters in our study seem to be making a similar distinction between *passion* and *drive*. The data suggest a different kind and/or level of drive that is effective and ineffective. As it turns out, *overdrive* or *over-passion* has associated leadership liabilities.

We also see that *Intelligent/brilliant* is 11 points higher for High-Reactive Leaders, which on the surface seems surprising. Is it possible to be *too* smart? Probably not, but how often have we heard, "He's too smart for his own good," or "She always has to be the smartest one in the room"? The issue here is not the strength itself but how the strength is deployed. *The over-extension of a strength becomes a weakness in most every case.* This is true for *intelligent/brilliant* as well as the other strengths on the list of smallest/negative gaps.

As we studied the data, we were astounded by another finding, displayed in Figure 5.3.

Six of the top 10 strengths for High-Reactive leaders are also on the smallest/negative gap list. As we pondered this finding, we came to a number of surprising conclusions.

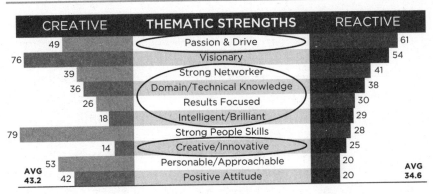

| CREATIVE | THEMATIC STRENGTHS | REACTIVE |
|---|---|---|
| 49 | Passion & Drive | 61 |
| 76 | Visionary | 54 |
| 39 | Strong Networker | 41 |
| 36 | Domain/Technical Knowledge | 38 |
| 26 | Results Focused | 30 |
| 18 | Intelligent/Brilliant | 29 |
| 79 | Strong People Skills | 28 |
| 14 | Creative/Innovative | 25 |
| 53 | Personable/Approachable | 20 |
| **AVG 43.2** 42 | Positive Attitude | 20 **AVG 34.6** |

Creative leaders endorsed **1.3 times** more often than Reactive leaders

**FIGURE 5.3** Non-Differentiating Strengths of High-Reactive Leaders

Reactive leaders are leading with what we now call *Non-Differentiating Strengths*. Think about it. High-Reactive leaders are described similarly to (if not more strongly on these strengths) High-Creative leaders, but they could not be more different in how they are experienced by others as leaders. High-Creative leaders have similar to lower scores on these strengths, and yet they are experienced by others as far more effective than High-Reactive leaders.

This led us to conclude that *High-Reactive leaders are leading with Non-Differentiating Strengths*—strengths that don't differentiate between the most-effective and the least-effective leaders. These Non-Differentiating Strengths comprise the bulk of the strengths for which High-Reactive leaders are endorsed.

Even *results focused* is a Non-Differentiating Strength, and if you push results too hard, it may make you less effective. How counterintuitive is that? The lesson? Not all strengths are equal as it relates to leadership, and if you overplay certain strengths, you get in your own way. You block your effectiveness as a leader.

This led us to another conclusion: Leading from Non-Differentiating Strengths is not scalable leadership, or at least these strengths scale only to a point. They are *necessary* but *insufficient* to leadership. You need to have them or you don't make it into leadership positions, let alone reach the top. But as you move up, they become table stakes. Effective leadership is something entirely different. That "something different" has to do with the strengths for which High-Creative leaders are most strongly endorsed.

As we reflected on this research, something else became obvious: *You don't get to the top of large organizations or any organization without being tremendously talented.* These are equally talented groups of people; High-Reactive and High-Creative leaders are rated similarly on Non-Differentiating Strengths. In fact, High-Reactive leaders are endorsed more often on most of these strengths. Based on that, we might conclude that they are *smarter*, have *more technical and domain knowledge*, and are more of an *innovative genius* than the High-Creative leaders. The data does not allow us to conclude that, however, so we will call it even. Instead, we conclude that High-Reactive and High-Creative leaders are equally and highly talented, but as leaders, they are experienced very differently by those they lead.

The Non-Differentiating Strengths are about getting results through one's own drive and capability (drive, intellect, technical capability, creative genius, and so forth). However, they are *not* about scaling capacity and capability in others and in the organization. When you are leading and driving results primarily through your own individual capability, your leadership has a built-in limit to scale. In fact, *you* are the limit to scale.

Again, we define leadership as *scaling the capacity and capability of the organization to create what matters most*. Non-Differentiating Strengths *limit* the scaling of capacity and capability. These are hindered by the High-Reactive leader's capacity that is, by definition, too limiting. Leaders who make their own capability the focal point of their leadership do not—*cannot*—scale leadership.

Remember, the leader's primary job is to *scale leadership within the organization and then to scale that even further by helping those leaders become collectively effective in the way they lead together and develop other leaders*. This is, in fact, a condition of scaling leadership.

As noted earlier, the organization will never perform at a level higher than the collective effectiveness of its senior leadership. High-Reactive leadership, with its reliance on leading through personal capability and Non-Differentiating Strengths, does not build the capacity and capability of the organization to create what matters most—precisely because it is not focused on *collective effectiveness* and thus does not scale leadership.

When describing a High-Reactive leader named Shari, one person stated this:

> Shari has to develop the ability to allow others' ideas to positively influence her thinking. She must realize that her superior intellect, the confidence she has in her abilities, and her experiential knowledge only make for a strong framework from which to begin in leadership; her view cannot be the whole picture.
>
> Unquestionably, her contributions are affirming to the organization's work and the realization of its goals. However, something is lost in translation in terms of her work, leading to Shari not being perceived as a leader among her peers. Ultimately it is less what Shari does—and that is excellent work—than the way she goes about doing her work and creating a sphere of influence around herself in the process.

Leading through Non-Differentiating Strengths doesn't mean you are *not* making a large contribution, but it does likely mean you are becoming a bottleneck. If you are not scaling leadership, then all key business decisions need to go through you. After all, you have been promoted because you are the one with such amazing intellect, brilliance, technical capability, domain knowledge, and creative/innovative genius. Right?

While this may well be true, as the organization grows and becomes more complex, there comes a point that too many tough, critical decisions are waiting on your doorstep. And waiting and waiting. The pipeline of innovation passes through your office and across your desk 24/7, yet no human being is capable of handling that volume of complexity alone. That means if you don't scale your leadership, *you become the limiting growth factor.*

That doesn't suggest you lack incredible passion or incredible drive nor does it mean you're not a technical domain expert. You may excel when it comes to knowledge in your field. What it does mean, however, is that these things alone won't get you where you need to go.

In fact, as you move up and take on more responsibility and complexity, relying on Non-Differentiating Strengths actually works *against* you instead of *for* you. When you are promoted into management and leadership positions, you had better quickly learn that what got you to this point in your career—your technical domain knowledge, skillset, and work ethic, for example—won't get you or the organization where you need to go.

## REDEFINING LEADERSHIP

Let's look at the strength picture again. Table 5.1 shows the strengths that were endorsed above a score of 20 for both High-Creative and High-Reactive leaders. All Non-Differentiating Strengths including *passion and drive* have been removed from both sides because this represented a negative gap, suggesting a liability for High-Reactive leaders. What do you notice about the results?

High-Creative leaders had 18 Differentiating Strengths with endorsement scores above 20 for a total score of 734. High-Reactive leaders had only four Differentiating Strengths with a total score of 122. The only strongly endorsed Differentiating Strength for High-Reactive leaders was *visionary* with a score of 54. High-Creative leaders scored much higher at 76.

**Table 5.1**  Total Differentiating Strengths for High-Creative and
High-Reactive Leaders

| High-Creative Leader Strengths | | High-Reactive Leader Strengths | |
|---|---|---|---|
| Strong People Skills | 79 | Strong People Skills | 28 |
| Visionary | 76 | Visionary | 54 |
| Team Builder | 61 | | |
| Personable/Approachable | 53 | Personable/Approachable | 20 |
| Leads by example | 49 | | |
| Develops People | 46 | | |
| Good Listener | 46 | | |
| Empowers People | 43 | | |
| Positive Attitude | 42 | Positive Attitude | 20 |
| Communicator | 33 | | |
| Motivator | 32 | | |
| Calm Presence | 31 | | |
| Person of Integrity | 29 | | |
| Open, Honest, & Forthright | 26 | | |
| Servant Leader | 24 | | |
| Courage-Assertive | 22 | | |
| Open-Minded | 22 | | |
| Good negotiator/ mediator | 20 | | |
| **Total** | **734** | **Total** | **122** |

High-Creative Leaders were endorsed **6 times** more often

Table 5.1 shows dramatically that High-Creative leaders are *six times* more strongly endorsed for strengths that make the fundamental difference between effective and ineffective leadership. This street view of leadership confirms a need to redefine how we select, promote, and develop leaders.

All the leaders in our study have been put through the wringer to get to where they are. They either created and grew a successful business, or they have earned their way to a top leadership position in an organization. All are extremely talented and successful. What does the data suggest about what gets us to the top and what we look for when promoting leaders? Too often we end up at the top *for what got us there* and not *for what will scale*.

Bill Adams learned this lesson early in life as he said:

> I was born and raised on a cattle ranch, and my father used to talk about this all the time. "How you get results is as important as the results themselves," he often told me. I didn't appreciate it at the time what he was trying to tell me, but now I do. If you're not treating people with the dignity and respect they deserve, and the results you get are over the top of them, you've got a problem. If you aren't listening to your people, if you aren't caring about them, if you're not building teamwork within your organization, you've got a problem. He was teaching me these lessons at an early age, and lo and behold, it shows up in the research.

Generally, when leaders get hired or promoted into their roles, they are expected—usually *implicitly*, but sometimes *explicitly*—to build relationships, create the right environment, grow personally, develop other leaders, and get the best out of people. We expect that because we know that's how it all comes together.

However, we seldom think about sorting for these strengths and developing them until leaders reach a point where they are in over their heads and starting to derail, if not fail. When we are called in to help a leader who is derailing, we usually find a leader who is talented and highly Reactive—someone who underuses his or her High-Creative strengths. These leaders are exceptionally bright and innovative, but they usually have weak people skills. They are not building teams or developing their people; they don't listen; they are poor communicators, and so forth. Furthermore, these leaders have been promoted any number of times through the ranks for their technical brilliance, yet they haven't been challenged along the way to learn how to effectively lead within a more complex role and context. This has to change.

One day, we received an emergency message from a consultant who was working with a professional sports team. He said, "I need you to look at a couple of Leadership Circle Profiles, and I need you to look at them *right now.*" The owner of the team was having a crisis—the team's head coach and its general manager were simply not able to work together. Consequently, the team's performance was coming apart.

After we looked at the Profiles for each of these men, the problem was immediately obvious. The general manager had an effective, High-Creative leader Profile while the coach's Profile was among the most Reactive we've ever seen. When people are promoted to the head coach position, they face a completely different set of responsibilities and requirements than they did as a position coach or a defensive or offensive coordinator. It's an executive position, and any ineffective leadership behaviors get quickly exposed.

In this case, the head coach had doubled down on his Non-Differentiating Strengths and was deploying them reactively such that they increasingly became weaknesses. His behavior became more controlling and more autocratic. Clearly, he was more focused on behaviors that had put him in his position. He wasn't open to new behaviors that would enable him to learn, grow, adapt, and build a team. The head coach was brilliant at what he knew (what got him there), but he was an ineffective leader. In his new position, he went from being an asset to having a tremendously negative impact.

We pointed this out to the consultant who conferred with the team owner. When it became clear this coach was unwilling to face his development gap and unable to make the move from a great technical coach to a team leader, he was let go.

Many leaders say, "Well, I'm good at my technical job. I network well. That should be enough." It's not! Those skills just get you in the door—they don't keep you there. The difference is your ability to lead people. Exceptional leaders spend a lot more time in people leadership, in team leadership, and in collaboration. The research clearly indicates that *effective relationships are an essential component of leadership. They drive desired results, agility, and innovation.*

To scale leadership, you need to establish all the conditions for scale by upgrading your leadership from Reactive to Creative. You start with yourself and step into the *radical humanity* and *vulnerability* of taking on your development gaps with those you lead. You let go and learn from each other. You do all this in *deep relationship* at all levels of scale (one on one, team, organization). You design together a learning organization that puts everyone in *generative and developmental tension*, and you do all this in service of a *higher purpose* and *strategic vision*.

The next chapter explores how High-Reactive leaders not only limit their ability to scale by relying on the strengths that got them promoted (and not on the strengths that create the conditions for scale), but they also compensate by doubling down on these strengths. This creates major liabilities for themselves and for the organization.

---

### REFLECTION

Take time to reflect on and answer these questions:

- How do the top 10 strengths *you* bring to the table as a leader line up with the list of High-Reactive and High-Creative leaders' strengths?

- Do you overly rely on Non-Differentiating strengths to lead? If so, how does this impact the way you show up as a leader?

- Do your answers to the above questions change your One Big Thing? If so, update your Leadership Development Plan.

# Chapter 6
# Leader Liabilities
*Most Reactive versus Most Creative*

None of us is a perfect human being; we all have limits and liabilities. Leaders live out loud and their strengths, weaknesses, and liabilities are on display all day, every day. This is just the way it is. In spiritual boot camp, weaknesses and liabilities go with the territory. There's no shame in that. They become invitations to transformation. We all have the ability to evolve and turn our weaknesses and liabilities into strengths and assets. And since each of us possesses that ability, it's in our best interest to take advantage of it.

## HOW WE INTERRUPT OUR EFFECTIVENESS

In our study, the leaders who provided feedback have much to teach about what interrupts effective leadership and how we can get in our own way. Here's an example:

John is an individual who, in his professional life, does not suffer fools gladly, who takes challenges to his authority personally, who does not allow real or perceived slights to his status to go without a vigorous and sharp reaction, and who demands public recognition for his ideas, work, and contribution to (shared or individual) successful outcomes.

John can go on the attack! When acting from the perception he has formed on an issue, his assault can be consuming. It becomes difficult, if not impossible, in the moment for him to see any other reality. His situational inquiry, ostensibly delivered as questions to inform, is actually designed to elicit responses that build a case for the conclusion he has already reached. Have that process go awry, and his ire only grows. So, it is easier to allow John to have it his way—the way he sees it.

John's greatest leadership challenge is learning to shift the focus away from himself and onto others. The situation always comes back to him. He is arrogantly confident in his opinions/conclusions. He does not listen. He is closed to and shuts down others' good ideas. He needs to learn that others have much to contribute. He needs to let go, learn to allow others' ideas to positively influence his thinking, and develop the brilliance of his team. He will never realize his significant leadership potential unless he can look through the lenses of others' experiences, see the world from their various perspectives, and use his power to lead for collective success.

This comment is only one of thousands of similar comments that point to the liabilities of Reactive leaders.

## TOP 10 LIABILITIES OF HIGH-REACTIVE LEADERS

Here are the top 10 High-Reactive leader liabilities in order from most frequently endorsed to least. The definitions are created from language used in the written comments gathered in our database from leaders all around the globe.

What strikes you about this list? What do you notice?

1. **Ineffective Interaction Style:** Off-putting verbal and nonverbal communication style, often described as arrogant, condescending, dictatorial, confrontational, or overly critical.

2. **Not a Team Player:** Operates independently and does not provide enough support for the team, or recognize its needs. Makes decisions in isolation and focuses on only his or her own goals.
3. **Team Not Fully Developed:** Does not provide development opportunities. Does not clearly define roles and responsibilities.
4. **Over-Demanding:** Drives others too hard, too fast, and sets unrealistic expectations such that others cannot keep up with their current capability. Is unforgiving and harsh when expectations are not met.
5. **Micromanages:** Does not trust others to get the job done or empower people to make decisions and resolve issues. Tries to do it all by himself/herself.
6. **Team Not Held Accountable:** Teams are not held accountable for quality results and struggle to execute against strategy to meet deadlines. Lacks quality focus by settling for "good enough."
7. **Inattentive/Poor Listener:** Does not listen to others' ideas, especially those ideas that do not match their own. Engages in other tasks while people are speaking or will interrupt them to present his or her own ideas.
8. **Too Self-Centric:** Puts personal agenda and gain ahead of the team. Boasts and takes credit for other's work.
9. **Lacks Emotional Control:** Has a temper and launches into emotional outbursts and tirades, particularly when things do not go as planned.
10. **Impatient:** Becomes easily frustrated when others are too slow to catch on. Tends to rush through things rather than giving them time for understanding and informed decision making.

Figure 6.1 shows the endorsement scores for the top 10 liabilities of High-Reactive leaders. Their scores are on the right side of the figure, and the corresponding scores for High-Creative leaders are on the left. The differences are clear and stark: *High-Creative leaders barely move the needle when it comes to the liabilities that High-Reactive leaders have, while High-Reactive Leaders have plenty to choose from.* The only liabilities mentioned for High-Creative leaders are related to overwork. Otherwise, there was little mention of liabilities for High-Creative leaders. A quick comparison of the numbers tells the story:

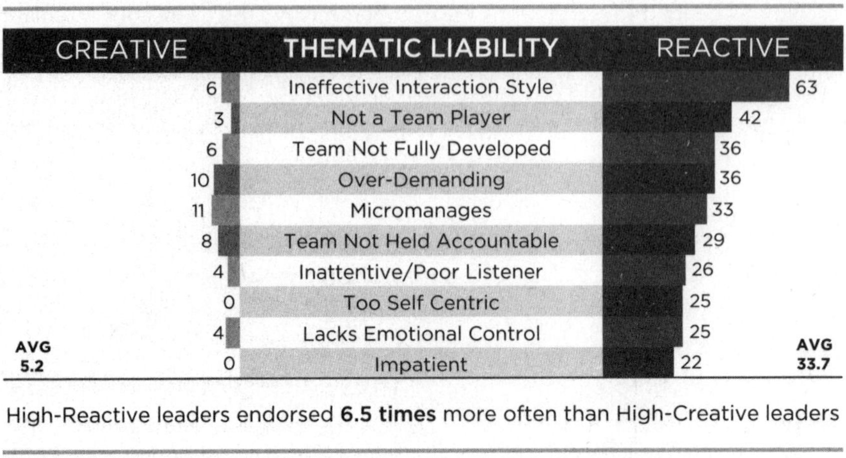

| CREATIVE | | THEMATIC LIABILITY | REACTIVE | |
|---|---|---|---|---|
| | 6 | Ineffective Interaction Style | 63 | |
| | 3 | Not a Team Player | 42 | |
| | 6 | Team Not Fully Developed | 36 | |
| | 10 | Over-Demanding | 36 | |
| | 11 | Micromanages | 33 | |
| | 8 | Team Not Held Accountable | 29 | |
| | 4 | Inattentive/Poor Listener | 26 | |
| | 0 | Too Self Centric | 25 | |
| AVG 5.2 | 4 | Lacks Emotional Control | 25 | AVG 33.7 |
| | 0 | Impatient | 22 | |

High-Reactive leaders endorsed **6.5 times** more often than High-Creative leaders

**FIGURE 6.1**  Top 10 Liabilities of High-Reactive Leaders

*Ineffective interaction style,* 63 to 6.

*Not a team player,* 42 to 3.

*Team not fully developed,* 36 to 6.

*Over-demanding,* 36 to 10.

*Micromanages,* 33 to 11, and so on.

If you average both columns, the average score for High-Creative leaders is 5.2 compared to an average score of 33.7 for High-Reactive leaders—a *6.5 times difference!*

Recall that the top 10 strengths of High-Creative leaders are 2.3 times more endorsed than High-Reactive leaders and that High-Creative leaders are six times more frequently endorsed on the Differentiating Strengths list. And here we see that with High-Reactive leaders, the liabilities are *6.5 times* more prevalent!

We notice that the top 10 High-Creative strength list is loaded with people strengths. Conversely, the top 10 High-Reactive liability list has to do with lousy human interactions. This list is the opposite of *deep relationship* and *radical humanity.* It is also highly unlikely to inspire *purposeful achievement.*

If you want a list of how to disrespect, discourage, and disempower people, this is a good one. In the way that antimatter annihilates matter, these anti-relationship behaviors cancel out a leader's relationships and therefore his or her effectiveness. Further, these Reactive behaviors disrupt and damage the conditions for scale, stunting the organization's growth.

High-Reactive leaders comprise 28 percent of our database. From our experience, this is also true of most Extended Leadership Teams. If your Extended Leadership Team is comprised of 28 percent High-Reactive leadership, think about the cost of this—and the missed ROI—because *ineffective* leadership offsets *effective* leadership.

### CASE EXAMPLE: PRESIDENT EDWARDO

Edwardo is the president of an organization. As you read the comment below, see if you can identify the towering strengths that helped him get promoted into his current position but have become Non-Differentiating. Also, see if you can spot the liabilities that Edwardo possesses as a leader.

> Edwardo is extremely intelligent and typically gets to the solution before everyone else. This is often his downfall as he moves quickly to implementing a solution when in fact the organization is two steps behind him. This creates a disconnect with the team. In his role as president, he should be "teaching people how to fish." Unfortunately, Edwardo gets frustrated with the lack of responsiveness from the organization and, as a result, hands over the "fish." This can create insecurity and frustration, with people feeling they cannot live up to his expectations.
>
> Edwardo does not leverage his team to create the desired vision. Because he is intelligent and gets to answers faster than most, he loses patience and decides to do all the work himself. By doing so, he misses out on the input of others and fails to garner support for the vision. When he becomes quickly entrenched in his position, he often ignores valid input and alternative points of view.
>
> Edwardo thinks he knows best (he does not listen to others), and he does not inspire confidence in his team. As a result, his

"professional arrogance" creates more of a dictatorial leader-ship style, which in turn produces adversarial relationships internally (Edwardo versus everyone). Over time, this out-come will also spread to external partners. In the end, we will continue to lose talent, which will eventually impact business performance.

Like many leaders we meet and work with worldwide, Edwardo is a classic example of a brilliant man reaching the limits of his development. He is facing his development gap. We suspect his leadership effectiveness has capped out or is steadily decreasing as a result.

While this comment does not provide us with Edwardo's business context, we can assume he is in over his head, under stress, and default-ing to reactivity, which undermines his effectiveness. The combination of Non-Differentiating Strengths (however towering) and the Reactive default behaviors that show up under pressure puts Edwardo at his limits to scale. Too much depends on him, and his working more, harder, and faster will make things worse.

Edwardo is not merely challenged to develop additional competencies, he has reached the limits of Reactive leadership and is challenged to evolve into a Creative leader, the first condition for scaling leadership.

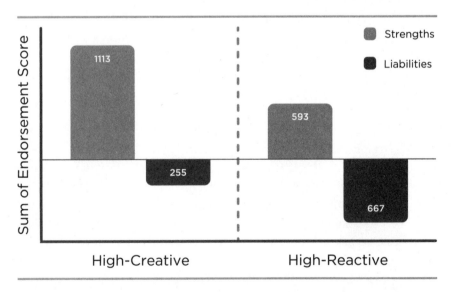

**FIGURE 6.2**  Sum of All Strengths and Liabilities

## LEADERSHIP RATIO

What is the balance of strengths to liabilities of these two groups of leaders? What is each group's *Leadership Ratio*?

Figure 6.2 illustrates the sum of all strengths and liabilities for both groups. These total scores are not based on the top 10 lists. Instead, we totaled the endorsement scores for all 40 strengths and all 37 liabilities identified in our study. High-Creative leaders had a total endorsement score for strengths of 1,113 versus 255 for liabilities. This gives High-Creative leaders a strengths-to-liabilities ratio of 4.4 to 1. Not surprisingly, High-Reactive leaders are endorsed more often for their liabilities at 667 compared to 593 for their strengths, which gives them a ratio of 0.9 to 1.

Think about that. If you have a Leadership Ratio of 0.9 to 1, it means *you are in your own way.* It also means the harder you go and the longer you work, the more you get in your own way and the less you accomplish. You may try to counter this by working even harder, but eventually you'll hit a wall, both personally and with your people. This does not mean you are not proficient at getting results. It means that, from a leadership perspective, you are not developing the capability and capacity (scaling leadership) of people and teams to create what matters.

Your Leadership Ratio gives you an indication of the effect you are having on people and your organization. As the complexity of your organization and environment increases, your multiple—the return on your leadership—must increase. For example, if you routinely give an hour and only get an hour in return, you are investing your time ineffectively. You won't be an effective leader of leaders. You can and must do better, *much* better.

How do you increase the multiple on your leadership? By increasing your Leadership Ratio. Extremely effective leaders get a 10, 20, even 1,000 to 1 return on their time and interactions, and they do this by maintaining a high Leadership Ratio. If your Leadership Ratio does not grow with the organization, *you* become the limit to scale. The same is true for your team of leaders. *If your team's Leadership Ratio does not grow, then the organization's leadership does not scale at the level required.*

Furthermore, if you are a High-Reactive leader, you likely lead with Non-Differentiating Strengths. This means you lead primarily with strengths that get results through your own drive and capability, *not* through developing capability and capacity in others. Hence, a Leadership Ratio of 0.9 to 1 is not going to scale. This is a serious liability. *You are dragging down and even cancelling out your own effectiveness and that of your leadership team.* Not only are you not putting in place the conditions for scaling leadership, you are actively *preventing* those conditions from emerging.

Erik Fyrwald, CEO of Syngenta, recalled when he learned he couldn't do it all by himself. He said: "Fifteen years ago, I realized I would not get any more operating P&L experience until I learned to let go, trust other people, and not need to be the smartest guy in the room—to always be right."

Erik's three-fold developmental agenda—to let go, trust other people, and not have to be the smartest guy in the room—created a greater capacity to meet complexity in himself while increasing his Leadership Ratio. This allowed him to increase the multiple on his leadership by behaving in a way that consistently created greater capacity in others and within his team.

Erik's deep learning is being absorbed by those around him. Today, we work with Erik and his Senior Executive Team, and with Jon Parr, the president who has responsibility for a large piece of Syngenta's business. After Jon had received feedback regarding his leadership, he pulled out a notebook, wrote down two words (Figure 6.3), and said, "This is the way I have to look at my leadership."

He continued: "I have to make decisions and lead in a way that's not driven by ego but in a way that builds the capacity and capability of my team to lead." Jon is recognizing that driving and pushing himself and

**FIGURE 6.3**　Let Ego Go

others harder, versus developing the leaders that work with him, reduces his Leadership Ratio. He has become focused on involving his entire team to develop its capability to lead the more than 20,000 people in Syngenta's Crop Protection Business. Jon is letting go, developing others, holding them accountable and, in the process, becoming more *radically human*. As a result, he is setting up the conditions for scale.

All things change when *we* do. As Erik does his leadership work, so does his entire team and the Extended Leadership Team—now a priority for Erik and for Syngenta. This is how scaling leadership works.

## WHAT IS YOUR RETURN ON LEADERSHIP?

Are your strengths a multiple of your liabilities, or are you getting in your own way? What is the return on your leadership? Does your Leadership Ratio give you a high return on your leadership or not? Are you increasing the multiple on your leadership by developing other leaders around you, by increasing the capacity and capability of your people in every interaction?

You scale leadership by being *radically human* and in *deep relationship* focused on *designing systems* for *purposeful achievement*. In other words, you scale it by finding the *optimal balance* between task and relationship focus in your individual and collective leadership.

## RELATIONSHIP-TASK BALANCE

Your Leadership Ratio is directly related to your ability to drive purposeful, strategic task accomplishment through deep, authentic relationship. In the LCP, the vertical axis of the circle points to the *Stage of Leadership* of the leader. The top half represents *Creative*; the bottom half *Reactive*. The horizontal axis runs from *Relationship* to *Task*. The left half measures how you are in relationship with yourself and others; the right half measures how you engage task. This creates the four-quadrant framework that underlies the Universal Model of Leadership and the Profile (see Figure 6.4).

A leader can manage people *Creatively*—with high self-awareness, emotional intelligence, and in a manner that engages, empowers, and

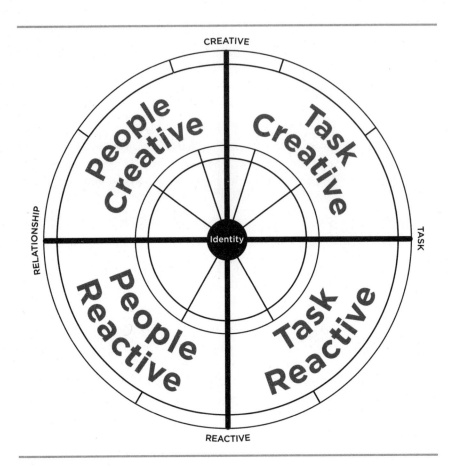

**FIGURE 6.4**   Four Quadrants of Leadership

brings out the best in people, teams, and organizations. Or a leader can engage people *Reactively*—in a way that gives up too much power in the pursuit of harmony and the need to be accepted. A leader can manage *Task Creatively*—purpose-driven and vision-focused, translating into effective execution on results and systemic improvement. Or a leader can manage *Task Reactively*—taking up too much power and becoming over-controlling, micromanaging, and driving the organization and people beyond sustainable limits.

The LCP measures the balance between task and relationship strengths. Good balance is far more effective than imbalance, and gaining this balance has everything to do with your Leadership Ratio. You decrease your Leadership Ratio when Relationship and Task are out of balance, and you increase your ratio when you balance Relationship and Task strengths.

The ability to lead people Creatively and focus them on purposeful task accomplishment is a key to effective leadership that scales. Alan Mulally is such a leader. He had achieved a great deal of success as the CEO of Boeing Commercial Airplanes. In 2006, he was hired as president/CEO of Ford Motor Company.

From day one at Ford, Alan applied his extraordinarily high Leadership Ratio to the company, and within two years, people all around the world felt a strong connection with him, whether or not they had personal contact with him.

Over the course of his career, Alan developed a set of "Working Together" principles and practices. As you review his principles listed below, note that at least half of them are on the High-Creative leader top 10 list. All of them can be found within the Creative half of the Leadership Circle Profile, which relates directly to creating the conditions for scaling leadership. The principles are:

- People first
- Everyone is included
- Compelling vision, comprehensive strategy, and relentless implementation plan [that builds Generative Tension]
- Clear performance goals
- One plan
- Facts and data . . . we can't manage a secret . . . the data set us free
- Everyone knows the plan, status, and areas that need special attention
- Propose a plan, positive "find-a-way" attitude
- Respect, listen, help, and appreciate each other
- Emotional resilience . . . trust the process
- Have fun . . . enjoy the journey and each other[1]

Alan Mulally's list of "Working Together" principles and practices is particularly powerful because it goes back and forth between people and plan, staying on task, and working together for execution. Not surprisingly, Alan was considered one of America's top CEOs while serving at the helm of both Boeing Commercial Airplanes and Ford Motor

Company. This is due in large measure to his own ability to optimize the balance between relationship and task.

There's one more thing, though. Alan makes no bones about his belief that leaders should love the people who work *for* and *with* them. As he said in an interview on *CBS This Morning:* "The purpose of our success is to serve others because that's the ultimate reward. The purpose of life is to love and be loved."[2]

When other CEOs look at Alan's example, they often ask: "Do you mean I've got to love my people?" His response would be: "Why *wouldn't* you? They spend three quarters of their waking hours helping you produce something amazing for the world." He naturally understood the importance of balancing task and relationship, and he was constantly in service to others.

Creative leadership is far more effective than Reactive leadership, *and optimal leadership is strong in both task and relationship capability.* We believe this is the primary reason women leaders are experienced by others as more Creative and effective—and why they get better results—than men. In effect, they better balance the yin and yang of leadership.

High-Creative leaders get a multiple on their leadership by optimizing the focus on results with developing their people. Their average Relationship-Task Balance (RTB) score on the LCP is quite high at the 87th percentile. High-Reactive leaders reverse this with an RTB score at the 10th percentile compared to our norm base. In addition, by disrespecting and disempowering people, High-Reactive leaders have a Leadership Ratio that's higher on liability than strength, thus canceling out their leadership and the contributions of others. Their leadership does not scale because it undermines the conditions for scale.

*Leaders have a moral obligation to get good with people at scale.* When you step into or are thrust into leadership, you are in the people business! You are tasked with scaling results through people, teams, and organizations. You don't lead *results*—you lead *people* to get results. The higher you go in an organization, the more you need to excel in relationships at scale.

**HOMEWORK**

You have already begun to improve your Leadership Ratio by identifying your One Big Thing. The next step is to identify your One Big Liability. Take a moment to:

- Identify your One Big Liability. Review the list of Top 10 High-Reactive Leader Liabilities and the dimension in the Reactive half of your LCP Self-Assessment. What Reactive behavior do you habitually run that interrupts your effectiveness and works against your One Big Thing? Ask yourself, "What thing, if I stopped doing it, would take my leadership to a whole new level?"

- Reflect on what your One Big Reactive tendency might be; also, solicit feedback from people who know you well and whom you trust to tell you about the One Thing that gets in your way of being an effective leader. (Suggestions for how to solicit feedback are in the Development Plan that comes with this book.)

- Write down your Reactive tendency in your Development Plan.

Telling the truth about your One Big Thing and your One Big Liability establishes generative *tension*. In doing so, you cultivate a gap between how you want to lead and how you are leading. This creates a force for resolution. If you continue to get feedback on how you are doing on both, you will naturally tend to become the leader you want to be.

# Chapter 7
# The Canceling Effect
*Are You Canceling Yourself Out?*

How many times have we heard people say, "He can't get out of his own way." "She keeps shooting herself in the foot." "He is canceling himself out." "Could you believe that conversation? It completely undid all that we've done for the last three weeks." Our personal favorite is, "He or she keeps *stepping on a rake.*" Not a pretty sight!

These statements are indicative of what we call the Canceling Effect. When leaders, or entire leadership organizations, experience the Canceling Effect, their strengths are canceled out by their liabilities. As a result, their leadership cannot and does not scale.

Here is feedback to Jim, a senior leader. In these comments, you can clearly see the Canceling Effect at work in his leadership.

> Jim is all over the map in his management style—from extremely professional and centered, to childish and petty. He needs to believe in the values he espouses and then align his behavior consistently with those values.

> Jim seems a bit disconnected on a personal level from those he should be mentoring. While I know he is often pressed for time, I suggest that he strive to connect with those in the

organization and be willing to share some of himself to develop a bond with them so they want to follow him.

Jim undervalues the power of relationships and the synergies those relationships can create in accomplishing his vision and those of others. He tends to go it alone, instead of working to figure out how to combine resources and efforts with his peers to be able to accomplish an expanded vision.

Jim is an example of a leader who is canceling himself out. He's a capable professional, but his leadership is neither scaling, nor is it scalable unless he changes his approach. He is pressed for time *all* the time, and he's not leveraging the power of relationships in his business dealings. As the organization grows, Jim is working harder and longer—certainly much more than if he leveraged those around him through better relationships and leadership development. Instead, he is capping out and reaching limits to scale.

With the best of intentions, Jim is also canceling out his own leadership and limiting the capacity of others, *and* the capability of his organization.

## THE CANCELING EFFECT

A picture is worth a thousand words, and Figure 7.1 shows the Canceling Effect—how the Top 10 High-Reactive Strengths are offset by the Top 10 High-Reactive Liabilities. (Strengths are on the left, liabilities on the right, and bar charts for each extend from the center.)

We invite you to read back and forth, from left to right and back again, directly comparing the High-Reactive Strengths and Liabilities. For example, he is driven and passionate (61) but ineffective in his interaction style (63). She is visionary and strategic (54), but she is not a team player (42). He is a strong networker (41), but his team is not fully developed (36). She possesses domain/technical knowledge (38), but she is *over-demanding* (36). And so on.

As you go back and forth, you'll notice that each High-Reactive Strength is canceled out by a corresponding Liability, and the endorsement scores between Strengths and Liabilities are almost equal. This is the Canceling Effect visibly in action. In fact, when you average the

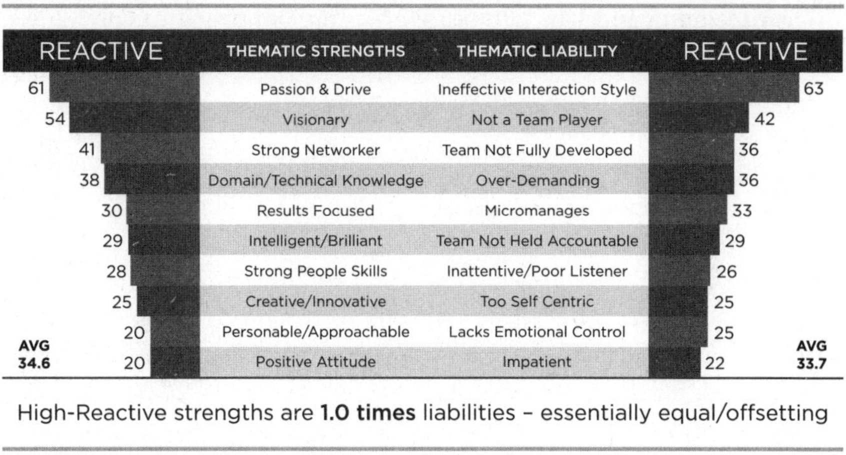

| REACTIVE | THEMATIC STRENGTHS | THEMATIC LIABILITY | REACTIVE |
|---|---|---|---|
| 61 | Passion & Drive | Ineffective Interaction Style | 63 |
| 54 | Visionary | Not a Team Player | 42 |
| 41 | Strong Networker | Team Not Fully Developed | 36 |
| 38 | Domain/Technical Knowledge | Over-Demanding | 36 |
| 30 | Results Focused | Micromanages | 33 |
| 29 | Intelligent/Brilliant | Team Not Held Accountable | 29 |
| 28 | Strong People Skills | Inattentive/Poor Listener | 26 |
| 25 | Creative/Innovative | Too Self Centric | 25 |
| 20 | Personable/Approachable | Lacks Emotional Control | 25 |
| AVG 34.6 | | | AVG 33.7 |
| 20 | Positive Attitude | Impatient | 22 |

High-Reactive strengths are **1.0 times** liabilities – essentially equal/offsetting

**FIGURE 7.1**   The Canceling Effect

scores for the top 10 Strengths and top 10 Liabilities, the ratio is 1:1. Highly Reactive leaders cancel themselves out.

When we show this information to leaders, they immediately nod their heads. They know exactly what we're describing—they've seen it in action. Everyone smiles and says yes when asked, "Do you know leaders who get in their own way or leaders to whom you might say, 'I wish you'd stop talking, because the longer you talk, the more you talk yourself out of a good deal?'"

When we share this idea of the Canceling Effect, people almost always say, "Yeah, that makes perfect sense." And when we help leaders see what they are doing that might be getting in their own way, they tell us, "Wow, I did not know. If I continue doing that, I will end up working harder and longer for less and less return on all that effort."

You can be very good at doing certain things—for example, creating an inspiring vision or networking with others—but depending on how you do them, you may ultimately cancel out your own impact. Given how talented you are to have made it into the senior leadership ranks, you may still be making a significant contribution to the organization. But, if you are a highly Reactive leader, your leadership is neutral at best. It likely has an overall negative effect on the organization's capacity to scale, as well as its capability to develop and execute on strategy and create its desired future.

The number-one reason for failure of vision and strategy is *ineffective leadership*, both individual and collective.

We recently worked with a young leader, Janet, about 40 years old, who is one of the sharpest leaders we've ever met. Janet works for a large, multinational corporation in charge of an entire business segment that generates about half of this company's $15 billion in annual revenue. Her people love her, but when she gets really busy, which is all the time, she doesn't notice how she cancels herself out as a leader.

One day, we were invited to tour one of her production facilities in Latin America. The facility has been a top producer for years—touted as a benchmark for the company's other production facilities to try to emulate. Soon after we arrived, we were shepherded into a conference room where the members of the production facility's leadership team made presentations to Janet—their boss—and to us. It was an important time for them to show just how much they had accomplished.

A few minutes after the first speaker started, we turned around to see what Janet was doing at the back of the room. She had her head down and was writing an email on her smartphone—obviously not paying attention to the speaker. This went on for 15 to 20 minutes until we took a break. During the break, we took Janet aside and said, "The symbolism of what you're doing—being inattentive and obviously not listening—is sending the unmistakable message to those on the leadership team that they're anything but valued and important."

Janet didn't notice she was canceling herself out with the leadership team at this production facility, which was very important to the bottom line of the company. In this, she is not alone. Ironically, as Figure 7.1 illustrates, one of the low but endorsed High-Reactive leader strengths is *people skills*, and it's right across from that is *inattentive/poor listener*. Janet was canceling out her people skills with her not paying attention to her people. To be effective, leaders have to focus on nuance—what it means to be attentive, to attend to others, and to actually listen deeply. When they don't, they cancel themselves out.

Another interesting pairing from Figure 7.1 is the strength of *results focused*, which is canceled out by *micromanages*. We often encounter High-Reactive leaders who are results-focused controllers who micromanage. They are sending a clear message to their people not only that "I can do it better than you," but worse, "I actually don't trust you to do it; therefore, you're not as capable and competent as you need to be." They don't intend to send this message, but they do, and it cancels them out as leaders.

Contrast this with the leader who understands what's required for people to feel inspired and motivated—a leader who knows how to get the best out of people so they offer their discretionary energy in service of an outcome greater than themselves. The difference is night and day.

Our Reactive tendencies may serve us well to the point when we hit a wall and realize (often too late) we are outmatched by what's required of us to lead effectively. As we experience the shift from Reactive to Creative leadership, we get a multiple on our strengths and leverage the capacity and capability of those around us. The farther we follow through on this shift, the more we can scale our leadership.

## DOES YOUR LEADERSHIP SCALE? THE IMPACT OF NON-DIFFERENTIATING STRENGTHS

Is your leadership built for scale? Will it scale into the next promotion or as your organization commits to four times growth? Is your leadership designed to enhance the creative capacity of the organization to thrive in a VUCA world? If you're leading reactively, we think not.

Figure 7.2 shows the Canceling Effect but with Non-Differentiating Strengths circled.

| REACTIVE | THEMATIC STRENGTHS | THEMATIC LIABILITY | REACTIVE |
|---|---|---|---|
| 61 | Passion & Drive | Ineffective Interaction Style | 63 |
| 54 | Visionary | Not a Team Player | 42 |
| 41 | Strong Networker | Team Not Fully Developed | 36 |
| 38 | Domain/Technical Knowledge | Over-Demanding | 36 |
| 30 | Results Focused | Micromanages | 33 |
| 29 | Intelligent/Brilliant | Team Not Held Accountable | 29 |
| 28 | Strong People Skills | Inattentive/Poor Listener | 26 |
| 25 | Creative/Innovative | Too Self Centric | 25 |
| 20 | Personable/Approachable | Lacks Emotional Control | 25 |
| AVG 34.6 — 20 | Positive Attitude | Impatient | 22 — AVG 33.7 |

Reactive strengths are **1.0 times** liabilities – essentially equal/offsetting

**FIGURE 7.2** The Canceling Effect with Non-Differentiating Strengths Circled

Again, Non-Differentiating Strengths are strengths that *do not differentiate* between the most-effective leaders and the least-effective leaders. In fact, most Non-Differentiating Strengths are more highly endorsed for High-Reactive leaders than for High-Creative leaders. This suggests that if they get too strong, they may be working against scaling your leadership.

Here we put the two concepts together. Highly Reactive leaders use strengths that don't scale well, and their liabilities more than offset the remaining strengths. The conclusion is obvious. High-Reactive leaders, at one point or another, get in their own way, and their leadership is not scalable. As you will see, negative system-wide damage can result from their leadership.

## SEVEN MULTIPLES, SEVEN CANCELING EFFECTS

The team of researchers that conducted the written comment study identified and highlighted seven key themes in the data where High-Creative leaders get a multiple on their leadership and High-Reactive leaders cancel out their effectiveness. Figures 7.3 through 7.9 show seven juxtaposing strengths and liabilities and the scores on each for both High-Reactive and High-Creative leaders.

Figure 7.3 contrasts two leadership behaviors that offset each other—strong people skills and ineffective interaction style. High-Creative

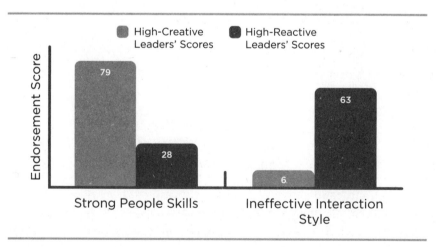

**FIGURE 7.3**  People Skills

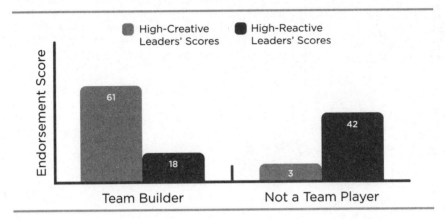

**FIGURE 7.4**    Teamwork

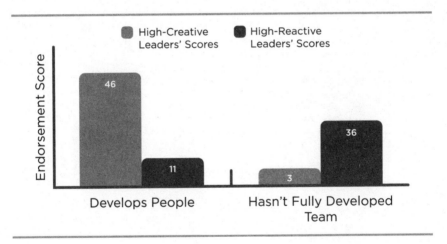

**FIGURE 7.5**    Developing People and Teams

leader scores are in light gray and High-Reactive leader scores are in dark gray. The conclusion is obvious: High-Creative leaders get a multiple on their leadership and scale the capacity and capability of those around them through *strong people skills*, whereas High-Reactive leaders cancel themselves out through their *ineffective interaction style*.

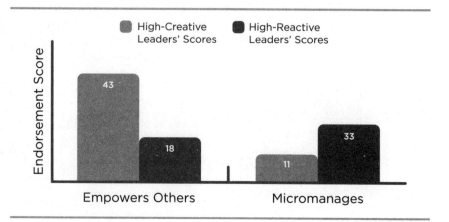

**FIGURE 7.6**    Empowerment

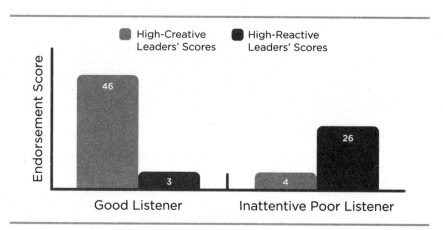

**FIGURE 7.7**    Listening

As we look at Figures 7.3 through 7.9, we see similar sets of strengths and liabilities, but High-Creative leaders get a multiple on their leadership and High-Reactive leaders get in their own way. High-Creative leaders get leverage through people, teamwork, developing and empowering others, listening, composure, and servant leadership. High-Reactive leaders are ineffective with people, not team players or developers, micromanaging, lousy listeners, emotionally unstable, and egocentric.

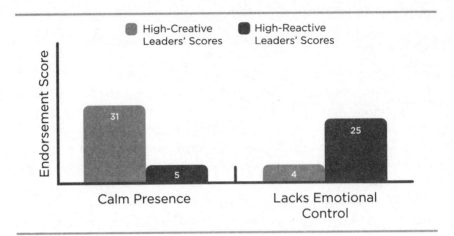

**FIGURE 7.8**  Composure

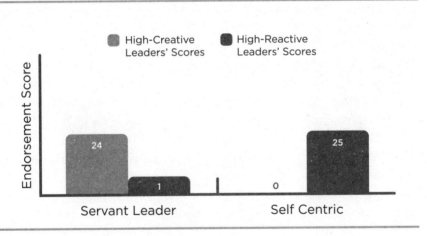

**FIGURE 7.9**  Servant Leadership

## SYSTEMIC CANCELING EFFECTS

Leaders bring the weather, and leaders who cancel themselves out bring weather that has a wide storm pattern.

The High-Reactive leaders in this study comprise 28 percent of the senior leaders on the Extended Leadership Teams (ELT) of large organizations in our norm base. Think about that weather pattern and how the people who work *with* and *for* these leaders are affected by it.

We know the negative impact just one highly Reactive leader can have on the tone, energy, and performance of a leadership team. The chilling effect created shuts down important conversations and has the entire organization doing "workarounds"—that is, finding ways to get things accomplished without upsetting a key leader. In extreme cases, members of the leadership team will seek ways to avoid dealing with the highly Reactive leader. This may mean seeking a transfer or leaving the company altogether.

One leader—and certainly a 28 percent cross-section of the senior leaders on the ELT—can have a huge Canceling Effect, not only canceling out him- or herself but seriously impeding the entire team and/ or organization. This is how the *collective intelligence* of a leadership team can drop below the team's average intelligence. The collective level of play drops to the lowest common denominator to accommodate the limitations of Highly Reactive leaders. Everyone "dumbs down" to accommodate this person, and rather than getting a huge multiple through synergy, where the collective intelligence rises well above the average intelligence, we cancel out one another.

We were once involved in a top-to-bottom transformation effort with a large company in North America. One member of the company's ELT was its top revenue producer, but he was also a leader who canceled out the people who worked for and with him. This leader had tremendous drive and passion, but his interaction style was ineffective. He was demanding, self-centric, impatient, and not a team player. Gradually, this leader canceled out the people around him. He left behind a complete wasteland of men and women he had burned out and burned up.

The organization had counseled him on many occasions, strongly encouraging him to behave in less Reactive and more Creative ways. But, his highly Reactive leadership style was deeply held; he would not change. Sadly, his leadership team finally had to let him go. The cost of his continued employment to the organization was too high. By canceling out others in his company, this leader had become an obstacle to the current performance and future growth of the organization. Letting him go was absolutely right.

Another client had decided the billions in revenue that one senior leader brought in annually was worth the wreckage that this genius left in his wake. Yet he was minimizing the organization's potential and keeping the other geniuses (some of whom left to find better working conditions) from fully contributing. The decision-makers accommodated his *genius* at the expense of their corporate values and purpose and, we would argue, at the expense of their company's long-term growth and prosperity.

Organizations face extremely difficult choices when they have a genius for a leader—someone who gets tremendous results but whose leadership seriously constrains growth. This puts the organization in an excruciatingly difficult dilemma. Its leaders cannot afford to let the person go (or so they think), yet keeping that person in leadership is costly. So, they ignore, accommodate, work around, and look the other way. This is a common but suboptimal decision because the negative impact Reactive *genius* leaders have on those around them may more than offset their contributions, especially as the organization scales. They choke off the growth and innovation in the organization.

When we talk with leaders, we often have them reflect about their experience over the years, all they've accomplished, and things that didn't work out. Specifically, we ask them, "What is the one thing, if you could do it all over again, you would like to have done differently?" The number one answer is almost always, "I would have made the difficult decisions more quickly to change out those leaders I *knew* were not leading effectively and were not going to develop." This is a tough lesson and one we can take to heart. If we do, it will make a substantial *positive* difference in accelerating the results we want to accomplish.

If you are a leader faced with peers who get results but are damaging people and your organization in the process, take quick and decisive action. Either help them upgrade their leadership or encourage them to step aside—even if that means out of the door. That's often the only way leadership can scale.

## ARE YOU AMPLIFYING YOUR MULTIPLE OR YOUR CANCELING EFFECT?

The data in this book have elucidated our experience working with Creative and Reactive leaders. We've concluded that Creative leaders get an Amplification Effect while Reactive leaders amplify their Canceling Effect.

As a leader's LCP becomes more and more Creative, we notice the person's effectiveness begins to amplify while energetic costs go down and leading becomes easier. In the written comments and when we interview people about a Creative leader, they mention liabilities, but they often do so by minimizing the impact of those liabilities. They might say, "She could listen better, but her leadership is so exceptional that it's a privilege to work with her."

Notice that liabilities that would be amplified in Reactive leadership are minimized in Creative leadership. High-Creative leaders have liabilities, but they are overshadowed by the amplification effect that has happened to their leadership effectiveness.

The amplification effect results from getting a few things right. As a measure, High-Creative leaders are *2.3 times* more endorsed by followers on their Top 10 strengths. They lead with the key strengths that differentiate effective leadership for which they are endorsed *six* times more often. They have a great leadership ratio (4.4 to 1, strengths to liabilities), and therefore are getting a significant multiple on their strengths. Further, they optimize the focus on results by developing people, having a high balance between task and relationship at the 87th percentile.

The combination of all these amplifies their leadership. It is like an equation:

*Differentiating Strengths × Leadership Ratio × Relationship-Task Balance = Amplification Effect*

Because each variable in the equation amplifies the others, we call it the amplification effect. High-Creative leaders amplify their multiple and effectiveness; Reactive leaders get the same amplification effect, but it works in the opposite direction. The more Reactive the leader, the more they double down on Non-Differentiating strengths—6 out of their top 10 strengths are Non-Differentiating. In addition, their Top 10 liabilities are *6.5 times* that of the High-Creative leader. This results in a low Leadership Ratio (< 1). This means they are disrespecting and disempowering people resulting in a low Relationship-Task Balance at the 10th percentile.

Reactive leaders use the same equations to amplify the Canceling Effect. Consequently, their leadership does not scale because it undermines the conditions for scale.

## A MATTER OF DEVELOPMENT (THE PETER PRINCIPLE REVISITED)

Figure 7.10 shows a collage of graphics. When we saw all that we were learning from this study so graphically displayed, we started asking a different question.

You've likely heard about the phenomenon known as the *Peter Principle*. It happens when managers eventually get promoted to a position that's beyond their capability to perform. Well, what if Peter got the principle wrong?

The Peter Principle appeared in a book of the same name published in 1969. When we ask managers if they know what the Peter Principle means, they'd recite in unison, "People are promoted to their highest level of incompetence."

There is some truth to it. However, as we considered our experience and the data in our study, we wonder if leaders cap out, not so much for their level of *competence*, but for their level of *development*. When leaders reach their limits to scale, hit the celling, cap out, or derail, are they meeting the upper limit of their *capability* or the upper limit of their level of *development*?

We think the correct answer (more often than not) is the latter—reaching the upper limit of their level of development.

We've concluded that the most Creative/effective and most Reactive/ineffective leaders in this study are equally talented. We also suggested that if you had to choose who was the most talented—based on leaders' comments about pure brilliance and raw intelligence—the Reactive and least effective leaders would get the nod. So, are these people ineffective as leaders because they lack the talent? Or are they running into something different, something less obvious?

In our experience, ineffective leaders at this level are capable of much more, but they have reached the limits, not of their *competence* but of their *development*. This conclusion redefines how we go about developing leaders for the future.

To understand how significantly this redefines leadership development, we need to understand how each level of leadership, described in this book, is underpinned by a progressively maturing Internal Operating System. *This inner game runs the outer game.* Creative leadership arises on a more mature inner game than does Reactive leadership. So, when an extremely talented leader is reaching his or her limits, years of working

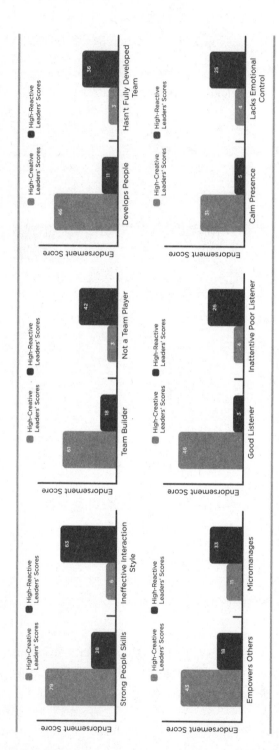

**FIGURE 7.10** A Collage of Graphics in This Chapter

with this type of the leader leads us to conclude that these limits are (more often than not) within their inner game. Their inner game is reaching its Peter Principle and needs to evolve. They are not reaching the limits of their level of competence but of the development and maturity of their *inner game*.

The second section of this book explains what's meant when we say a leader has reached the limit of his or her development. It then describes a universal path of development. The next chapter turns your attention to how leaders transform their organizations by scaling Creative leadership.

**REFLECTION**

- Are you canceling yourself out? If so, in what ways?

- Specifically, which Reactive Strengths are canceling out your Creative Strengths?

- Are Non-Differentiating Strengths impacting the way you show up as a leader? In what ways?

- Have you experienced the Peter Principle, either in others or in yourself? What happened?

# Chapter 8
# How Leaders Scale Leadership
## *Learning from One Man's Example*

People often wonder if leadership is something you're born with or if it can be learned—improved with knowledge, practice, and feedback. The answer is an unequivocal *yes.*

We are all differently gifted. Some us may be born to lead; still, the leadership ability we are born with must be developed, coached, and exercised regularly, just as natural abilities or talents in athletics, the arts, and other pursuits can be fully realized through practice. Regardless of what natural leadership traits you bring to the table, your leadership ability can and should be developed.

However, to have a developmental (if not transformative) effect on your people, your teams, your organization, and the world around you, you must scale your leadership. This chapter takes a close look at just how to do that.

### CASE IN PONT: JEFF HILZINGER

Jeff Hilzinger has shown us that leadership can be learned, honed, developed, and scaled. Jeff is the CEO of Marlin Business Services, a commercial finance company that provides commercial equipment financing and working capital loans to small businesses across the United States so they can acquire new equipment and technology while preserving capital. Marlin's value proposition is centered on providing excellent service and delivering on commitments made to equipment dealers, manufacturers, resellers, distributors, brokers, and their customers.

Jeff is a High-Creative leader, but he wasn't always that way. More than 10 years ago, when we began our engagement with his organization, Jeff was considered to be a *great* businessperson but just a *good* leader. He had strong technical, industry, and financial knowledge. He was an excellent strategist with a thorough understanding of business and organizational processes. And while he was very successful, sometimes that success came at a high cost—to himself and to the people around him.

When Jeff completed his first LCP in 2007 (see Figure 8.1), he was rated as a highly Reactive leader. However, his Leadership Effectiveness score was at the 80th percentile. Jeff scored relatively high on Leadership Effectiveness because his leadership brought tremendous upside—his intelligence, decisiveness, strategic capability, financial acumen, business knowledge, and courageous authenticity (he tells it the way it is). His leadership had a clear downside, however, given the tendency of his Reactive traits to cancel out his strengths. His autocratic, arrogant, critical, and distant way of relating made it difficult for others to fully embrace his leadership.

In 2007, we did not know that the Great Recession was just around the corner, and that his leadership would be tested as never before. Jeff needed to upgrade his leadership, let go, and vulnerably face his development gaps, but he resisted changing his approach. Instead, he would do what he had always done as a leader.

The good news is that Jeff did eventually realize he needed to upgrade his leadership and then scale it to his Executive Leadership Team and throughout the rest of the organization. That is exactly what he did. Today, Jeff Hilzinger is a tremendously successful all-round leader. How did Jeff make this fundamental transformation? He put in place all the conditions needed for scaling leadership, and you will soon see how.

## SCALING LEADERSHIP BEYOND YOURSELF

Over the years, we have worked with thousands of leaders in hundreds of organizations—large, small, and in between. How do the best of these leaders change themselves, scale their leadership, and in so doing, transform their organizations? We have learned a lot about

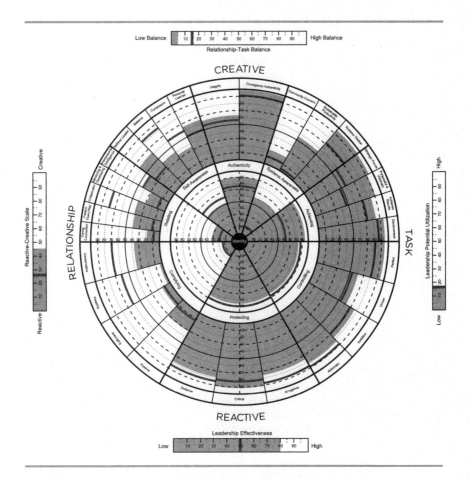

**FIGURE 8.1**   Jeff's First Leadership Profile (2007)

how to do this from the leaders with whom we have worked. In our experience, three key steps will get you there:

**Step 1: Start with yourself.** Take a deep look within yourself to understand your strengths and liabilities as a leader. Review and reflect on the list of strengths and liabilities from earlier chapters. Take the Leadership Circle Profile to see where you sit in the spectrum between Creative and Reactive, and Relationship and Task. Specifically:

- Awareness first: acknowledge your gap
- Harvest your feedback-rich environment

- Focus on the One Big Thing
- Reach out for help

**Step 2: Develop leadership teams.** Once you have an understanding of your own strengths and liabilities as a leader, the next step is to shift the focus to your leadership teams. This begins the process of scaling leadership beyond yourself. Specifically:

- Lead the development agenda
- Assess individual and collective effectiveness
- Get the right people in place
- Build alignment around what matters

**Step 3: Build leadership systems.** Creating long-term organizational change that will survive those who catalyzed it requires building systems that develop Creative or higher leadership throughout the organization. Specifically:

- Create a developmental organization
- Focus on measuring results
- Institutionalize the development agenda

### Step 1: Start with Yourself

Jeff got serious when he received a second LCP about two years after the first. It revealed that he'd become even *more* Reactive—a High-Reactive leader. (See Figure 8.2.) His scores had significantly decreased across the Creative half of the Profile, his Relationship-Task balance was near zero, and his Leadership Effectiveness had dropped to the 30th percentile. Jeff was seriously canceling himself out as a leader.

The combination of seeing this second picture of his increasing reactivity, learning from a great mentor/leader, and being a part of a committed leadership team encouraged Jeff to face his development gap. He went to work and never looked back.

As mentioned, one key factor in Jeff's progress was learning from a great mentor/leader. Jeff had the good fortune to report to a remarkable boss, the late Jim McGrane—one of the best leaders with whom we have

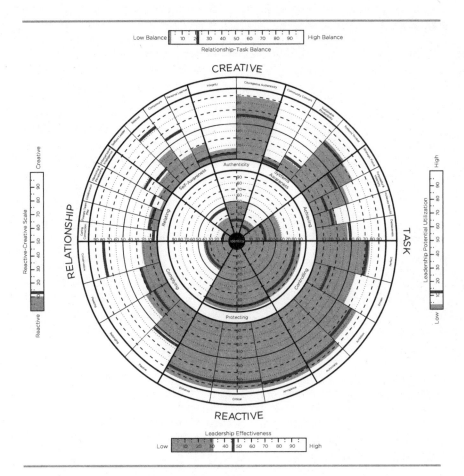

**FIGURE 8.2**   Jeff's Second Leadership Profile (2009–2010)

ever worked. Jim was the CEO of US Express Leasing (USXL) and Jeff was his number two and the company's CFO/COO. They supported each other to improve their individual and collective leadership effectiveness.

In *Mastering Leadership*, we tell the story of the time Jim received his second round of LCP feedback and discovered how he had slipped from being a High-Creative leader to one of average effectiveness during the Great Recession. When we met with Jim a week after he'd received the Profile, he had already held 25 meetings with 40 of his key leaders. He showed both Profiles to these leaders and asked a simple question: "What happened to me, and what do I need to do about it?" Jim was a role model of being radically human and starting with oneself.

### Awareness First: Acknowledge Your Gap

You can't make the first step of your journey to great leadership until you admit there's a gap between your current leadership and the leadership you aspire to attain. Jeff acknowledged that he was in a development gap—that he needed to travel a distance before he could become a great leader. Making this journey would require significant self-awareness, development, skill building, and practice. As Jeff became more self-aware, he put himself in the generative tension that results from telling the truth about who you are and who you choose to become.

How then do you become more self-aware? You have a conversation with yourself. Ask: "How self-aware am I?" "What do I pay attention to?" "What impact do I create across the organization?" Then widen your circle. Ask colleagues you trust in your organization, including team members and others: "What is my impact in every context in which I am required to lead?" Knowing your impact or influence is vital. You can't lead effectively unless you are self-aware of how you deploy yourself into circumstances and what impact you are having.

### Harvest Your Feedback-Rich Environment

The fastest way to become more aware is to get feedback from those around you on an ongoing basis. Many leaders are not clear about their impact. We saw this in the discrepancy between rater scores and self-scores on the LCP. The more Reactive leaders are, the more likely they are to assume they have a more positive impact than they actually do.

If you're not clear about what your impact is as a leader or have reason to believe what you think you know is wrong, then gather feedback via the Leadership Circle Profile or another 360 instrument. After digesting the feedback from the assessment, have a conversation with your team about the impact you're having and what they need from you. Listen, respond nondefensively to the feedback you receive, and fully appreciate it.

Next, build a feedback system for yourself so you are regularly able to receive input. You want to always know the effect you're having and whether it's consistent with the way you want to show up as a strong leader in your organization. If you don't know how to do this well, get help from a trusted advisor. To succeed as a leader, you must be willing to build, maintain, and use a robust feedback system. And, of course, you must be open to what you learn and to act upon it.

We helped Jim, Jeff, and their team design to harvest their feedback-rich environment. Now Jeff gets feedback all the time. He asks for it; he demands it. His arrogant and critical manner is still apparent, but he is conscious of this. He mitigates the impact of these behaviors by saying something like, "I know this is going to come across as arrogant and I apologize. I'm really trying to learn how *not* to have that happen. I don't mean to be critical here. Please give me feedback about anything you see that I need to improve."

### Focus on the One Big Thing

As you put in place a way of harvesting your feedback-rich environment, the one or two big things you need to change will become clear to you. Jeff did exactly this. He asked those around him, and he asked us. Jeff told us he wanted to become a more effective leader. We told Jeff that the combination of variables in our assessment most predictive of effectiveness are Purposeful Vision and Teamwork. When Jeff heard that, he said, "Okay, that's pretty clear. That's what I'm going to do." He chose to become a leader who leads from a clear sense of purpose and translates that into a strategic vision for the organization. And since vision catalyzes alignment and teamwork, those two go together perfectly.

Jeff focused on the One Big Thing (building teams aligned on vision) that would completely transform his leadership and his organization—to unlock it and take it to the next level. As he did that, he continued to get clearer about how he was getting in his own way and canceling out the very things he was focused on improving. He continued to ask for ongoing feedback. And when he found himself leading in old, less effective ways, he looked inside himself—getting to the core drivers of less-than-effective leadership. He wanted to understand why he needed to keep showing up this way.

By getting really clear on the One Big Thing that would take his leadership to the next level and continuing to notice when he got in his own way, Jeff put himself into a transformative structure—generative tension.

A few years later, Jeff's Leadership Profile had changed considerably. (See Figure 8.3.) His high Controlling scores had come way down. He had reduced his Arrogance and Critical scores. His Relating scores were on the rise and the rest of the Creative half of his Profile was in full bloom. His Leadership Effectiveness had gone from the 30th to the 70th percentile.

Tragically, in 2014, Jim McGrane passed away. Jeff was the natural successor and stepped in to lead the organization. He told us at that time, "Well, I guess we'll find out if we are serious about collective leadership." And, as it turned out, Jeff was. He committed fully to developing his leadership and that of his team. They continued engaging the people around them. These made a quantum difference in the business's performance.

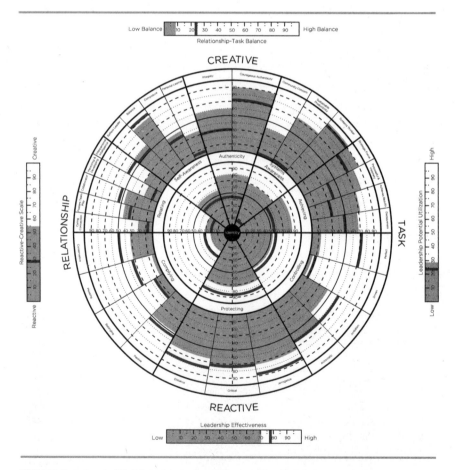

**FIGURE 8.3**    Jeff's Third Leadership Profile (2013)

Jeff has become an example of someone who proves that leaders are not just born, but they can actually grow and be developed. He's *that* guy. Jeff has taken his natural ability and built on it, mitigated his liabilities, and adopted new leadership practices that make him a highly effective leader. Jeff is part of Jim's legacy, leading in a way that's unique to him and, in that way, Jim lives on. With all Jeff has learned from other leaders, he has truly carved out his own leadership brand and is now passing on that legacy. This is the spiritual beauty of great leadership.

### Reach Out for Help

Scaling leadership can be a tremendous challenge for any leader, executive team, or organization—so much so that it often cannot be done from within your current expertise. You may know, individually and collectively, all that's required to run many aspects of your business, but you may not know all you need to know about how to improve your own leadership and scale that throughout the organization. When you find yourself in this situation—you keep running into obstacles and taking two steps back for every step forward—it may be time to reach out to an outside consulting firm for help. Instead of trying to run portions of the business for which you do not have subject matter or content expertise, either find it within the organization, hire the expertise you need, and/or bring in outside consulting help.

Bill received the email below from Paul, the chairman of a $100 million family business. (The chairman's name has been changed to protect his identity.) In his thirties, Paul is a strong young businessman tapped to step in and run the company for his father.

Bill,

I hope you're well.

I run a family-owned business that's approaching 100MM in revenue this year. Our leadership effectiveness is deplorable, and we are succeeding in spite of ourselves. I'd like to get certified in the Leadership Circle Profile and cascade the assessments and development processes throughout our company. We have to upgrade our leadership if we are going to grow this company and thrive.

*(continued)*

> Also, as we continue to have advisory relationships with companies both big and small, I see a unique opportunity to apply these tools in the small-to-mid business arena.
>
> I am ready to take on the responsibility of developing our leaders as well as bringing in leaders that are effective and can do the job. I need to be more effective and need effective leaders in the organization for this business to grow and thrive. Please share your thoughts with me, so we can get started.
>
> Thanks
>
> Paul
>
> Chairman of the Board

Paul is not only smart, he is humble. He knows when he needs help and is big enough to let go (*let ego*) and admit it. He doesn't want to squander his father's hard work and lose a company that benefits his family and the people who work for them. Recognizing the leadership in place won't get them where they need to go, he reached out for help. The best leaders we know who have transformed and scaled leadership, have done so with expert help.

Jeff, Jim, and Paul all began putting in place the conditions for scale by starting with themselves, modeling the radical humanity it takes to succeed. If you don't start with yourself, you become an obstacle to the very transformation you're trying to lead. You cancel yourself out. But when you start with yourself, you take hold of the organization's development agenda, you lead it personally, and you do it openly, vulnerably, and in deep relationship and trust. As you put in place all the conditions for scale, you put the whole organization in generative tension. This is what transforms.

### Step 2: Develop Leadership Teams

Your most important job as a leader—Job 1—is to develop other leaders. To that end, stop thinking about your team as a random collection of individuals. Instead, start thinking about your team as a *team of leaders*.

Knowing you have a team of leaders orients you to your primary job, which is to develop other High-Creative and effective leaders. Jeff

Hilzinger realized that his primary responsibility was to develop effective individual and collective leadership throughout the organization, and so should you.

### Lead the Development Agenda

What makes Jeff's story complete is that he continued to work on himself. But, more than that, he took on the development agenda of scaling individual and collective leadership development across the entire organization. By doing so, he took it to new, unprecedented levels of performance.

Jeff's success led to his next opportunity, accepting the role of CEO at Marlin Business Services. This was the first time he had the opportunity to punch that ticket.

In 1997, Marlin Business Services was a startup, operating primarily as a micro-ticket lessor since its inception. When the founding CEO left in 2016, the board used that event to look for somebody who could lead a business transformation at Marlin. The platform was sound but under-leveraged, and the primary goal was to accelerate growth in profitability and enterprise value.

Jeff took on the organization and leadership development agenda personally before he even landed in the new company. A month before he started his new job, he reached out for help and called us. He said,

> I know what I've got to do here when I come on board. I've got to make sure that we do the work around setting vision and strategy. The Marlin platform has several strategic directions it could pursue, so an important early part of this evolution will be a re-visioning of "Marlin 2.0." I will use this process to create alignment within the senior team and the board about where we want to go.
>
> Most of the current senior team is relatively new to Marlin, and I like them all. So, I'm hoping, as we re-envision the company, to coalesce the team around a common view of our collective leadership responsibilities. We need to be clear on our values and who we are. I've got to build a top team of effective leaders. Not only do they have to be effective leaders individually, we've got to be a team. We've got to work well together in

leading the organization. I'm going to take on the development agenda. I want to come in and start working with these folks from the very beginning.

Jeff owned the development agenda from day one. He started with himself and did so transparently, leading by example. He knew he had more to learn and asked for help, feedback, and input from those around him. His letting go in this way and being radically human encouraged everyone around him to do the same.

There is no faster way to develop other leaders and high-performing leadership teams. When you lead the development agenda, you do so personally. If you are willing to learn out loud, let go, be vulnerable, and do it all in deep relationship, the organizational transformation accelerates.

Scaling leadership starts with your team. Do you have the right team in place? Are you treating your team as a team of leaders? Are your leaders self-aware—do they know how they show up as leaders on your team? Is your team of leaders team-aware? If you answered "no" to any of these questions, you've got work to do before you can scale your leadership beyond yourself to the rest of the organization.

In developing your team of leaders into a collectively effective leadership team, you will be doing many of the same things you did for yourself, but all team members will do it together. So, it's a great idea to have individual conversations with all leaders on your team to help them determine how self-aware they are of their impact. Do they know what's working for them and what's not? Is the way they show up individually as leaders *enabling* the organization to become more effective and get better at what it does, or is it *disabling*? Are they open to feedback and able to respond in a way that creates an organization with greater capacity and capability, or do they defend themselves and continue to diminish capacity and capability?

In summary, you want to help every leader on your team start with him/herself and get on a development path.

### Assess Individual and Collective Effectiveness

Next, assess the collective effectiveness of your team and then your Extended Leadership Team. How does your team show up collectively to lead the organization? Gather the necessary information and feedback. Get open to it. Build an "on the table" culture. Create a supportive, feedback-rich environment in which you hold each other accountable for improving your leadership.

Develop the business case for transformation and determine what that requires of your team. How will the team need to show up in order to accomplish it? For example, if your leadership team chooses to strategically focus on stronger business results and increasing revenues, the question becomes this: How do you need to lead differently— individually and together—to get those results? If you choose to build an organization that's more engaged, then how will you go about that engagement process? Who do you need to be so that the culture of engagement actually takes root and results in the outcomes that the leadership team desires?

Once you build the connection between business outcomes and the leadership required to achieve them, put the entire group into a development process. Work that process until it becomes part of who you are and how you lead the organization. The development agenda needs to be highly focused and comprehensive. Develop it together but lead it personally. Say, for example, "Here's how we will transform our business by shifting from *who we are now* to *who we want to be a year from now*. This is going to be a major focus."

Everything you take on as a leadership team needs to be thought about from two distinct perspectives. One, what are the results you want to achieve and over what period of time? Two, who do you need to be, and how do you need to show up and lead together to create those results? Those two agendas go hand in hand. If, as a team, you can lead more effectively, you will get better results.

### Get the Right People in Place

To effectively scale leadership within your team, you absolutely have to get the right people in place. Do you ever find yourself accommodating the performance of a member of your team? You might find yourself saying something like, "You know, Frank's a really good guy, and I want to keep him on the team even though he's not really pulling his weight." Well, guess what? Frank may not be the leader you need. If he's not doing what you require of him, and if you adopt an accommodation or compromise strategy, he could keep the entire team from being as effective as it could be. One or two poor leaders on a team can seriously cancel out the effectiveness of the entire team. Frank either needs to get on an aggressive development agenda or leave.

When we started working with one of our clients, the company had an 11-member senior team that functioned ineffectively together. Two years later, the team has only six people. There is, in fact, only one member left from the original team, but the team itself is much stronger. The CEO and members of the team are working together on their leadership effectiveness. They're becoming more effective as a team in their collective leadership of the organization.

As you upgrade the leadership talent and leadership effectiveness of your organization, some people will fully embrace the development agenda. They'll be willing to take themselves on, to develop beyond where they are, and make development an ongoing part of who they are. You will need to change out people who aren't willing to develop and bring in people who embrace what you're doing. You cannot afford to have ineffective leaders who are not going to develop. As you consider each of the leaders you have in place, ask: "Does this person have the desire to develop? Does he/she really want it? Is he/she capable of what you are asking?" It is a matter of both the desire as well as the capability. You *have* to know. And then you must decide.

### Build Alignment Around What Matters

Once you have your team of leaders in place, you have to build strong alignment around your organization's purpose, vision, and strategy, which is a condition for scaling leadership.

This is what Jeff did when he stepped in as the new CEO of Marlin. We started working with him right away to access the effectiveness of each individual top leader as well as the top leadership team. We helped him get his entire team on a development agenda. Then, within his first 60 days on the job, he brought his leadership team together to set the organization's direction. Together, they clarified and aligned around the purpose, vision, values, and strategic agenda of the company.

If a team of leaders has responsibility for a business unit or for the whole business, they have to understand and commit to the organization's higher purpose. They must ensure that the right mission, vision, and strategy are in place. If any of these things need to be refreshed or completely redone, then tasking them to work together to do that will pull them into alignment. It will create the case for their continued leadership and team development, as well as set the stage for each of them doing the same within their teams. They will also be able to communicate the vision, mission, and strategy to the rest of the organization in a way that others are able to understand them, align around them, and know how they can contribute, individually and collectively.

### Step 3: Build Leadership Systems

Once you have started with yourself and have begun to develop your leadership team, you need to put in place the structural pieces for scaling leadership throughout the organization. This is the systems awareness condition for scaling leadership. It includes making development a strategic priority, a permanent part of what you do, and institutionalizing it throughout the organization. You are never truly done with creating a system and culture designed to develop leaders.

#### Create a Developmental Organization

You can and should create a developmental organization. You do this by cascading all the above steps through the organization and institutionalizing it. How? By starting with yourself and owning the organization's development agenda; by developing the team of leaders you have, changing out those leaders who are not effective and can't make the shift, and promoting or bringing in talented people who you assess capable of being effective leaders; by creating a feedback-rich environment; by measuring and tracking development to provide feedback for everyone's ongoing development; and by continually upgrading the entire system over time. You will also ask all the leaders on your team to do the same with their teams, who will do the same with their teams, and so on.

#### Focus on Measuring Results

What gets measured gets done. If you want to scale your leadership, then you need to measure the results and outcomes of your efforts. This requires creating systems to generate the data you need to assess if you are succeeding. Jeff became aware that he needed to measure the results of his efforts to scale his leadership. He asked his team these questions:

> What do we have to do from a measurement standpoint? What do we have to do from an accountability standpoint? What's going to be important from a process standpoint? How do we need to reorganize for us to do that? How do we continue to tell the truth about our performance—where we are in relationship to where we said we would be? How do we create a feedback-rich environment where we're all getting feedback?

Jeff got it—100 percent. To scale his leadership, he realized he had to completely transform himself and his organization. He had to work with his people to create systems that would support leadership at scale, including measuring results and outcomes. Anything less would not be enough to move the needle on performance.

### Institutionalize the Development Agenda

Fast forward 12 months. We brought Jeff's entire team together for the second time in just a little over a year. We spent three days together in Gettysburg on that hallowed battlefield learning leadership lessons that could be directly applied. We worked with the team on their own leadership—individually and collectively. We upped their feedback quotient, improving how they could give each other direct feedback. We put all the learning into leadership development plans, capturing what every member of the team needed to do for the next phase of his or her development.

Fast forward another five months. We followed up with the team by measuring its improvement and identifying what needed to be done to further improve.

Fast forward to today. We are going to the next round—institutionalizing the development agenda. As we do this, we're bringing in the leadership teams underneath them to build and extend the organization's leadership. We are cascading this work in Marlin's Extended Leadership Team (the Business Leadership Team). It is now time to scale leadership beyond the top team and engage the organization. Without scaling leadership and building bench strength in leadership, the business will not continue to thrive. Scaling leadership *at* scale and *for* scale.

Jeff is extremely methodical in his approach. He understands what works, and he's data driven. He took what he knew would give him the biggest bang for his buck in turning around the organization and has created leadership systems to perpetuate it. In his two years as CEO, Jeff has built a team that has literally taken the cap off the company, with the stock price going up 120 percent. They're knocking it out of the park. Marlin is achieving the highest performance in its entire history and is rapidly growing to become a billion-dollar organization.

## JEFF HILZINGER: A TRANSFORMATIONAL LEADER

When Jeff Hilzinger decided to take the CEO position at Marlin, the first thing he did was coalesce his team by aligning all the elements of organizational identity—purpose, vision, strategy, culture, and values. In parallel, he assessed his leadership team over several months. Within a year and a half after taking the helm, he had upgraded his team by installing talented leaders and removing those who weren't performing at a high level. He had everyone, including himself, working to develop their individual and collective leadership effectiveness. They have gone from a team of leaders that was performing at five or six on a 10-point scale to operating at seven or eight.

Jeff has extended this approach to the next level of leadership to upgrade the leadership system of the entire business. Team members are in the process of completely redesigning the organization and its processes. They have put metrics in place with key business indicators and accountability systems and redesigned the compensation and performance system. The results are telling.

Jeff is constantly raising the bar on leadership. As he scales his leadership further, he continues to look at his ELT and ask a variety of probing questions:

> Are we all aligned? Are we all on the same page? Can we have the tough conversations well? Do we speak with one voice? If you hear from one of us, do you hear from all of us? Are we consistent? When we're inconsistent, do we actually get clear about it?

In 2017, Jeff received his fourth LCP in 10 years. (See Figure 8.4.) It shows what a remarkable CEO Jeff has become, improving on all

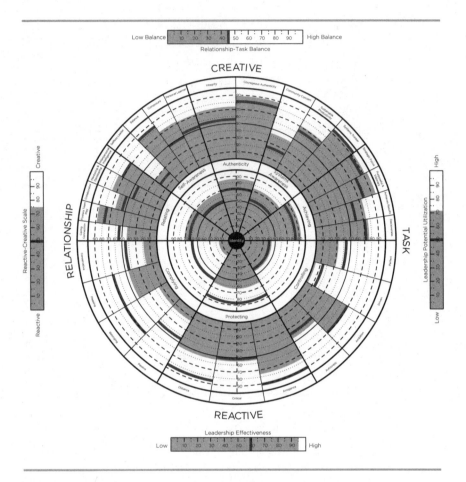

**FIGURE 8.4**   Jeff's Fourth Leadership Profile (2017)

fronts. He is now capable of deep relationships to complement his other tremendous strengths. His Reactivity is greatly reduced, and his Leadership Effectiveness is at the 95th percentile.

When we first gave Jeff feedback in 2007, he struggled to understand the value of this feedback and accept it. However, over the past decade, Jeff has transformed himself as a leader in almost every way possible. He has gone from being a bottom-quartile leader in effectiveness to the top-quartile, if not a top-decile leader. Not only that, but Jeff has learned how to scale leadership in his organization, amplifying his own leadership many times over through the people who work with him.

We asked Jeff how he managed to make the shift from the leader he was 10 years ago to the great business leader he is today. He explained:

It was actually fairly simple—I took to the bank what you guys told me and what I had learned from other great leaders like Jim. You told me that, from your research, the two most highly correlated dimensions for a leader's effectiveness are Purposeful Vision and Teamwork. So that's what I focused on. I focused on building a high-performing leadership team that is really clear on vision, strategy, and performance. I focused on the collective effectiveness of our Executive Leadership Team. Then, I built a feedback-rich environment and took on the development agenda for our business.

We recently spoke with Laura Anger, the CHRO at Marlin, and she described the tremendously powerful effect that Jeff's leadership has personally had on her.

When I interviewed for the position, I had the opportunity to interview with two other CEOs in addition to Jeff and choose among them. When I sat down with Jeff, I knew I was going to have one of those quality leadership experiences that would become a hallmark in my career.

That's not what she would have said about Jeff 10 years ago. In fact, people who knew him then would have suggested she not take the job. But Jeff did hire her—one of the best people in her field. Great leaders attract, retain, and further develop great talent.

So, what is Jeff tasked with doing, going forward?

He has to grow leadership capacity and capability as the leaders go into the other lines of business and grow the company. They need the capacity and capability to lead these new business lines as effectively as they are the core business. Jeff has gone from doing the work on self and the work on team to doing the work on his Extended Leadership Team. Then he'll do the same work on the organization's entire leadership system.

By following Jeff Hilzinger's example and the steps laid out in this chapter, you can scale your own leadership and grow leadership capacity and capability throughout every level of your organization. Make no mistake about it, the transformation will not be easy, and it won't happen overnight. It's an ongoing process that will take many years, and it's never really done. However, if you're willing to follow this process and take on the development agenda, which we hope you will, leadership will become a competitive advantage and asset—both for you personally and for your organization.

Because none of this happens unless you start with yourself, the rest of this book is focused on the universal path of development for shifting from Reactive to Creative and Integral leadership. Chapter 12 discusses in depth how to navigate this journey together.

## HOMEWORK

Take time to reflect on and answer these questions:

- Are you taking responsibility for scaling leadership in your organization? If yes, exactly what are you doing to accomplish this task? If not, why not, and what will you do to change this?

- What do you need to do to become more self-aware of the impact of your leadership?

- Are you leading a team of leaders? How does your team show up?

- Do you have the right team in place? If not, what will you do in the coming weeks to get the right team in place?

- In the Leadership Development Plan that comes with this book, write a vision statement for your leadership and for leadership in your organization. What will exist in two years that does not exist now?

# Chapter 9
# Full-Spectrum Leadership
## *Four Levels of Leadership*

In the preceding chapters, we explored how senior leaders describe, in written feedback to each other, what differentiates the most effective leaders from the least effective ones. We also explored how the senior leaders, with whom we have worked, have successfully transformed their organizations by scaling leadership. This chapter focuses on the deeper transformational journey each of us takes to become a more consciously effective leader. It also shows how the leaders in our study map out the journey.

In *Mastering Leadership*, we introduced a *Universal Model of Leadership*, and we took our share of criticism for being so audacious. The Universal Model integrates most of the best theory and research on leadership and its development over the past 70 years. (See Appendix E.) It integrates this knowledge into a model that captures something universal about leadership and how it develops. More important, it has been road-tested with more than 150,000 leaders over an 18-year period. The results achieved are phenomenal. We were surprised and pleased that, in their comments, the leaders in this study described the entire Universal Model the way we articulated it in *Mastering Leadership*. And, in doing so, they pointed to a unique pathway of development for each type of leader. This indicates that the street view of leadership validates the Universal Model and provides a practical path on which you can walk to evolve your own leadership.

In essence, the pathway is *Up* and *Across*. For most of us, *Up* means making the shift from Reactive to Creative leadership. For others, it means moving from Creative into Integral leadership. *Up* always means upgrading your Internal Operating System to match to the complexity of the challenges we face in leadership, now and in the future. *Across* means optimizing the balance between the yin and yang of leadership, the feminine and masculine, the relationships and tasks—thus moving toward better balance and greater optimization.

But first we must make the *Up* move. This *Up* move enables the move *Across*. Let's start by exploring how leaders describe the move up—the Full Spectrum of Leadership.

## THE MIDDLE GROUPS

To illustrate the Full Spectrum of Leadership, we introduce the middle groups in our study that had been left behind earlier. (See Figure 9.1.) If you recall, we sampled our database into four groups. So far, we have only discussed the two ends of the bell curve—the High-Reactive, Low-Creative end and the High-Creative, Low-Reactive end. But we wondered if those providing feedback about their leaders could also discern the middle groups between the two extremes.

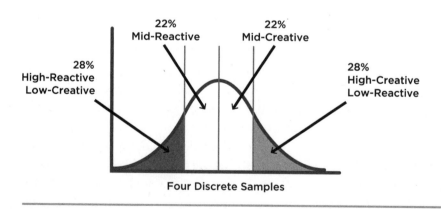

**Four Discrete Samples**

**FIGURE 9.1**   The Four Leadership Samples

The answer is a definite "Yes." People can see the Full Spectrum of Leadership—from High-Reactive/Low-Creative through the middle two groups to High-Creative/Low-Reactive—and they can describe the differences between these groups. For ease of discussion we call these four groups (1) High-Reactive, (2) Mid-Reactive, (3) Mid-Creative, and (4) High-Creative.

For each of the two middle groups we performed the same quantitative and qualitative analysis (matrix content). We think these astonishing results are game changing.

The first important finding is how statistically different these four groups are. As we explained, statisticians use the metric *effect size* to indicate if the measured difference among these groups of leaders is likely to show up as a noticeable difference. The *effect size* scores between these groups were between 1.2 and 2.8.[1] That means we should expect to see substantive differences in the way High-Reactive and Mid-Reactive leaders lead. The same is true for differences between Mid-Reactive and Mid-Creative, and between Mid-Creative and High-Creative leaders. Each progressive level of leadership measures differently and shows up with different effects.

This framework gives us a *pathway of development*—from Low-Creative, High-Reactive all the way up to High-Creative, Low-Reactive. It suggests that a Creative leader has a higher level of consciousness and competence, awareness and effectiveness than a Reactive leader. This framework represents an accelerated and lifelong pathway of measurable development for leaders.

## A PATHWAY OF DEVELOPMENT

Currently, we are working with an entire generation of European leaders, some of whom came from the former communist Eastern Bloc countries once in the firm grip of the Soviet Union. To a person, these men and women were raised in conditions that have led them to constantly seek security and safety today. As a result, they keep their heads down and build walls that their colleagues and employees can't penetrate. While they no longer operate in that controlling communist environment, they still behave as though they do.

We recently met with Anna, a female leader born and raised in Romania. During World War II, both of her grandparents died in concentration camps, and she was raised in a solidly communist country ruled with an iron fist by dictator, Nicolae Ceauşescu. Fellow citizens suffered poverty, food shortages, and late-night visits from the secret police. As a direct result of her upbringing, Anna is naturally highly Reactive. It resides deep in the DNA of her Internal Operating System.

When we first met her, Anna led with dictates and orders, seldom asking for suggestions or input from her employees. She was a closed book—no one got to know her. As a result, she had built few relationships with her team members. The feedback represented in her LCP was tough, even brutal, but she accepted it. Anna acknowledged that her leadership was reaching limits to scale, so she committed to a development path that would eventually take her to a High-Creative level of leadership. It would take time, and she would need to work through the middle levels first—no small task for this woman, whose habits would not be easily changed.

We began by coaching Anna to start requesting input from her people and soliciting their involvement by asking them questions instead of giving them orders. In this way, there would be a gradual shift in her behavior toward inviting inclusion and participation by her people. Not a huge leap, but small steps forward.

The second suggestion was for Anna to start opening up and letting people get to know her better. "Talk to them about your background," we said. "Give them some perspective and share details about what shaped you into who you are. Create a more open forum." Then, we gave her suggestions on how to do that. As a result, we were able to help Anna move from High-Reactive to Mid-Reactive leadership. Today, she is firmly on a path of development toward Mid-Creative leadership and, one day, to High-Creative leadership. But, it's not easy to change when, for years, she's been leading in a way that has brought a large measure of success and rewards—both financial and psychological.

## A DEEPER DIVE INTO THE DATA

Let's look at our findings, starting quantitatively. Figure 9.2 shows the aggregate Leadership Circle Profile for each of the four groups.

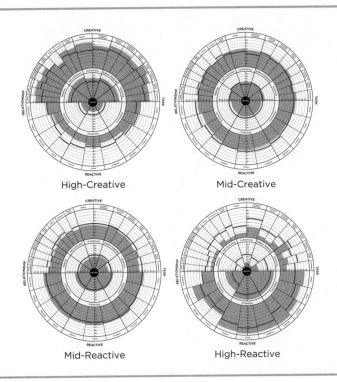

High-Creative

Mid-Creative

Mid-Reactive

High-Reactive

**FIGURE 9.2**   Leadership Circle Aggregate Profiles for the Four Leader Groups

You can see the progression from one Profile to the next. This is not surprising as we sampled for it, but the *effect size* differences between these Profiles are large. This suggests that these four groups of leaders bring different weather to their people and their organizations. Our independent researchers were surprised by how well the Profile measures the differences between these four groups of leaders. The LCP is a finely honed instrument, and it measures large, meaningful differences as leaders progress along the Full Spectrum of Leadership.[2]

Figure 9.3 provides another view of this data. The bars in this chart show the average percentile score (provided by raters) for the leaders in the sample of each level of leadership. The Creative (top-half) Competency score on the LCP for each of the four groups is shown by the light gray bars. The darker gray bars represent the associated *Leadership*

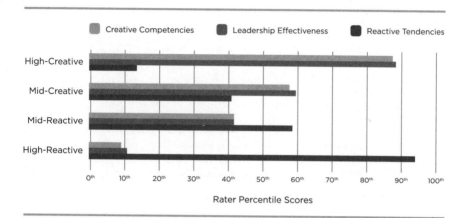

**FIGURE 9.3** Creative, Reactive, and Leadership Effectiveness Scores

*Effectiveness* scores, and the very dark bars are the scores for average Reactive Tendencies.

Notice how closely the Creative Competency scores correlate with the Leadership Effectiveness scores. They are completely in sync. Also notice how the Reactive Tendency scores are also in sync but move in the opposite direction and provide an inverse mirror image of the Creative Competency and Effectiveness scores. The Creative Competency and Leadership Effectiveness scores, in round numbers, move from the 10th to the 40th, 60th, and 90th percentile. By comparison, the Reactive Tendency scores move in the opposite direction—from the 90th to the 60th, 40th, and 10th percentiles. This data clearly suggests that each progressive level of the Spectrum of Leadership is quite different, and each is more effective as it moves from High-Reactive to High-Creative.

Next, we wanted to see how the written comment scores for each level of leadership tracked to these measures. Figure 9.4 shows the results.

In this graphic, the comment scores were overlaid on the Profile percentile scores. For each group, we used the Net Strengths scores (number of endorsed strengths minus the number of liabilities), then converted those numbers to a percentage in which the High-Creative leaders' Net Strengths score—because it was the largest—becomes 100 and the other scores are a percentage of that. This conversion allowed us to see the relationship between Net Strengths endorsement scores and Profile percentile scores.

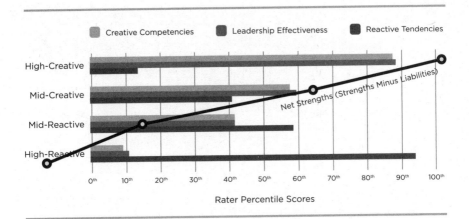

**FIGURE 9.4**  Creative, Reactive, Leadership Effectiveness, and Net Strengths Scores

As we see, the written comments parallel the quantitative data to a remarkable degree. From this, we concluded that leaders are precise when providing written feedback. They see and describe with precision, quantitatively and qualitatively, the Full Spectrum of Leadership.

As leaders, we bring the weather, and the people around us can accurately describe the weather we bring. Another set of graphics demonstrates how precisely others see us in action and can describe what we are doing that is working, and not working, and how all this impacts our effectiveness as a leader. Figures 9.5 through 9.8 display the relationship between endorsed strengths, endorsed liabilities, Leadership Effectiveness percentile scores, and Leadership Ratio.

These graphics display the stunning difference between each level of leadership. The light gray bars are the endorsement scores for the High-Creative leaders' top five strengths. The dark gray bars show the endorsement scores for the top five liabilities for High-Reactive leaders. The large arrow shows the average Leadership Effectiveness score for each group.

As you scan sequentially through each graphic, you can see how the endorsement scores for the top five strengths decrease with each level of leadership (from High-Creative to High-Reactive). You can also see how Leadership Effectiveness scores follow suit and how the top five liabilities grow, moving along the Full Spectrum of Leadership from High-Creative to High-Reactive.

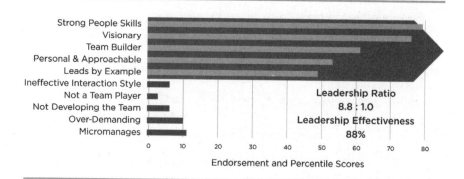

**FIGURE 9.5**    High-Creative

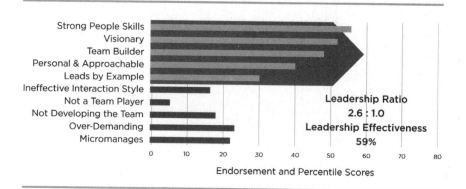

**FIGURE 9.6**    Mid-Creative

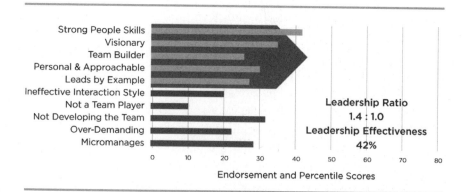

**FIGURE 9.7**    Mid-Reactive

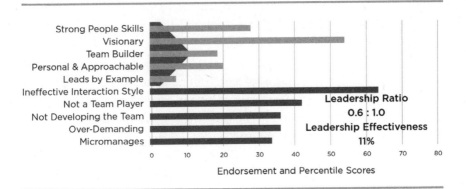

**FIGURE 9.8**  High-Reactive

The Leadership Ratios reported in these graphics are the ratio of strengths to liabilities in the top five lists. High-Reactive leaders have a Leadership Ratio of 0.6 to 1. The Canceling Effect is obvious. They are getting a 0.6 multiple that, because it is far less than 1, means that the harder they go, the more they cancel themselves out. This is why their Leadership Effectiveness scores average at the 11th percentile.

Mid-Reactive leaders have a Leadership Ratio of 1.4 to 1. This suggests that while these leaders are not getting in their own way as much, they are still not getting much of a multiple on their leadership. It may be worth noting that raters in this study are more likely to provide positive feedback than negative feedback. When we look at all the comments from all 4,113 raters, we find they are 1.7 times more likely to comment about strengths than liabilities. We see the same response bias in quantitative data. Given this tendency, we believe Mid-Reactive leaders are likely canceling themselves out more than their 1.4 Leadership Ratio would suggest. This is confirmed by their Leadership Effectiveness score, which averages at the 40th percentile.

The Leadership Ratio for the Mid-Creative group is 2.6. These leaders have a competitive advantage, and they get a multiple on their leadership. Their average Leadership Effectiveness score at nearly the 60th percentile is above average.

The High-Creative group is truly an astounding group of leaders. Their leadership is clearly getting a multiple with a Leadership Ratio of 8.8 to 1. The Amplifying Effect of this ratio is huge as Leadership Effectiveness scores are nearly at the 90th percentile. These High-Creative leaders could not be more different than their High-Reactive colleagues, who have a ratio of 0.6 to 1 and Effectiveness scores down near the 10th percentile.

In Figures 9.9 through 9.12, bubble charts show the endorsement scores. For these charts, we took all endorsement scores higher than 20 for both strengths and liabilities and combined them into one chart. The size of the bubble corresponds to the magnitude of the endorsement score. Strengths are shown in white. Liabilities are in dark gray. Non-Differentiating Strengths are shown in light gray. Browse through these four charts and visually take in how progressively different each level of leadership is described in writing.

Notice that as leadership becomes less Creative and more Reactive, the bubble charts become less white and increasingly more dark gray. Key strengths—such as *strong people skills*—diminish as you move down the spectrum while the corresponding liabilities—such as *ineffective interaction style*—grow dramatically. Liabilities and Non-Differentiating Strengths become more prevalent as leadership becomes more Reactive. These images dramatically show the declining Leadership Ratio and the increasing Canceling Effect as the leadership becomes more Reactive. These figures create a clear visual of the kind of weather each level of leadership brings, running from smooth sailing to extremely stormy and choppy.

## SO WHAT? KEY CONCLUSIONS

From this research come these key conclusions:

- The Leadership Circle Profile is a nuanced assessment capable of measuring effective differences in leader behavior and impact across the Full Spectrum of Leadership. This confirms that we are providing meaningful feedback to leaders.
- There is indeed a measurable Full Spectrum of Leadership. We pulled out four levels for research purposes, but given the magnitude of the *effect size* scores, the LCP could distinguish even more levels with remarkable granularity. So, it is possible to know, with accuracy, where you land on this spectrum and where your organization's collective leadership lands. Do you think this might be important for you to know?

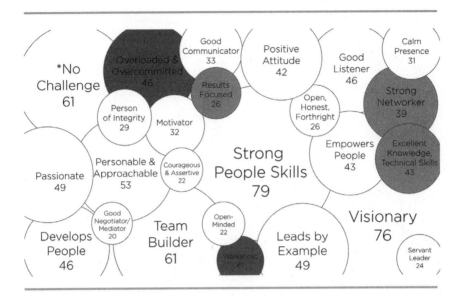

**FIGURE 9.9**   High-Creative Endorsement Scores

\*No Challenge means that, when asked, raters either cited no liabilities or actually commented as such.

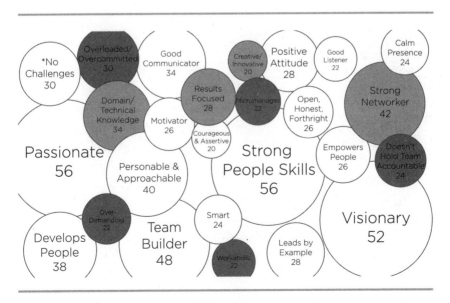

**FIGURE 9.10**   Mid-Creative Endorsement Scores

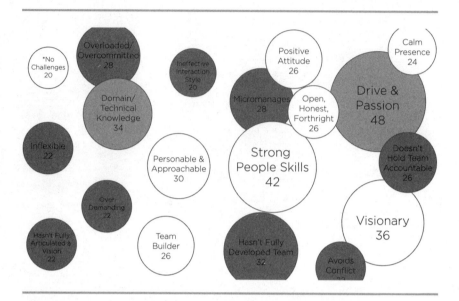

**FIGURE 9.11**    Mid-Reactive Endorsement Scores

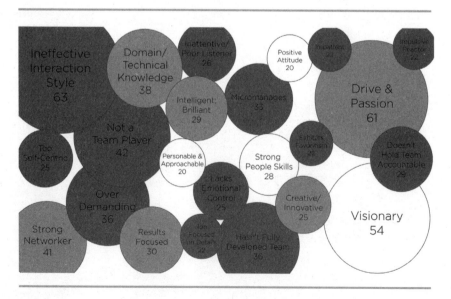

**FIGURE 9.12**    High-Reactive Endorsement Scores

- We know that leadership is a primary contributor to organizational performance and we know what it looks like. We also know what Effective Leadership is (and is not) and how to describe it. The leaders around you can describe the Full Spectrum of Leadership—from High-Reactive to High-Creative, from very ineffective to very effective, from what works and what does not and how it correlates to performance.
- The wisdom is in the system—it's all around you! As a leader, you are in a feedback-rich environment whether you realize it and use it, or not. Leaders around you experience and can describe (quantitatively and qualitatively) how you are behaving, what makes you effective, and what is limiting your effectiveness. This question remains: *Do you take advantage of the feedback-rich water in which you swim every day?*

## WHERE ARE YOU?

Where do you land on the Spectrum of Leadership? How do you know? Where does your Extended Leadership Team land? How do you know? Can you answer these questions?

How clearly do the leaders around you actually *see* you? If you took a moment to ask them, how precise would their feedback be about how you show up as a leader, what is working for you—and what is not—and the kind of effect your leadership has on people in the organization?

Would you want to know? Unfortunately, most leaders don't.

Organizations are feedback-poor when they need to be feedback-rich. The higher we go in the organization, the less feedback we get. Why? Because the higher we go, the more cautious (and afraid) people are to tell the truth, especially when the news is not good. This is how the emperor gets to the point where he or she has no clothes. Most leaders don't take advantage of the feedback-rich environment in which they work because feedback is not something we naturally request. We must learn to do this.

Since the organization cannot perform at a level higher than the collective effectiveness of its leadership for any sustained period, it's critical to know the answers to these questions. The more Reactive you are as a leader, the more likely you do not see your development gap and see yourself as more effective than you are. The more Creative you are, the more likely you see and acknowledge your development agenda.

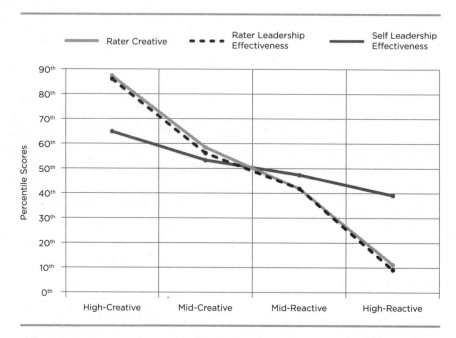

**FIGURE 9.13** Self-Scores Compared to Rater Scores

Figure 9.13 shows the relationship of Self-Leadership scores (how a leader evaluates him/herself) compared to the Rater scores.

The average rater Leadership Effectiveness percentile scores for each of the four groups are remarkably similar to the average Rater Creative Competency scores. The Leadership Effectiveness scores that leaders give themselves tell a different story. Notice that High-Reactive leaders tend to *overrate* their effectiveness by almost 30 percentile points while High-Creative leaders tend to *underrate* theirs. This is what Jim Collins found in his book *Good to Great*.[3] The highly effective leaders in his study (*Level 5 leaders*) are a counterintuitive mixture of fierce resolve and humility.

The most effective leaders are oriented toward development and aware of where they need to grow. Their High-Reactive colleagues resist getting ongoing feedback and facing their development gap. Consequently, they cancel themselves out in ways they do not know, and more often than not, in ways they do not want to face.

Since you already are in a feedback-rich environment, the only question is this: *Are you taking advantage of it and capitalizing on it?*

Setting up methods and processes for harvesting feedback and learning from it will determine the kind of leader you become. Each of us dwells in a more feedback-rich environment than we recognize. People see us with amazing, nuanced precision. They can see the subtle but substantive difference between a High-Reactive and a Mid-Reactive leader, and between each of the levels of leadership.

What would prevent someone from giving *you* feedback? If you can honestly answer this question, you can also identify what it would take for you to receive more feedback. If you're not getting a great deal of feedback from your people, there's a reason. We know that High-Reactive leaders don't get much direct, honest feedback because they don't do well with it, and those who provide it often pay a price.

The precise feedback you need to grow is all around you. While Creative leaders harvest it, Reactive leaders repel it and their people eventually give up.

## IT'S TIME FOR AN UPGRADE

Each level of leadership is likely equally and highly talented. However, each is different in how their leadership is experienced with different levels of impact and scalability. Movement up the spectrum means going from Reactive Liabilities to Creative Strengths; from canceling out talent to getting a multiple on it; from deploying personal technical, intellectual, and creative talent to amplifying that through people and teams. This movement up the spectrum is less a matter of adding to or improving on a competency and more a matter of development.

The Full Spectrum of Leadership is related to the Stage of Development of the leader. If you want to master the art and practice of leadership, then the first move in the Universal Pathway of Development is *Up*. That means upgrade your Internal Operating System, so higher levels of leadership effectiveness and mastery can boot up. The next few chapters explore this vertical move as described by the leaders in our study.

**HOMEWORK**

- Where on the Full Spectrum of Leadership are you as a leader? How does this affect the way you lead?

- Where on the Full Spectrum of Leadership is your Extended Leadership Team? How does this affect the effectiveness of your organization?

- What is your pathway to development as a leader? What are the pathways of development for your direct reports?

# Chapter 10
# Reactive Leadership

*Strengths Run Reactively Cancel Themselves Out*

The Universal Pathway of Development is *Up* and *Across*. The first move is vertical (*Up*) and the second is to augment your core capability with a complimentary competency (*Across*).

Let's start with the vertical move first. Counterintuitively, you must go down to go up, so if you want to go higher, you must go deeper. Here's an example from our lives.

＊　＊　＊

A few years ago, when I (Bob) received my LCP 360 feedback, what I learned was unexpected and even hurtful. I had high scores on *Arrogance* and low scores on *Collaboration* and *Teamwork*. This pattern in my leadership hamstrung the organization's ability to develop strategy and translate it into execution on results. It wasn't a pretty picture.

My first inclination, like many of our clients, was to explain it away. I called Bill over and tried to talk him out of the scores he had given me. The conversation went something like this:

**Bob:** Bill, you scored me 4.5 on a 5-point scale on *Arrogance*.
**Bill:** Yes, I did.

**Bob:** Well, Bill, the average score on *Arrogance* in our norm base is 2, maybe slightly less. The standard deviation is about 0.5. So, you scored me 5 standard deviation units above the mean on *Arrogance*. That would mean you see me as one of the most arrogant persons in the world, if not the most arrogant person you know."

**Bill:** Right.

**Bob:** Ouch.

That hurt. I did not want to accept Bill's feedback, but eventually I did. After receiving similar feedback from my business partners, I made a choice. I declared to the group that if my arrogance was getting in the way of our working relationships, then I wanted to change. I chose to know *more* about that behavior, not less. So, I asked my partners for continued feedback about how I get in my own way, and how I can play more collaboratively.

Over the next couple of years, I had plenty of experiences that enabled me to see myself in action. At one point during a heated conflict, I went for a walk to reflect on how I was showing up in this disagreement. As I dropped into how I was feeling and thinking, I suddenly fell all the way to the bottom. Insights come when they come, and clarity came in this moment. It was startling. "Oh, my God, I am my ideas," I realized.

In that moment, I saw yet another hidden layer in the core of my Reactive Operating System. I saw how I define myself based on my ideas. "These ideas (and I have created a career around my ability to craft ideas) are not ideas I have; instead, they have me. Who am I without my ideas and my intellectual brilliance? I *am* my ideas."

I had no idea I was so defined by my intellectual capability. But once I saw it, I started to laugh. "All these years, I have been angry at Bill for his arrogance. All the while, *I* am the one who is arrogant. It has all been my projection. I see myself in him and then blame *him*. Wow!"

I went home and wrote Bill the following email: "Bill, I am wrong. Furthermore, I have been wrong in our partnership for a long time. I am ready to talk." Bill wrote back: "I feel your heart, brother, let's talk." A week later, we met for breakfast on the morning before a day of work with a key client. We had an extraordinary and healing conversation and then went into our day with the client and did the best work we've ever done together.

\*　\*　\*

The core of Reactivity is *identity*. We define ourselves by having to be seen or experienced in a certain way, to know ourselves as good, worthy, and successful. Not to be seen that way is to lose oneself—not to be or exist at all. Of course, this is an illusion, not the truth. But it sure feels true, and since we have a lifetime of living *as if it were true*, we have made it true.

The first half of the vertical movement into Creative leadership is this: Drop into and see the Reactive illusion at the core of how we define ourselves and how that illusion has us deploying ourselves into circumstances in ways that are ineffective. We need to see the core organizing assumptions beneath how we are canceling ourselves out.

Different types of people have designed their Internal Operating Systems around different organizing assumptions that form the core of their identity. The Universal Model of Leadership maps out three different core types of leaders, each organizing their identity around a different corresponding leadership strength:

1. Heart—people strengths
2. Mind—intellectual strengths
3. Will—results strengths

Each of us is a unique combination of heart, mind, and will.[1] However, one of these strengths usually dominates, meaning we are uniquely heart-centered/relationship-oriented, mind-centered/idea-oriented, or will-centered/results-oriented. Likely while growing up, we tended to develop our primary strength to a high degree and our other gifts to a lesser degree, if at all.

As we develop into our Socialized Self[2]—the Internal Operating System of Reactive leadership—we leverage our core strength, whether it is relationship (heart), intellect (head), or results (will). Although we have all these strengths to some degree, we tend to organize around one and make it core to our identity. When we become identified with our strength, we believe it defines who we are. Therefore, we have to be seen as nice, likable, agreeable, supportive (heart); or as smart, wise, brilliant, analytical (head); or as the one who drives results and gets things done (will).

Because we identify with a core strength as who we are, we slip into a compulsive relationship with our strength—we *must* be this way or else. We tend to overuse, overextend, and overplay our strength until it becomes a liability. Overdeveloping our strengths usually means under-developing the other strengths, which brings additional liabilities. Likely, we are unaware of how we turn our strengths into liabilities, thus playing right into the Canceling Effect in which our strengths are offset by the associated liabilities.

We tend to pack our best strength into our Reactive strategy. When reacting under threat or pressure, we default to our strength. Hence, three types of Reactive leaders emerge:

1. Complying (heart)
2. Protecting (head)
3. Controlling (will)

At the Socialized level of development, one of these three behavioral tendencies is usually central to our identity and how we deploy ourselves as leaders.

## CANCELED GIFTS AND COMPETING LIABILITIES

As Reactive leaders cancel themselves out, they remove or cancel their gift in a way that introduces *Competing Liabilities*. These come with the underdevelopment of other strengths and further limit a leader's effectiveness and scalability.

To summarize, Reactive leadership does these three things: It cancels its gifts and strengths; it introduces Competing Liabilities; and it does not scale.

Because each type of leader has designed his or her Internal Operating System around different gifts and strengths, each reacts in a unique way. Each type brings different strengths to the table and then uses certain liabilities to cancel out those strengths. They simultaneously introduce a set of Competing Liabilities that is unique to that type.

*If you want to go higher, you must go deeper.* The first move on the Universal Path of Development is up. But up from where? An important first step in closing your development gap is to drop into your Reactive self to understand the strengths and weaknesses that come with your type. This includes seeing how your current Operating System is designed, its core organizing assumptions, and how you, therefore, deploy yourself into the circumstances. Seeing this locates you within the Universal Model, orients you, and charts your specific path of development.

## HEART-CENTERED LEADERS

Heart-centered leaders move toward others to form relationships and build their character around their gift of heart. They are relationship oriented. At the Socialized level of development, they are identified with that gift—their self-worth and security depend on others liking, loving, or accepting them. Their core belief is, "I'm okay if you like, love, and accept me." In their version of playing not-to-lose, they pursue safety over purpose by tending to give up too much power because they want to be liked. More than that, they fear rejection—not being accepted, loved, and liked feels like death to them—so they avoid controversy and conflict, tending toward Complying leadership.

The leaders in our study described Complying leaders similarly. In the Leadership Circle Universal Model of Leadership, the dimension of *Complying* is opposite the Creative dimension of *Achieving* because they are contradictory tendencies. The more power a leader gives up to feel accepted (Complying), the less likely he or she will use power to champion a vision, then translate vision into strategy and execution into results (Achieving). Figure 10.1 shows the correlations between these dimensions based on our database of 1.5 million surveys.

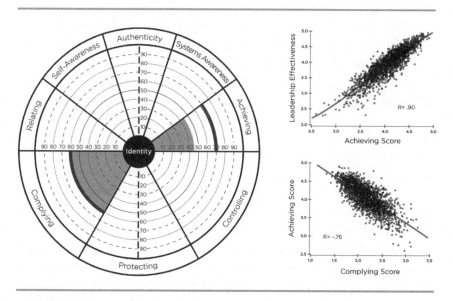

**FIGURE 10.1**   Correlations between the Dimensions of Achieving and Complying

Achieving is positively and strongly correlated to Leadership Effectiveness ($R = 0.90$). Naturally, a leader who is high Achieving would be seen as effective. As purpose-driven leaders, they create a clear and compelling vision, translate that vision into strategy, and execute well on their strategy by getting results. By contrast, Complying is strongly and inversely correlated to Achieving ($R = -0.76$). Complying leaders interrupt their Achieving, which limits their effectiveness.

To see how leaders describe Complying leadership, we turned to our database, isolated High-Complying leaders, and then sampled the comments those leaders received from their raters. Figure 10.2 shows the aggregate Leadership Profile for 50 High-Complying leaders.

As you can see, this is a High-Complying group of leaders with average Complying scores at the 99th percentile and Achieving scores that are essentially nonexistent.

How were these leaders described in writing? Here are some typical comments:

> Jim needs to stop worrying about what others think, stop being wishy/washy with his decisions, focus on team improvement and results, and let opinions fall where they may.

> He needs to take a stand on his business position/feelings and support them with facts. He shouldn't change positions to please others when controversy happens.

> Many of his employees and peers believe that he is more a "yes man" than a person who will actually commit to making things change for the better.

When we sampled the written comments on this group of leaders, here is what we found (see Figure 10.3).

In column one, Strength, High-Complying leaders are described by other leaders as having *strong people skills* (55). They are calm, easy to work with, good listeners, and they tend to develop teams and collaborate. Their strength scores are moderate to low because these heart-centered leaders lead in a highly reactive manner. Remember, whenever we run our strength reactively, we limit that strength.

Column two in Figure 10.3, Strength Removed, lists the liabilities most strongly endorsed that go beyond limiting the gift and/or removing

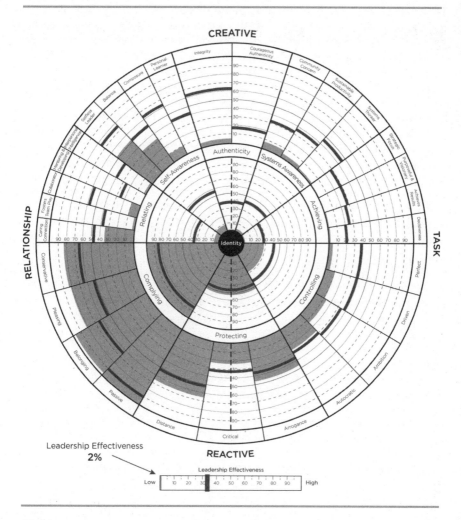

**FIGURE 10.2**    Aggregate Leadership Profile for High-Complying Leaders

it. Leaders who have a Reactive strategy of Complying are seen by other leaders as too reserved, too differential, lacking in confidence, insecure, conflict averse, too worried about what others think, and distant. These liabilities nearly cancel out all strengths. The total score for strengths is 216, which is nearly equaled by the liabilities that come with playing not-to-lose by giving up power (181).

| STRENGTH | | STRENGTH REMOVED | | COMPETING LIABILITIES | |
| --- | --- | --- | --- | --- | --- |
| Strong People Skills | 55 | Too Reserved | 50 | Poor Decision Making | 43 |
| Calm Presence | 45 | Too Deferential | 38 | Vision Not Fully Articulated | 30 |
| Easy to Work With | 38 | Lacks Confidence, Insecure | 25 | Doesn't Hold Team Accountable | 20 |
| Good Listener | 33 | Too Worried About What Others Think | 25 | Doesn't Engage with Staff | 23 |
| Team Builder | 25 | Avoids Conflict | 23 | Not a Team Player | 23 |
| Strong Collaborator | 20 | Aloof/Distant | 20 | Lacks Passion | 8 |
| **TOTAL** | **216** | **TOTAL** | **181** | **TOTAL** | **147** |

**FIGURE 10.3**   Strengths and Liabilities of High-Complying Leaders

Competing Liabilities in column three in Figure 10.3 lists additional liabilities that were endorsed. We call these *Competing Liabilities*—strengths that are underdeveloped due to the overreliance on the strengths that are core to a leader's type. Competing Liabilities are deficits in the opposite direction of their strengths, in this case Achieving. When Complying gets too strong, Achieving suffers and High-Complying leaders are described as poor decision makers, lacking vision, not holding team members accountable, disengaged, not being a team player, and lacking passion. These Competing Liabilities total 147. When combined with the liabilities that take the strengths off the table, the total liabilities (328) more than cancel out the strengths (216).

The leader-raters in this study described Complying leadership with great precision in the same way we do in the interpretation manual of our LCP 360 assessment. Complying leaders have the strengths of forming relationships with people, supporting and developing others, approachability, listening, and connecting. These are heart-centered folks.

When the heart gets overused, however, and these skills are run Reactively, these leaders are experienced as conventional, cautious, submissive, self-centric, not holding the team accountable, too focused on pleasing others, indecisive, and failing to achieve results. When we provide this kind of feedback to High-Complying leaders, they often tell us, "Wow. I have no voice. I've lost my power." Why? Leaders lose voice and power when their strengths are turned into liabilities by running them through a Reactive structure.

In another example, we recently worked with Joan, a leader who was very High Complying, and the feedback she received reflected that. Some of the comments were:

> I don't know what you stand for, I don't know what's important to you.

> I really wish you'd just let me know and understand what it is you really want.

> It feels like what you're doing is telling me what you think is important to me, versus what's important to you, and you're my boss.

Toward the end of her debrief, we asked Joan, "Where does that come from?" She explained, "My parents did everything they could for us as children, but my brother was a real problem, so I never wanted to cause any trouble for my parents."

Joan was the perfect little girl who turned into the perfect grown woman, and she carried this persona right into her leadership. By trying not to be a problem, she swallowed her voice and gave up her power to other people. People consistently and constantly wondered what's important to her and what she really thought, but Joan wouldn't put it out there.

At the end of our conversation, we told her, "We see that you've worked incredibly hard your entire life to not be a problem."

Joan thought about it for a moment. And then her eyes opened wide as she responded: "You're right. I spend every day of my life trying to figure out how not to cause problems for anyone, and as a result, I'm causing problems all over the place. And I'm doing this in a big way. I'm holding myself back by holding myself back."

She then described how some of the ways she conducted herself as a leader at work carried over to her personal life. As a single mom with two teenage sons, Joan knew she needed to provide them with guidance through this difficult time because their father was no longer in the picture. But she wasn't able to have the conversations with them that *they* needed. She couldn't open up to them and share experiences from her own challenging life. And because she was unable to connect with herself, Joan was unable to connect deeply with her boys.

High-Complying leaders can lose their voices to such an extent that they no longer know who they really are—at work and home.

To help Joan better understand what her people needed from her, we scheduled a session with her and 12 of her associates. We then asked each of them to provide one another with feedback. Surprisingly, they had plenty of feedback for their coworkers but none for Joan. When we asked why, they said that, while they liked Joan, they didn't feel they knew her.

Insidiously, Complying leaders are relationship-oriented, but in a way that ultimately undermines relationships. They are heart-centered, but give up power in the deferential way they talk and how they lose their voice. Because they are caring human beings, people love being around them, but they take their gift off the table. They undermine their relationships by being *too* concerned about relationships.

## WILL-CENTERED LEADERS

Will-centered leaders are the opposite of heart-centered leaders. If heart-centered leaders are the *yin*, will-centered leaders are the *yang*. Rather than moving *toward* others, will-type leaders move *against* others. They compete in order to triumph over others. Rather than giving up power, they take up power and use it to get ahead. In fact, their core strength is their willpower—their inner drive to make things happen, get results, and create what they want. They are born to lead and drive things forward.

At the Socialized level of development, will-centered leaders organize their identity around their gift of will and use of power to drive results. Their core belief is, "I'm okay if I am the one who gets results, am perfect, am moving up, am in charge and in control." They fear failure because failing at anything feels like death. Their strength is driving results forward. Since they often seek and gain power at the expense of others— seeing others as resources to be used to achieve what they want—they can leave a host of maimed bodies in their wake. They do not delegate, develop teamwork, build trust, or mentor others gracefully. They are Controlling types.

Figure 10.4 shows the dynamic relationship between Controlling and Relating in the Universal Model of Leadership. These are opposite

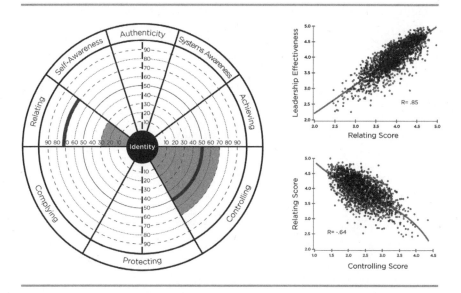

**FIGURE 10.4**   Correlations between the Dimensions of Relating and Controlling

behavioral tendencies. High-Controlling leaders tend not to excel at relationships and teamwork. Relating (connecting with people, mentoring them, developing high-performing teamwork, collaborating, and strong interpersonal skills) is highly correlated with Leadership Effectiveness (0.85). Given what we saw in the most endorsed strengths of High-Creative leaders (people, people, people), this makes sense.

Controlling, however, is solidly inverse to Relating (-0.64). As Controlling leadership increases, Relating decreases. This is how Controlling leaders get in their own way.

We also isolated and sampled the comments of a group of High-Controlling Leaders to get a street view on their leadership. Figure 10.5 shows the aggregate Profile for this group of leaders. This group of leaders has average Controlling scores at the 87th percentile and low Leadership Effectiveness scores in the 17th percentile.

Let's see how they were described in writing. Here are a few examples:

John is passionate about the success of our company. But he sometimes lets this passion get the better of him. He pushes others too hard, demanding more than they can deliver.

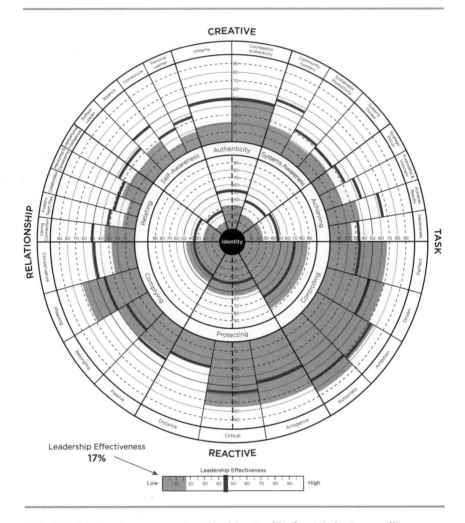

**FIGURE 10.5**    Aggregate Leadership Profile for High-Controlling Leaders

Sara's greatest challenge is to trust and rely on her team in a way that empowers them to do their jobs and creates trust. She wants to free her time to focus on matters that really require her attention (and not get bogged down in little details that can be handled by others).

Barry does not foster team play or create a collaborative culture. He can be disrespectful, selfish, arrogant, and scornful.

He uses a directive, authoritative, command-and-control style. He sees everything as WIN-LOSE and distances others through his judgments. He is not an inspiring leader.

Figure 10.6 summarizes the written comments for the sample of High-Controlling leaders.

High-Controlling leaders scored moderately on passion, drive and technical/domain knowledge; they were also described as being visionary, positive and easy to work with. This is a strong set of skills with a total strength score of 222. But too much drive, especially *self-centric* drive, has liabilities associated with it. These strengths are more than canceled out with High-Controlling leaders being described as over-committed, micromanagers, over-demanding, inflexible, impulsive and impatient. Again, these descriptions show how the overextension of a strength (drive) becomes a liability and cancels out the strength.

The Competing Liabilities show up on the opposite side—the under-developed Relating strengths. These leaders are also described as being ineffective in interactions, poor team players, lousy listeners, self-centric, and emotionally uncontrolled. These Competing Liabilities also more than cancel out the strengths.

Total endorsed strengths are 222, but the overextension of those strengths removes the task gifts (164), while the Competing Liabilities (128) further cancel out the effectiveness of these leaders. Obviously when we run the strengths of will and power reactively, Strengths are canceled, and Competing Liabilities introduced, resulting in un-scalability.

| TASK GIFTS | | TASK GIFTS REMOVED | | COMPETING LIABILITIES | |
|---|---|---|---|---|---|
| Strong Technical/Domain Knowledge | 45 | Overloaded/Overcommitted | 38 | Ineffective Interaction Style | 28 |
| Passionate | 45 | Micromanages | 35 | Doesn't Engage with Staff | 23 |
| Driven | 38 | Overdemanding | 33 | Poor Listener | 18 |
| Easy to Work With | 33 | Inflexible | 28 | Unaware of Impact on Others | 18 |
| Positive Attitude | 33 | Impulsive | 15 | Lacks Emotional Control | 18 |
| Visionary | 28 | Impatient | 15 | Doesn't Hold Team Accountable | 23 |
| TOTAL | 222 | TOTAL | 164 | TOTAL | 128 |

**FIGURE 10.6**   Strengths and Liabilities of High-Controlling Leaders

The leaders in our study describe the strengths and liabilities of Controlling leaders exactly as the theory and research predict. It is also similar to how we describe it in our Leadership Circle Profile interpretation manual. From an early age, Controlling leaders develop the strengths that use power to get results. The strengths include passion, drive, results-focus, and decisiveness. When they're used reactively, Controlling leadership results.

The strengths are often experienced by others as overdrive, perfectionism, "workaholism," excessive ambition, "dictatorialness," ineffective interaction style, poor listening, micromanaging, and over-demanding. This pits will against will, strength against strength. The beauty is that *will and power for creating results* are a core strength; they're unique gifts. But when they're run through a Reactive Operating System, it creates liabilities and outcomes that cancel out strengths.

## HEAD-CENTERED LEADERSHIP

Head-type leaders are people who move away from others in rational, analytical distance. They are usually intellectually brilliant and quite rational. They seek knowledge and truth, and they identify with those gifts.

At the Socialized level of development, they establish their sense of worth and security by demonstrating their analytical and critical capabilities. They remain in their head—staying above the fray—and provide rational explanations for events. Their self-worth and security depend on others seeing them as smart, knowledgeable, and superior. Their core belief is this: "I am okay if I am smart, self-sufficient, superior, above it all, and can find flaws in others' thinking." Their strength is remaining composed and rational amid chaos and conflict, analyzing what's going on from a safe, rational distance, and providing brilliant analysis to complex and conflictual situations. They are often experienced as cold, distant, disengaged, overly analytical, critical, or arrogant. Because their core fears are irrelevance and vulnerability, they tend to stay in their heads and provide analysis, but often they come across as being harshly critical, finding fault, and feigning superiority. They are Protecting types.

If Complying is *yin* and Controlling is the opposite energy, *yang*, then Protecting is *neutral* (staying calmly and critically above it all).

Consequently, Protecting is placed in the center position of the Universal Model of Leadership. Because it is neutral, it has no opposite. It is, however, inverse to its own strengths. Figure 10.7 shows this relationship. Protecting is opposite to its own core strengths and orientation: Self-Awareness, Authenticity, and Systems Awareness.

The Awareness dimensions (Self-Awareness, Systems Awareness, and Authenticity) are strongly and positively correlated to Leadership Effectiveness (0.88) while Protecting is inverse to these dimensions (–0.59). As Protecting leadership becomes more highly Reactive, it undermines Self-Awareness, Authenticity, and Systems Awareness. In fact, Protecting has strong inverse correlations to the entire Creative top half of the circle.

Figure 10.8 shows the aggregate Profile for the High-Protecting leaders sampled. Protecting is high at the 95th percentile and Leadership Effectiveness is low at the 10th percentile. As you can see, scores across the Creative top half of the circle are quite low.

Figure 10.9 shows the summary of written comments for the High-Protecting group. As you look at it, keep in mind that this group is at the 85th percentile on Protecting, but it's also high (65th percentile)

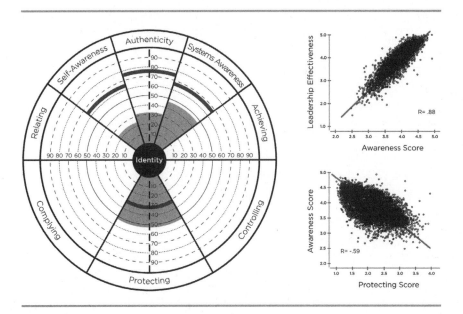

**FIGURE 10.7**   Correlations between Protecting and Awareness (Self-Awareness, Authenticity, and Systems Awareness)

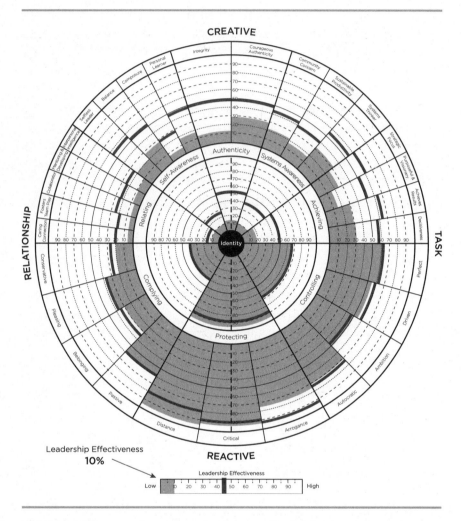

**FIGURE 10.8**    Aggregate Leadership Profile for High-Protecting Leaders

on Controlling. Thus, we should see a mix of both rational and willpower strengths.

As expected, the strengths most endorsed are *highly rational* and *driven*. High-Protecting leaders are visionary and strategic, technically strong with good domain knowledge, driven, results focused, smart, and passionate. Again, most of these scores are moderate to low because the

| STRENGTH | | STRENGTH REMOVED | | COMPETING LIABILITIES | |
|---|---|---|---|---|---|
| Visionary | 45 | Over Demanding | 35 | Ineffective Interaction Style | 58 |
| Strong Technical/ Domain Knowledge | 30 | Vision Not Fully Articulated | 33 | Not a Team Player | 35 |
|  |  | Inflexible | 30 | Doesn't Engage with Staff | 25 |
| Driven | 30 | Doesn't Hold Team Accountable | 23 | Exhibits Favoritism | 25 |
| Results Focused | 28 |  |  |  |  |
| Smart/Intelligent | 25 | Impulsive Reactor | 23 | Puts Others Down, Publically Humiliates | 25 |
| Strategic Thinker | 25 | Avoids Conflict | 19 | Doesn't Develop Directs | 18 |
| Passionate | 20 | Aloof/Distant | 18 | Poor Listener | 15 |
| TOTAL | 203 | TOTAL | 181 | TOTAL | 201 |

**FIGURE 10.9**   Strengths and Liabilities of High-Protecting Leaders

strengths are being run reactively, which limits them. They are also being canceled out by the overextension of these strengths.

High-Protecting/Controlling leaders are experienced as over-demanding, not clear about where they are heading, inflexible, not holding the team accountable, impulsive, conflict averse, aloof, and distant. These liabilities largely offset the strengths (203 to 181). The Competing Liabilities show their underdeveloped strengths. They are ineffective in their interactions with others, not team players, low on engagement, play favorites, put others down, publicly humiliate people, don't develop their direct reports, and don't listen well. This is the unique form of the Canceling Effect for leaders who are high on Protecting and moderately high on Controlling.

Consider the following story in which Bill was harshly critical of his son Chase.

\* \* \*

I score high on Protecting, and I often lead with a kind of critical arrogance. But if you think the words I say are critical, you ought to hear what's going on inside my mind. You're actually getting only about 1 percent of my Critical.

The strength of my Critical is that I'm able to see what others don't see. For example, during one quality improvement initiative, I saw every possible error in the 2 percent that needed to be improved and was able to completely tune out the 98 percent of what was right—which was just noise. Being critical works well in those situations, but at times it definitely does not.

Such was the case with my oldest son, Chase. About 15 minutes after he arrived home from his first year of law school in California, we were sitting in the living room, and my Critical started kicking up in a big way. It was kicking up because, frankly, Chase looked like he had crawled out from under a freeway viaduct. He was unshaven, and his clothes were a mess. I held myself back for 15 minutes, then suddenly these words came spilling out of my mouth: "Chase, you look like crap. I guess looking good is just not important to you."

Chase quickly replied, "No, that's not it. The reality is, I don't have money to buy new clothes. You told me and my siblings that you'd get us through undergraduate school, which I am grateful for. Then, if we went on for a graduate degree, we would need to figure out how to pay for that ourselves. I'm not going to ask you for money, for clothes, or for anything else. You work way too hard as it is. Out of my love and respect for you, I am doing this on my own. So, yes, I can't afford new clothing."

I had thought the greatest value I brought to the relationships with my children was being able to point out what they did well and what they could improve on. But, I was coming across as being harshly critical, finding fault, and feigning superiority—all the hallmarks of the Protecting type. With Chase, I realized that what I thought was a strength and core to my own identity had no value to my son. At this stage of my life, I never imagined that the Canceling Effect would happen to me—not only at work, but also at home.

Instead of being arrogantly critical of Chase, I should have led with Courageous Authenticity—that is, telling the truth with an open heart. It's the same strength, but it's telling the truth in a way that levels *with* you rather than *levels* you. This move would have made me more radically human—the quality my children, my family, my work colleagues, and my clients need most from me.

\* \* \*

As with each of the types, High-Protecting leadership over utilizes its strengths, in this case, its brilliant critical and analytical capability. And it does so at a cost.

## THE UNIVERSAL MODEL MAPS CORE PATTERNS

We regard the Universal Model of Leadership as universal because it maps out core patterns that are common for all. Moreover, when we sample our database to see if the model holds up on the street, it does. Leaders describe these types and their behavior patterns with the same precision as the theory and research suggest. There is something universal to all this; leaders see it and can describe it the world over.

Nothing is more helpful than a good model that informs and instructs for a lifetime. It orients you to reality in such a way that you can navigate within it more effectively. The Universal Model of Leadership is such a model. It is validated, not only quantitatively (correlations are strong and in the expected direction), but qualitatively (by the way leaders see and describe what is happening on the street). Leaders can describe the Full Spectrum of Leadership (*Up*) and the direction of development for each core type (*Across*). Therefore, this model can help you see where you are in your leadership journey of development and plot a precise path forward. It is a Universal Model of both Leadership *and* Development.

This strength-based approach assumes that leaders have developed considerable strengths that have carried them far. Yet strengths can be run Reactively or Creatively. Strengths running Reactively actually remove the strength, introduce Competing Liabilities, and do not scale well, while strengths running Creatively have the opposite effect.

The first move in the Universal Model of Development is *Up*, which means upgrading your Internal Operating System and moving up the Spectrum of Leadership. The two are related. The research reported in *Mastering Leadership* suggests that moving up and into the higher levels of the Spectrum of Leadership is greatly supported by upgrading your Internal Operating System from Socialized to Self-Authoring.[3]

So, the first move is *Up*, but up from *where*? Your first move is to liberate your core gift, to free it from the Reactive structure that limits and cancels it. In doing so, you can then bring that strength into a Creative structure where it gains its true power in multiples. Therefore, as a leader facing development gaps, it's in your interest to know precisely how you are deploying your strengths. Are they being run Reactively or Creatively? If they're being run Reactively, which specific Reactive type are you? Which specific Reactive strategy and behavior do you habitually deploy? Although they're difficult to face, knowing the answers to these questions is critical to charting a specific pathway of development for you. To get where you want to go, you need to know precisely where you are in relationship to a good map (model) that can help you navigate the journey.

The second move in the Universal Model of Development is *Across* but across from *where*? Once you know your core type, you know where *Across* lies—it's in the opposite direction of your core strengths, the strengths that have gone underdeveloped.

Closing development gaps requires that you move *Up* and *Across* by:

- Upgrading your Internal Operating System, bringing the embedded strengths into a higher order of impact.
- Moving across to develop underutilized strengths, thereby turning Competing Liabilities into Complementary Competencies.

The leaders around you can describe all of this with precision. After all, you are swimming in a feedback-rich environment, and the wisdom is all around you. All you need to do is ask.

It is not enough to know how you are deploying yourself into circumstances. You must see this essential first step with the specificity represented in this chapter. The second essential step is to learn how to work within yourself, to interrupt the pattern by which you habitually cancel yourself out, and then go deeper into your Internal Operating System to change the core internal assumption that's running the whole pattern.

This is the gritty, hard, spiritual boot camp work of leaning into your development gaps and transforming yourself. All leaders need to do it— for a lifetime.

**HOMEWORK**

- Reflect: Do you tend toward one of the three types of Reactive leadership, Complying, Protecting, or Controlling? How does your type affect your effectiveness as a leader? What might you want to do about this?

- In the Development Plan that comes with this book, write down one action step you will take or state one new behavior that will propel you toward your One Big Thing.

- Write down one action step you will take or new behavior in which you will engage that will mitigate your One Big Liability.

# Chapter 11
# Transforming Reactive into Creative Leadership
*A Fundamental Shift of Mind and Heart in Three Movements*

Chapter 10 showed how Reactive leadership takes its unique, core strengths off the table, introduces Competing Liabilities, cancels itself out, and consequently fails to scale. Creative leadership is a level of leadership built for scale.

In this chapter, we describe the shift of mind that boots up Creative leadership and allows it to get a multiple on its core strengths, access Complementary Competencies, and scale well.

The primary development gap leaders face is that they are leading amid a level of complexity that requires Creative leadership or higher, yet most are leading Reactively. And since Reactive leadership has built-in limits to scale, and tends to cancel itself out, Reactive leadership is outmatched by the complexities that leaders face. The resulting development gap is an adaptive challenge.[1] Its solution is not a technical one (such as learn a new capability, add some knowledge, improve a skill, add a competency). Its solution cannot be found, neither from within our known solution set nor in our current Internal Operating System.

Rather, its solution requires evolving to a higher order of thinking and being. From there, we can solve the challenges that come with complexity. As Einstein noted, "The solutions to our current problems cannot be found from within the consciousness that created them." The development gap we face *individually* requires that we evolve or fall behind, that *organizationally* we evolve or become less and less relevant to our customers, and *globally* we evolve or perish.

Since this gap is vertically developmental, it requires evolving from the inside out and booting up a new way of deciding, acting, and making meaning. We must deconstruct our current level of adult development, and reconstruct it at the next higher order of design—a design more fit for purpose in a world of escalating complexity.

In the Universal Path of Development, the first move is *Up*. It is a vertical evolution of your current self for a more evolved self.

In *Mastering Leadership*, we made the case that your level of leadership is related to your level of adult development. (See Figure 11.1.)

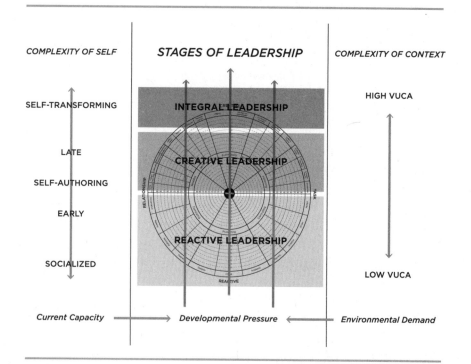

**FIGURE 11.1**    Stages of Development and Stages of Leadership[2]

We relied heavily on the seminal work of Robert Kegan, a psychologist and professor at the Harvard Graduate School of Education, and arguably the foremost researcher on adult development. His research shows that when adults evolve, they move through three progressive stages of development:

1. Socialized Mind
2. Self-Authoring Mind
3. Self-Transforming Mind

In Chapter 1, we suggested these progressive stages of mind and heart result in these different levels of leadership: Reactive, Creative, and Integral. We also showed how the Universal Model of Leadership and the Leadership Circle Profile are built around this framework. The Leadership Circle Profile is designed to accelerate a leader's development from one level to the next.

Since leadership is the deployment of self into circumstances, the question then is this: Which self are you deploying? If your self is constructed from Socialized Mind, you likely lead Reactively. If you do the hard, spiritual work of transforming Socialized Mind into Self-Authoring Mind, you more likely lead Creatively. Likewise, Self-Transforming Mind tends to boot up Integral leadership. Each level of mind and leadership is developmentally more adapted to meet complexity and thrive within it than the one before it. This leadership evolution has become a business and global imperative—our future depends on it.

Here, we focus primarily on the shift from Reactive to Creative leadership. *This is the shift most leaders are challenged to make.*

## SHIFT FROM REACTIVE TO CREATIVE IN THREE MOVEMENTS

Most great symphonies have three movements. Each movement builds on the one before it to make an artistic whole. Metaphorically, this is also true of the shift from Reactive to Creative leadership. This shift is nothing short of a transformation—a fundamental shift of mind *and* heart.

We describe this evolution in three movements. As we make this shift, we move from:

- Authored by others to authored by self ·
- Safety to purpose
- Ambition to service

**The First Movement**

The first movement is from a person who is *authored by others to one who is authored by self*. The leader authored by others is running a Socialized Mind—the conditioning we were given in our youth and the identity we constructed over the years. It is the self most people routinely deploy into circumstances. However, when we deploy ourselves from a Socialized mind, we are more likely to lead and live Reactively, because our behavior is being authored by outside circumstances and expectations. We are living from the outside in. We are doing our best to live up to the expectations of others—key stakeholders and authority figures in our lives, significant others (some of whom are long dead), cultural norms, political and religious beliefs, and messages from our past and current environment about who we must become to be successful, good, and worthy. We depend on outside validation for our security and self-esteem.

When this is the case, we are managing our behavior, mostly unconsciously, to meet these expectations. We do so out of fear—the fear of not measuring up to others' expectations, of disapproval, of falling short, of failing to be what we think others are expecting us to be. We are working hard to advance our objectives, but as Larry Wilson described it, we are doing so in a play-not-to-lose game.

The structure of this game is self-limiting—it is not mature enough for the kind of complexity most of us face as leaders.

Leadership is a crucible of transformation, a spiritual boot camp that creates the evolutionary pressure needed to dismantle our Socialized, Dependent, Reactive self and construct a Self-Authored, Independent, Creative self.

Jeff Hilzinger—the CEO introduced earlier—is a sterling example of a leader who, over a period of 10 years, learned to let go of his need to be seen as the smartest person in room. He shifted to focus on what mattered more: *creating the conditions for scaling leadership, building other leaders, and creating a vision-focused team*. Jeff became a Self-Authored, Creative leader.

Out of all the many external messages, the Self-Authored leader has discerned what is most important and what he or she chooses to stand for. From this move, we derive our definition of self-leadership: *creating outcomes that matter most.* What matters most defines the Self-Authored leader. Stephen R. Covey called this stage *independent,* not because those in it act independently (lone wolf), but because they no longer depend on outside validation for self-worth.

Self-worth is granted internally by discerning and living up to the internal dictates of an emerging and deeply felt sense of purpose. That purpose is translated into a vision of the future. *Authenticity*—acting in a manner consistent with that vision in every encounter—is the leader's hallmark. In the wake of their action, Creative leaders are focused on leaving an organization in which they would want their children to work. They are no longer run by fear—playing not-to-lose—but they are playing "on purpose," acting in service to something larger than themselves.

If you don't stand for something that's important for you, you're in danger of not standing for *anything.* It's about asking these questions: "Who am I?" and "What's important to me?" It's not about being against something or living in compliance with something or someone.

Fully Self-Authored leaders know they have come through a shift in their leadership, and they now focus on developing that in others. They become a leader of leaders—a person who develops other leaders. By doing so, they get a multiple on their leadership by building the capacity and capability of others and the organization. Such leadership is more adapted to the complexity of the intense challenges leaders face today. It is built for scale. Leadership at scale requires Self-Authored, Creative leadership.

## The Second Movement

The movement, from *safety to purpose,* is imbedded in the first movement. The primary tension in adult life is between *purpose* and *safety.* We want to be part of something great, but at the end of the day, we still need to pay the mortgage. Both are important. If we ignore safety, we put purpose at risk. If we focus too much on safety, we also put purpose at risk.

Some of today's most successful entrepreneurs and company founders are noted for their ability to balance safety and risk. As senior leaders we work this balance constantly. If we play it safe all the time and avoid taking risks, we won't benefit from the tremendous growth opportunities (and learning opportunities) that reside outside our comfort zone. If we take too much risk and fail to stay in contact with what is prudent, we put *everything* at risk. That's the ongoing balance required, and it's never easy to get it just right.

Most leaders live inside the pyramid, a hierarchal organization as illustrated in Figure 11.2. We have a sense of purpose for our work. We want to make a contribution to the world in which we live. We have a vision for what that would be. We want to create what matters most. And we work for financial freedom as well as to put a financial safety net beneath our own future and the future of our family.

Leaders working their way to the top are motivated to move up *safely*. The more we want to move up safely (knowing the fall gets farther and harder with each promotion), the more we need approval of those around us, especially those above us. To fall from grace with bosses is a frightening proposition. Most of us would do almost anything to avoid losing the confidence of key stakeholders. Here's the rub: *You can't pursue purpose and safety at the same time.*

Courage is required to address most of the complex, difficult issues we face. The future lives and dies in those moments, and the self we deploy

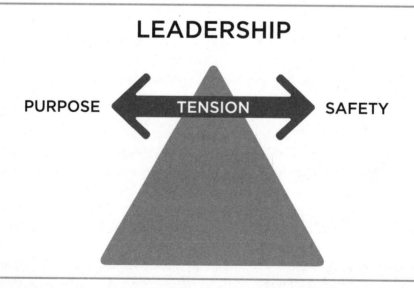

**FIGURE 11.2**   The Core Tension between Purpose and Safety

either contributes to the status quo or helps usher in the organization of our own choosing—canceling out or building our vision.

If we play not-to-lose too often, we are not leading; we are canceling ourselves out.

In the first movement, we let go of being constantly driven by the voices from our past and the expectations of others. As we do so, we play the second movement—we re-optimize the tension between purpose and safety. We move from playing not-to-lose to playing on purpose and what matters most. There is no safe way to be great!

Living on purpose is risky, but paradoxically, by taking the future into our own hands, individually and collectively, we create a different kind of safety—the kind that comes with creating the life and future we were born to create.

### The Third Movement

The third movement, from *ambition to service*, is interconnected with the first two movements. To distinguish between passion and drive, we turn to the written comment study to learn how High-Creative and High-Reactive leaders are motivated differently. This motivation is at the core of the inner game and moves us into action or non-action. It determines how we deploy ourselves into circumstances moment to moment, and it shapes the kind of weather we bring.

What do the leaders/raters in our study say about that? Figure 11.3 shows how they experience the difference between a High-Reactive leader's motivation and that of a High-Creative leader. Both are visionary and strategic, but High-Creative leaders bring more of that. Remember, Creative leadership is focused on *purpose and vision* over *safety*. The hallmark of the Self-Authored Mind, and leader, is an abiding focus on a future that matters. It is, therefore, no surprise that High-Creative leaders are experienced as more visionary (with a gap of 22 points) than High-Reactive leaders.

Figure 11.3 tells us a lot about the different motivational structure of High-Reactive and High-Creative leaders. We see that passion and drive are higher in High-Reactive leaders than in High-Creative leaders. Earlier, we suggested it's possible to be too driven, which appears to be the case for High-Reactive leaders. More important, look at these details about their drive:[3]

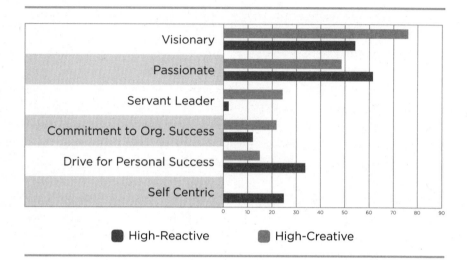

**FIGURE 11.3**    High-Reactive and High-Creative Motivation

- Reactive leaders are seen as more self-centric, or egocentric, than High-Creative leaders (25 to 0). If you follow the bubble charts from Chapter 9, you will notice that ego/self-centric leadership drops out by Mid-Creative—it does not show up as leadership transitions from Reactive to Creative.
- Self-centric drive is replaced by servant leadership and commitment to the organization's success. While self-centric leadership drops to zero (as leadership becomes less Reactive and more Creative), servant leadership grows from 0 for High-Reactive leaders (none of the 100 High-Reactive leaders in this study were described as servant leaders) to 25 for High-Creative leaders.
- *Commitment to organizational success* is also higher by 10 points in High-Creative leaders. *Drive for personal success* in High-Creative leaders is less than *commitment to personal success*, whereas the reverse is true for High-Reactive leaders.

In this view from the street, senior leaders are describing the third movement from *ambition* to *service*. As our leadership transforms from Reactive to Creative, we become less ego/self-centric and more focused on what is good for the whole. We become a servant of bringing into being what matters most. Our drive for personal success moderates and becomes maturely balanced with the success of others and with the success of organization's mission.

As this shift happens, leadership is freed up to scale. If we look at the biggest strength gaps between High-Creative and High-Reactive leaders (see Figure 11.4), we can see the kind of leadership that naturally emerges with this transformation.

Notice what comes along for the ride as this shift of mind and heart happens. Leadership becomes less self-centric and more about developing the capacity and capability of the organization. It becomes more approachable and skillful in working with people, listens well, builds high-performing teams, mentors, and develops capability in others and then empowers them. High-Creative leaders embody their vision calmly and with integrity.

## THREE MOVEMENTS, ONE SYMPHONY

Leaders can see and describe the Full Spectrum of Leadership from High-Reactive to High-Creative. In *Mastering Leadership*, we reported research conducted with the University of Notre Dame Stayer Center for Executive Education. (See Figure 11.5.) We found that with each progressive Stage of Adult Development

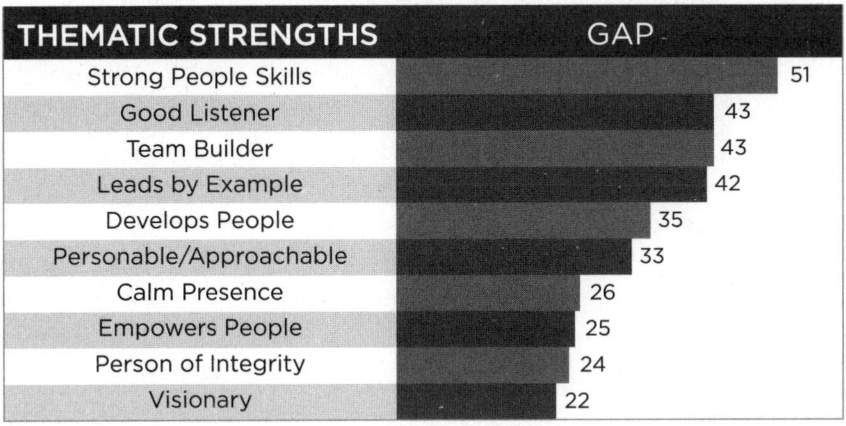

| THEMATIC STRENGTHS | GAP |
|---|---|
| Strong People Skills | 51 |
| Good Listener | 43 |
| Team Builder | 43 |
| Leads by Example | 42 |
| Develops People | 35 |
| Personable/Approachable | 33 |
| Calm Presence | 26 |
| Empowers People | 25 |
| Person of Integrity | 24 |
| Visionary | 22 |

**FIGURE 11.4** Biggest Gaps between High-Creative and High-Reactive Leaders' Strengths

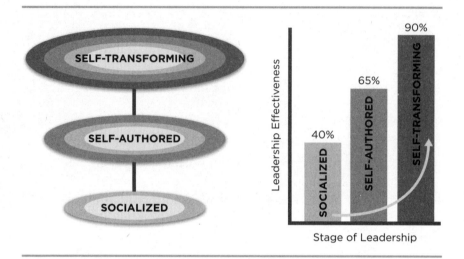

**FIGURE 11.5**    The Stages of Development and Effectiveness

(Socialized, Self-Authoring, and Self-Transforming), leaders were rated as increasingly more effective. Leaders who measured as Socialized had Leadership Effectiveness scores at the 40th percentile of our database. Those measured as functioning out of Self-Authoring Mind had Leadership Effectiveness scores averaging at the 65th percentile, and those at the Self-Transforming stage of development had Leadership Effectiveness scores averaging at the 90th percentile.

This study, combined with the comment research, has profound implications. While we did not assess the leaders in our comment study for Stage of Adult Development, we would expect to find an upwardly biased sample of Self-Authoring and Self-Transforming leaders in our High-Creative leader group. Therefore, the senior leader raters in this study are providing a description of what happens to Leadership Effectiveness as the mind of the leader transforms. And as leaders transform their inner landscape—right down to the core of what drives them—they become more effective and more capable of scale.

What the leaders in this study suggest is profound: *As we move from being Authored by Others to being Self-Authored, we become far less self-centric.*

This may seem counterintuitive, but it makes sense. If we are primarily motivated by the fear of not meeting the high expectations of key figures in our life, we drive others to perform for our purposes—to move up, to get ahead, to succeed personally, to never fall short or lose face. Such drive makes a lot happen, and so these leaders tend to move up.

However, as they grow into greater responsibility, this kind of drive develops tremendous liabilities, as indicated by very low Leadership Effectiveness scores, as well as the list of the top 10 liabilities of High-Reactive leaders. Leaving casualties in its wake, it often drives an organization into what Kaplan called "destructive productivity"—driving results in a way that exhausts the physical, emotional, and spiritual reserves of the organization.[4]

When we drive others for our self-centric purposes, we do so most often out of fear and playing not-to-lose. We lose sight of the larger purpose (perhaps we never had it in sight), and our self-centric purposes rise to the fore. We focus less on making a contribution, and work hard to meet the expectations given to us by others in our past and present. As we move from Authored by Others to Self-Authored, we move from driving *for our purposes* to leading *for contribution*. We move from the self-centric ambition to serving something larger than ourselves.

The three movements, one symphony of transformation, are shown in Figure 11.6.

## COMPLEMENTARY COMPETENCIES

As you move up the Spectrum of Leadership, not only do you get your core strengths (heart, head, will) in multiple, you also gain access to Complementary Competencies. In their book, *Extraordinary*

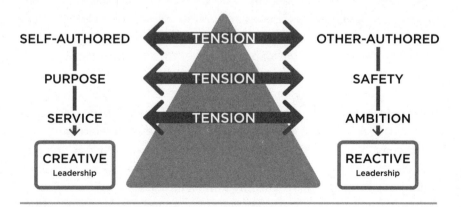

**FIGURE 11.6**   Leadership Mindset Shift

*Leaders*, Jack Zenger and Joe Folkman develop the framework of Complementary Competencies—competencies that differ from each other but also complement and amplify each other.[5] They show how certain pairs of competencies that both are well-developed, work together to make a leader even more effective. One competency multiplies the effectiveness of the other.

However, Zenger and Folkman failed to discuss that Reactive leaders tend to default to their core strengths and overuse them because they are identified with them. For example, Complying leaders may have the strength of *listening,* but lack the *courage* to advocate authentically and strongly for what they want. For this reason, Reactive leaders are far less likely to develop competencies that are different (opposite) from their core strengths.

When leaders rise up the Spectrum of Leadership, Complementary Competencies become more accessible. Leaders develop the agility to move between competencies in a way that Reactive leaders cannot. Here's an example comment:

> Mary inspires people to enjoy working harder and smarter. She fosters an incredible team atmosphere, and she does it while maintaining a strong sense of honesty and directness (as opposed to just a rah-rah type of leader). She is not afraid to point out areas that need improvement, so when she endorses another's idea, that person feels a true sense of accomplishment and a strong desire to do it again.

Notice the *both-and* quality of Mary's leadership. She can hold people accountable with her directness and honesty while fostering an incredible team atmosphere. These are Complementary Competencies—the capability to be direct *and* do so in a way that builds teamwork and trust. She can also support *and* challenge others' work in a way that is motivating.

Mary exemplifies a Creative-level leader who draws on a whole set of competencies, using the best one in any given moment or circumstance. She deploys herself into circumstances in a way that optimizes the situation and scales her leadership by fostering teamwork and developing other leaders. Yet she remains strong on results.

One client mentioned earlier, Gerard, has always had a superhuman capacity to know a remarkable amount of detail about any given situation. This has given him tremendous confidence. However, all that changed last year when his level of responsibility increased. His superhuman capacity to know everything that's going on is no longer possible. Now that strength is outmatched by what is required of him.

To continue succeeding in the future, Gerard needs to develop Complementary Competencies that naturally come when shifting from Reactive to Creative leadership. He must up his game (vertical development) and let go. As he does, he will stop compulsively doubling down on his core strength while gaining full access to competencies that complement his core strengths. He will use his core strengths and Complementary Competencies when appropriate—no more, no less.

When strengths are overused, they turn into weaknesses. And when strengths become outmatched and we double down on them, we can fail. To succeed in his new world of business, Gerard needs to develop new Complementary Competencies. Since one of his core strengths involve driving for results and knowing everything, he must develop strengths in the opposite direction—relationships, teams, and developing capacity in other leaders. To scale his leadership, Gerard needs to develop these strengths within himself and then develop these capacities within his Extended Leadership Team.

There are many "Gerards" at senior levels in every organization—successful, talented leaders who are promoted beyond their level of development and who are doubling down on what got them there. They are unable to access or develop the Complementary Competencies needed to be effective in a more complex context, and they are challenged to evolve their Internal Operating System from Reactive to Creative and Integral. If they don't make this move, they will be outmatched. It's just the nature of the game we're in.

Figure 11.7 illustrates the kinds of complementarity that permeates the written feedback of High-Creative leaders. As you read back and forth, you gain a sense of the power of developing Complementary Competencies.

High-Creative leaders are technically competent *and* approachable. They are results focused *and* they develop and empower others. They are visionary *and* they develop teamwork. (*Purposeful Vision* and *Teamwork* are the two competencies that have the highest correlation to Leadership Effectiveness on the LCP). They are passionate *and* highly driven while being good with people. And so on.

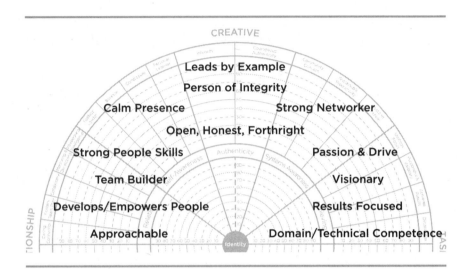

**FIGURE 11.7**  Leverage Strength and Develop Complementary Competencies

*Leadership mastery is the agile and fluid movement between strengths.* High-Creative leaders can mix and match competencies to optimize their leadership in any circumstance. This capability is built for scale and emerges naturally as leaders evolve from Socialized Mind into Self-Authoring and Self-Transforming Mind—and as leadership matures up the Spectrum from Reactive to Creative to Integral leadership.

## DEVELOPING CONSCIOUS LEADERSHIP

Leadership may be the most studied, but it is no longer the least understood subject. We now know what makes for Effective Leadership and the pathways to it. The leaders in our study have described the pathway with great precision. When we first saw how precisely they describe the Full Spectrum of Leadership—High-Reactive, Mid-Reactive, Mid-Creative, and High-Creative leadership—we said, "Wow! There is a complete development path here, and leaders see it!"

The Universal Model of Leadership was validated when we saw how leaders actually map out the entire model in the way they think and talk about leadership. This confirmed what we've said all along—that the Leadership Circle Model is a universal three-in-one framework. It is: (1) a model of leadership, (2) an in-depth leadership assessment against that model, and (3) a framework or path for development. It is built on universal developmental principles and pathways. Not only do leaders map out the vertical, developmental, Full Spectrum of Leadership, but they describe, with great clarity and precision, the unique developmental pathway for each different type of leader. They map out the up-and-across move for each type of leader. They show us that the development question becomes: *How do you take your unique set of strengths, free them up, leverage them, augment them, and scale them?*

So, let's turn to what works. How do leaders accelerate their development? What practices actually work to create profound and lasting shifts in a leader's individual effectiveness and the collective effectiveness of the leadership team?

This development agenda is a business imperative.

---

### REFLECTION

- What stage of development are you in personally: Socialized, Self-Authoring, or Self-Transforming? How do you know?

- How does your developmental stage affect those around you? How does your developmental stage impact your effectiveness as a leader?

- Assuming you are not yet at the Self-Transforming stage, what do you need to do to make the move to the next highest stage?

# Chapter 12
# Practices That Transform Leadership

*Change Is Simple, Change Is Hard*

If you want to change yourself, your leadership, or the leadership system of your organization, we know what works. It is straightforward to explain and understand the basic mechanisms of changing oneself, and that's what we do in this chapter. But don't be fooled: *It is hard to change deeply grooved patterns in how we show up every day in our lives, and our leadership.*

Transformation—fundamental change—is an acquired taste. It is not for the faint of heart. It is, in the mythic traditions, a heroic journey, a spiritual boot camp. It takes hard work individually, and it takes more hard work to do it collectively and at scale. If we pull it off, our leadership becomes a competitive advantage. Change and transformation are only worth the effort if there is something more or higher to gain or create for which our current level of leadership is too small. Then it is not only worth the effort; it is worth committing our lives to.

We are currently working with two leadership teams within one large corporation. These two teams combined are responsible for all the organization's revenue. One of these leadership teams has fully embraced its collective development and the challenge of increasing its capacity and capability to transform the organization. The team's momentum is palpable and synergistic as each member lifts the entire group's effectiveness.

What are they doing? They are experiencing the amplifying effect as they move toward greater effectiveness. They are scaling their leadership, moving it from one leader to 19 leaders and from 19 to 10,000. This is scaling leadership at the beginning stages.

The second team is coming along more slowly and its members, in some cases, are in deep resistance to what's required. The leader has consistently requested the team take on the collective leadership agenda, but that invitation has not been embraced. They still are working more on individual development than on their effectiveness as a team of leaders. And, therefore, they aren't getting the lift that the other team is experiencing.

This second team is internally focused and is having a hard time getting out of its own way. Sometimes, its members are working against each other and canceling out each other. As a result, the leader of this team is fighting an uphill battle with them before he can scale leadership to the next level and beyond—to the more than 25,000 employees and hundreds of thousands of customers depending on them.

Working internally, and privately, on individual leadership effectiveness is necessary but not sufficient to transform your organization. Yes, you must start with yourself; this is essential. But then you must learn out loud together if you want to scale your leadership (as discussed in Chapter 8) to your team and to your team's teams, and so on. If individual development does not become collective leadership effectiveness, then the organization's transformation is compromised.

We recently worked with the Senior Executive Team (SET) at Syngenta. During this session, each member of the team provided feedback to every other member. They were all given these questions to focus feedback back to each team member:

- What is the single most important contribution each of your peers makes to the SET?
- What is the one area that your peers must eliminate or improve upon for the good of the team?[1]

- What do you admire in each of your peers' leadership qualities that he or she should continue to contribute?
- What are the key things we must achieve as a team?

It was an open, direct, and powerful meeting. Each member left feeling clear about what he or she was doing that helped the team. It also revealed what needed to improve to increase the team's collective effectiveness in leading Syngenta. Each member also left feeling challenged by, supported by, and in deep relationship with all team members. Together, they were more focused on creating the outcomes that mattered most.

Jon Parr, who you recall, is working on the transformation of his own leadership and scaling it beyond his own brilliance, was involved in this session. Afterwards, he took us aside and said, "This is what I need to accomplish with my team." This is scaling leadership! Erik, the company's CEO, had scaled his leadership to the top team. Now it's being further scaled throughout the organization. The teams are well on their way.

How leaders can accomplish this in an organization was the focus of Chapter 8. In this chapter, we build on that. We discuss the principles and practices embedded in what great leaders do to scale leadership using the Universal Model of Leadership and the Universal Path of Development. Every one of the principles and practices in this chapter applies at the individual (as you start with yourself), team, and organizational level. (Note: In this chapter, we use "we" language to speak to you both individually and collectively.)

## HOW TO CHANGE

Effective leaders create the conditions for leadership at scale in themselves, in others, and in the organization by engaging in these four practices that work to establish and hold generative tension:[2]

1. **Tell the truth about what we want.** Create vision. Focus attention on the outcomes we want to achieve together. Set our intention to create them. Choose to have this become our current reality. Hold and reaffirm this intention daily.

2. **Tell the truth about how you are creating your current reality.** Tell the truth about the results we are creating right now, especially those that are inconsistent with what we want. Get underneath how we are creating our current reality, individually and collectively, until we see the embedded beliefs driving the behavior that gets us what we don't want. Surface those beliefs within yourself and within your team members. Delve into these beliefs deeply enough to see the falseness in them.

3. **Rinse and repeat to continue to hold generative tension.** Do this as an ongoing practice—that is, telling the truth about what we want and what we've got.

4. **Practice every day.** Make daily experiments. Take small steps every day to move toward what we want. Learn from your experience. It helps a lot if you . . .
   - Get feedback all along the way.
   - Have a practice of daily reflection.
   - Trust your intuition and develop the openness to intuitive insight in your teams.
   - Do all this publicly, transparently, and with the support of those around you.
   - Take a long-term, systemic approach to all of the above within the organization.

If we do this, individually and organizationally, we increase the chances that generative tension resolves by moving our current reality toward our vision. This is also how we shift our mindset, upgrading our individual and organizational Operating System from Reactive to Creative, and beyond that, to Integral. It is how we make the vertical move *Up* and the horizontal move *Across*. It is how we move from canceling a strength to multiplying it, and then amplifying it further by gaining access to the underdeveloped strengths that complement our core strengths. In short, this is how we become the leader, team, and organization capable of serving something larger than ourselves and creating outcomes that matter most. This is how we become the leader that scales the capacity and capability in the organization to create its desired future. It is how organizations transform.

It's that simple. Now, let's break it down—which is where it gets tough.

## ESTABLISH GENERATIVE TENSION

Generative tension (see Figure 12.1) is a mental model at the heart of Creative leaders' Operating System. It is how we change if we so choose; it is how we become ourselves. People who create a lot with their lives—entrepreneurs, artists, scientists, leaders, and so on—use tension to provide the energy that drives the act of creation itself.

Generative tension is established by cultivating a gap between what we want and what we've got. It's the resulting gap between the two ends that creates the tension. Tension seeks resolution—that is, to resolve to a state *without* tension—pure physics. Generative tension is a structure, and structure determines performance. The natural tendency of the structure of generative tension (if we continue to tell the truth about what we want and what we've got) is for our current reality to move toward our vision.

## TELL THE TRUTH ABOUT WHAT WE WANT

The starting place for creating anything we want is *knowing* what we want (and *why* we want it) with enough specificity that we would know if we did, indeed, create it. At this point, we don't need to know

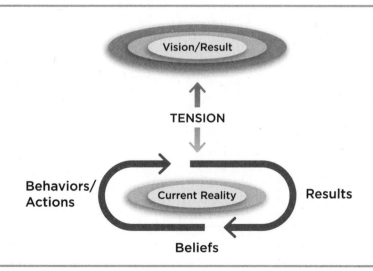

**FIGURE 12.1**   Generative Tension

how we will create what we want. To get started, we only have to care about something and focus that into an outcome we want to create.

Not any vision will do. What we want either matters or it doesn't. The soul does not invest itself in a compromise. This is as true for you personally as it is organizationally. The energy that fuels generative tension is our *passion*, our *love*, for achieving the result. If it does not matter, we won't build generative tension, and we will not stay the course. We will not persevere together.

Again, our definition of self-leadership is *creating outcomes that matter most*. Leadership scales this capability individually and amplifies it collectively. So, the first step in establishing generative tension is to focus on results that matter. This clarity can happen at multiple levels—purpose, vision, outcome, and behavior. The clearer and more aligned we are about each of these levels, the more powerful the generative tension will be.

## DISCERNING PURPOSE

The deepest and most profound level of clarifying what we want is to discern our purpose for being. In *Mastering Leadership*, we outlined six practices that reliably boot up the Creative (and higher) leadership. Discerning purpose is the first of those practices.

Purpose is the deep source of our passion, our true north. It is why we care about what we care about. Our life, if we pay attention, is constantly speaking to us about *why* we are here and *what* matters. It remains for us to connect the dots, but as Steve Jobs said in his 2005 Stanford University commencement speech, "You can't connect the dots looking forward."[3] And so, the task of discerning purpose requires a deep listening to our lives, and a profound trust that the events of our life are purposeful. Transformational leaders have done this work. They are purpose driven, and through their leadership, they encourage others to figure out what they stand for.

Discerning *higher purpose* is an organizational must, the core organizational identity. It is the top leadership's primary job to discern this and clarify it. How are the marketplace and all stakeholders leaving clues about how they want to be served? How do we discern a purpose that optimally serves all stakeholders and grabs our hearts, pulling us into alignment? If we do that well, we unleash tremendous energy in the organization.

## DISTILL VISION

Without vision, purpose cannot be realized. Purpose provides the direction—north—and vision provides the destination—a specific destination. Any compelling vision is infused with purpose.

Vision catalyzes generative tension by providing a description of the desired future reality. If Creative leadership is Self-Authored leadership—the capacity to create outcomes that matter most—then vision is its central tenant. *Purposeful vision* is the beating heart of Self-Authoring and Creative leadership, the true north of generative tension. Without it, there is no tension.

One fundamental aspect of leadership is to ensure the organization is focused on a purposeful vision. In fact, on the LCP, the dimension of *Purposeful & Visionary* is the most highly correlated dimension to Leadership Effectiveness. To create vision, you spend the time required to clarify what will exist down the road that does not exist now. You describe the life and the business you most want. You clarify it enough that you would know it if you achieved it. You do this by reflecting individually and together, as well as conversing with key stakeholders. Simply stated, if you do not build the leadership team around a purposeful vision, you are not leading.

We recently had the privilege of sitting with members of a senior leadership team of a large health care system. In the meeting, they discussed the future of the organization entrusted to them. From our pre-meeting interviews, it was obvious there was pent-up demand among them to gain clarity on where they were taking the organization. They all knew that the health care industry in their country was heading into a long period of significant disruption. So they needed to envision an organization that, if it existed in their country, would thrive in the exploding VUCA environment.

After a day and a half of meetings and two rounds of envisioning/designing their future, they stood astonished at the description of their organization that had emerged. None of them had walked in with this vision. Each had components of it, but what emerged was way beyond their expectations. They knew they were capable of pulling off what they envisioned. They also knew that if they did, not only would they thrive in what was to come, but they would dramatically transform the industry and health care outcomes in their country. They stood with tears in their eyes feeling more aligned than ever. The vision they had created together so fulfilled each of their personal purposes for getting into health care that they were "all in" to create it. It was an extraordinary meeting that established generative tension, both individually and collectively, around a higher purpose and compelling vision.

## OUTCOMES AND BEHAVIOR

Vision is distilled into strategies and goals—*outcomes*. Often over-looked in the literature is this fact: *If we hope to create a different future, we need to embody it now—act it out in every encounter.* We need to *be* the change, meaning we need to change ourselves and how we deploy ourselves into circumstances. We need to show up differ-ently, from moment to moment, in the way we lead individually and collectively.

To better compete, many leaders are trying to build more agile, cre-ative, engaged, and innovative structures and cultures. These transfor-mation efforts are less effective and more likely to fail if led Reactively. Creative leadership is required. The leaders in our study described for us the kind of leadership that is needed and were behaviorally specific about what works and what does not.

Figure 12.2 provides a list of what senior leaders worldwide say *does* work. It's a combined list of the top 10 High-Creative leader strengths and additional strengths that have the biggest gaps between High-Creative and High-Reactive leader strengths. This lists the biggest differentiators between the most and the least effective leaders.

We think this list, along with the Creative Competencies outlined in the top half of the LCP, provides a strong starting place for identify-ing the kind of leadership behavior that works.

The fastest way to change our leadership to become more effective is to establish generative tension around one of these behaviors/competen-cies. Chapters 4 and 8 discussed the One Big Thing—the one thing that, if we improve it or develop it, will take our leadership to the next level. We call this the *unlocking move*.

What *one* move will unlock our leadership? The unlocking move may be a strength that is embedded in a strong Reactive tendency. Remember, the first move in the Universal Pathway of Development is *Up*—freeing core strength from Reactive structure. For example, what is the difference

# What Works

- Strong People Skills
- Visionary
- Team Builder
- Personable/Approachable
- Leads by Example
- Passion and Drive
- Good Listener

- Develops People
- Empowers People
- Positive Attitude
- Motivator
- Calm Presence
- Person of Integrity
- Servant Leader

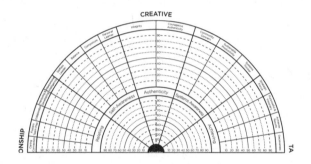

**FIGURE 12.2**    Biggest Leadership Differentiators

between power *over* people and power *with* people? Both are using the core strength of will, drive, and power for results, but there are different outcomes associated with each. The One Big Thing can often be an emerging strength (e.g., listening) that, as you leverage it, propels your leadership to the next level. Feedback and input from others can help you discover what your One Big Thing might be.

Once you identify your One Big Thing, create a direct line of sight between it and your purpose and vision. When you see that how you most need to change behaviorally is linked to realizing what you most care about, you establish the motivation of generative tension.

In Chapter 4, we encouraged you to begin work in the Development Plan provided with this book by defining your One Big Thing. If you have not done so, we strongly encourage you to do so now. We also encourage you to work on this together. In the feedback meeting discussed above, this is exactly what happened. The goal is this: *We build our teams, improve our collective effectiveness, and scale our leadership by doing this work together—transparently and vulnerably—and at every level in the organization.*

## TELLING THE TRUTH ABOUT CURRENT REALITY

Telling the truth about current reality unleashes energy. Sometimes current reality is quite positive. How often have you watched people dismiss a compliment? All too often we do not acknowledge what we have accomplished, and this does not serve us. Acknowledging what we have accomplished is a strong reinforcement to the belief that we can create whatever we set our minds to create. Acknowledgment builds momentum as we move toward manifesting what we envision.

How often is the honest, unvarnished truth told in meetings? In our experience, not often enough. One reason meetings take so long is that we spend time trying to have the discussion and avoid anything that is a political landmine or undiscussable. As leaders we are often surprised, even shocked, by 360-feedback results because we have not practiced giving and receiving feedback. If the feedback is uncomfortable, we avoid it. The higher we go in organizations, the less feedback we get because it feels risky to speak truth to power. We know that getting the honest, unvarnished truth about what is going on challenges us, but it's an *essential* practice for long-term success.

If we practice shading the truth about our current reality, we compromise the creation of generative tension. Generative tension often leads to *anxious tension* within us, as it highlights the gap between where we are and where we want to be. It creates doubt, stress, fear, and other forms of inner conflict. Reactive behaviors respond to this inner conflict by acting to remove it. The Reactive strategies of Controlling, Protecting, and Complying are designed to get rid of fear and inner conflict quickly.

If we have a habit of reacting to our doubts and fears by getting rid of them as fast as possible, we generally employ these two strategies: (1) lie about what we want—chop the vision down to size, get realistic, think inside the box, reject possibilities; and (2) lie about the current reality— avoid difficult conversations, manipulate, deny science because it is an inconvenient truth.

Both strategies work well for attenuating inner conflict and conflict among team members. However, both compromise generative tension and seriously undermine our ability to create what matters most. This makes telling the truth about *what we want* and *what we've got* essential.

Feedback helps articulate the truth about the current reality. Once we see how we are showing up in ways that are ineffective, we can do something about them. If we don't know we are off course, we may be making good time but going in the wrong direction.

The senior leaders in our study also provided us with a perceptive list of what does not work. Table 12.1 includes a list of the top 10 High-Reactive leader liabilities combined with the biggest liability gaps between the most effective and least effective leaders.

**Table 12.1** What Differentiates and Cancels Out Leadership

| What Works | What Doesn't |
|---|---|
| • Strong people skills | • Ineffective interaction style |
| • Visionary | • Not a team player |
| • Team builder | • Team not fully developed |
| • Personable and approachable | • Overdemanding |
| • Leads by example | • Micromanages |
| • Passion and Drive | • Team not held accountable |
| • Good listener | • Inattentive poor listener |
| • Develops people | • Too self-centric |
| • Empowers people | • Lacks emotional control |
| • Positive attitude | • Impatient |
| • Motivator | • Too detail/tactically focused |
| • Calm presence | • Impulsive decisions/judgments |
| • Person of integrity | • Vision not articulated |
| • Servant leader | • Inflexible |

Again, when we combine the Reactive tendencies in the bottom half of the LCP, and the list of what does not work in Table 12.1, we have a good idea of what is canceling us out—how we compete with our intention. To make an unlocking move, to establish generative tension around your One Big Thing, these two lists—what works and what does not—are helpful guides.

The bottom section of the generative tension model is a loop. Figure 12.3 shows the relationship between our current reality and our

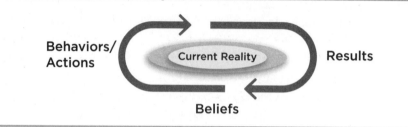

**FIGURE 12.3** The Generative Tension Loop

Internal Operating System. Behavior is driven from within—by our Internal Operating System, which is a set of well-established beliefs and assumptions. The way we behave gets certain results; these results reinforce our beliefs. When we come together, we do this collectively and create culture. We will always have more than enough evidence to prove that our beliefs are true. We have been acting, individually and collectively, as if they were true for a long time and getting results that reinforce the seeming validity of our beliefs. So, from our perspective, our beliefs are always true—that is, until we run into the limits of this Reactive structure and begin to inspect and reflect on our beliefs. Only then do we have other options that can get us different results.

Physicist David Bohm once said, "Consciousness creates reality and then says, 'I didn't do it.'" Our beliefs run beneath the surface. We don't see them, and so they manage our behavior in unseen ways. We are creating our reality in ways we may not realize. To tell the truth about current reality is to see all of this: to own up to how we are showing up; to see the weather we bring as leaders; to see and acknowledge the impact of our behavior on others, on the culture, and on results; and finally, to get underneath our habitual behavior to see the beliefs that are running our leadership. More than that, we need to see the falseness, the illusion, at the core of our beliefs.

Reactive beliefs equate our individual identity with a strength/gift we have. "I am defined by my ideas." "I am safe if you accept me." "High performance makes me a worthwhile person." These beliefs are all false. It is untrue that our safety, worth, and goodness are defined by anything or anyone. Rather, we are inherently good, safe, and worthy.

When we deconstruct these beliefs, we free our strengths (gifts we come by naturally) from the burden of using them to establish our self-worth and identity. As we do this, we lose our compulsive relationship with our strengths—for example, always controlling the conversation to have our ideas win out. Then we can choose how we might show up more effectively—for example, by listening deeply because we have something to learn. In short, we become better able to interrupt the behavior that cancels out our leadership effectiveness and experiment with something else. It's the One Big Thing that can unlock our leadership and take our effectiveness to the next level, the place where we get a multiple on our strength.

To summarize, by focusing (individually and collectively) on the One Big Thing—the thing that matters to create what matters—and identifying how we get in our own way—the relationship between our beliefs and behavior and our results—we establish generative tension. If we continue to tell the truth about this over time, we up the probability of changing in ways we intend. Generative tension is thus established in the precise way that can help us move *Up* the Spectrum of Leadership and/ or move *Across* to develop Complimentary Competencies.

In Chapter 6, we encouraged you to describe in your development plan the One Big Reactive tendency you have that cancels out your leadership and/or may interrupt your One Big Thing. We again encourage you to revisit what you wrote and *listen* to the story you tell yourself about why you have to behave this way. What is at risk for you if you don't behave this way?

See if you can track your inner conversation to a core fear and belief that drives this behavior. If you can, then examine that belief and seriously inquire into its truth or falseness. You will likely see the belief is false and needs an upgrade. *This is the deeper work of making fundamental shifts in how you lead.*

We also strongly encourage you to make this a collective practice, done in two ways: (1) Together, we inquire into the Internal Operating System that runs our culture by asking, "What assumptions influence the way we organize work, design our organization, make the strategic choices we do, and have us engaging each other the way we do?" (2) We build the kind of trust that allows us to make our Reactive tendencies, as well as the fears and beliefs that underlie them, public. When this happens in a team of leaders, we are quickly and compassionately able to interrupt the ways we cancel out our effectiveness and amplify what works.

## BE INTENTIONAL

Intention is more powerful than willpower. Willpower, the power of the ego, gets results, sometimes unintended. By comparison, intention is soul power, a spiritual commitment and energy. It elicits unseen forces in service of the purpose and vision that wants to come through us and through our leadership. As Johann Wolfgang von Goethe said:

> Until one is committed, there is hesitancy, the chance to draw back, always ineffectiveness. Concerning all acts of initiative (and creation), there is one elementary truth, the ignorance of which kills countless ideas and splendid plans: that the moment one definitely commits oneself, then Providence moves too.

> All sorts of things occur to help one that would never otherwise have occurred. A whole stream of events issues from the decision, raising in one's favor all manner of unforeseen incidents, meetings, and material assistance, which no man could have dreamed would have come his way.

> Whatever you can do or dream you can, begin it. Boldness has genius, power, and magic in it. Begin it now.[4]

When we set our intention (aligned with purpose) on what matters most, we elicit powerful forces and put them in play. As Joseph Campbell said, "When we are on purpose, all the doors open." This is the magic of the Creative mindset. As consciousness evolves—from Socialized to Self-Authored to Self-Transforming and even into Unitive Awareness—our intention becomes more and more powerful. We become a catalyzing force for creating what matters most and developing that capability in others. In effect, our evolution catalyzes the evolution of others. Together, we become the condition for scaling leadership.

## STOP, CHALLENGE, CHOOSE[5]

There is a simple, practical, and expedient way to work with generative tension in the heat of the moment. In the press of daily activity, it is rarely possible to take a time-out and track down what's running a

Reactive behavior. In the moment, it is enough to interrupt the pattern of the old behavior. There are three quick steps for doing this—*stop, challenge, choose.*

When we catch ourselves (or are about to be) behaving in a way that's contrary to our intention (One Big Thing) and collective agreements, the first step—and the best thing we can do—is simply *stop.* We interrupt and notice what's happening within and among us. We don't make ourselves wrong or beat ourselves up; we just stop and notice. We take a time-out, take a breath, and create space between what is happening and our impulsive reaction to it.

In that space, *challenge.* We ask ourselves, "Is this consistent with what we want for our future?" If we continue to think and behave as we always have, we will continue to get the kind of results we always have. But if we want something different, we need to think and behave differently. *Challenge* means questioning old patterns of behavior and reminding ourselves where this behavior leads. It also means refocusing on behavior that's consistent with the future we want.

Next, simply make a choice—*choose* to engage differently. "Let's dialogue, listen, and learn for a while before we dismiss ideas out of hand." That's it. Move on. Notice what happens. By doing this simple practice, we've re-established generative tension.

It is also a good practice to later observe more closely what happened—that is, examine how you fell back into an old pattern. Feel what was happening within you in that moment. Listen to the voice of fear, anger, and doubt present in your reaction. Track that voice. Listen to its story. Notice the assumptions you make that give the story a feeling of truth. Challenge those assumptions. See through their illusion. The more familiar you get with the story, as well as with the thinking and beliefs beneath the story, the faster you can interrupt the entire pattern. Then share what you learn with your team. By being radically human, you build trust, and everyone learns. As we become intimately familiar with how we cancel ourselves out, we become more effective at *stopping, challenging,* and *choosing* in the moment.

We will find it easier to interrupt an old pattern and refocus on what we want when (1) we are clear about what we want and how we want to show up to create it, and (2) we become more familiar with the illusory story we tell ourselves when we run a behavior that cancels out our effectiveness.

## PRACTICE

Establishing generative tension needs to become an ongoing practice. As it evolves into a habit, what remains is to experiment our way forward with the One Big Thing. We try one new behavior, take baby steps, make safe-to-fail experiments, watch the impact, adjust and try again. We notice when we fall back into old patterns, and we use those experiences to learn more about our internal beliefs and how they are running the show.

We reestablish generative tension by refocusing intention on what we are creating. We move on to the next experiment. We reinforce generative tension by acknowledging small successes. We build new beliefs that get reinforced by the new results that flow from new, more effective ways of behaving and leading. That's it. Practice-observe-reflect. Rinse and repeat. And seek supportive, ongoing feedback.

## INTUITION

None of the ideas stated above are purely rational. That's because we don't discern purpose and create vision solely with the rational mind. Inspiration is required, and our intuition is the gateway to being "in-spired." It is a built-in capability that enables us to draw on the unseen dimensions of ourselves (subconscious and superconscious) for information that's required if we want to break through.

Where does inspiration come from? How do big ideas get created? Do we invent them, or do they come to us exactly in accordance with our intentional and rational commitment? In the film, *The Man Who Knew Infinity*, the famous Cambridge mathematical genius (and the most rational of human beings) Thomas Hardy reports to his colleagues this startling conclusion: "We do not invent these formulae, they already exist and lie in wait for only the very brightest of minds . . . ever to divine and prove."[6]

Albert Einstein put it this way:

> Intuition is the father of new knowledge, while empiricism is nothing but an accumulation of old knowledge. Intuition, not intellect, is the "open sesame" of yourself. Indeed, it is not

intellect, but intuition which advances humanity. Intuition tells man his purpose in this life. I do not need any promise of eternity to be happy. My eternity is now. I have only one interest: to fulfill my purpose here where I am. This purpose is not given to me by my parents or my surroundings. It is induced by some unknown factors. These factors make me a part of eternity.[7]

Generative tension is a force field, and as the Goethe quote suggests, the clear intention that establishes generative tension sets much (seen and unseen) in motion. It establishes a gravitational field that attracts breakthrough. Some of this we rationally figure out, but some of it surprises us. It seems to come in a moment, in a flash. Purpose and vision require flashes of (if not sustained) inspiration. Intuitive knowing often shows up as we get close to unearthing a core self-limiting belief. It brings a sudden flash of insight into ourselves.

What we apprehend in intuitive moments can change how we live and lead. When we slow our meetings down and drop into team dialogue, we make room for intuition to work. System design and technical solutions to big challenges can come in an instant. Knowing what to do in the moment, even though we cannot explain why, is often the very action that helps us break through. Intuition and rationality work hand in hand to provide the insight and learning needed to resolve generative tension. Using our intuitive capability accelerates our development as leaders and as a team of leaders. Intuition works best in times of rest, relaxation, mindfulness, and dialogue after periods of intense conscious, rational commitment. Having a still center helps.

## REFLECTION

A few years ago, two of our business partners, Roma Gaster and Padraig O'Sullivan, conducted a research study on the daily practices of highly effective leaders. We sorted our database to find senior leaders whose LCPs measured at, or beyond, the 80th percentile—an extraordinary group of leaders. We invited them to be part of the study, and 25 leaders agreed to participate. Figure 12.4 shows their collective LCP (one similar to the High-Creative leader group).

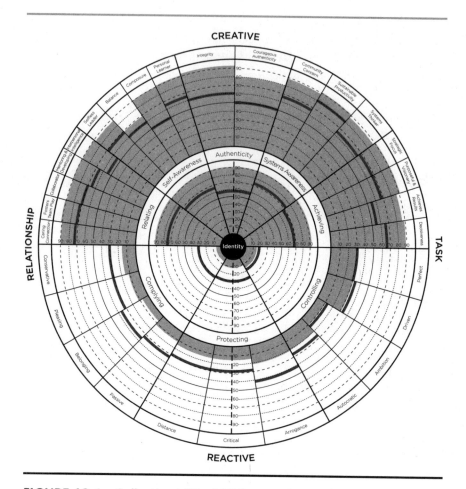

**FIGURE 12.4** Collective LCP of 25 Extraordinary Leaders

Then we created an app to be downloaded to their smartphones or tablets and asked them to log the daily practices they used to develop themselves and to stay at peak performance. Surprisingly, we found these leaders had the habit of morning and evening reflection and reported that their morning reflection had the following benefits:

- It prepares me for the day ahead and to be better *organized*.
- It helps me be more *intentional* for how I show up.
- It increases my level of *appreciation/gratitude*.

- It gives me to time to *reflect on* and process the previous day's events.
- It prepares me for the emotional load of the day through *awareness of my emotional/physical state.*
- It creates *mental alertness.*
- It provides me with *perspective.*

These leaders also told us that evening reflection allowed for completion, follow through, reviewing what worked and what did not, acknowledging successes, expressing gratitude, and staying focused and present. Reflection to start the day, during the day, and in the evening helped them become more conscious of how they were showing up and interacting. As a result, they were more present and skillful in supporting, challenging, and developing other leaders. In short, they led more effectively and were able to scale capacity and capability around them.

To close your development gaps, scale your leadership, and continuously perform at high levels amid volatile and complex work environments, we suggest you have a practice of daily reflection.

## FEEDBACK

This book has said a lot about the value of feedback. All dynamic systems require feedback loops. Why should we as leaders, and teams of leaders, be any different? Feedback facilitates development because people around us see us with great precision. They see the Full Spectrum of Leadership and can place us in it. They see the strengths and liabilities that come with our uniqueness. They see *us.* We are in a feedback-rich environment. It only remains for us to take full advantage of it.

One time, we were brought in to coach and save the career of a CFO who was "killing" the people around him. People hated working with him. He was canceling out the effectiveness of the entire top team, and the CEO brought us in to help him change, or he would be fired. Given that this CFO's job was on the line, he was open to working with us. Once he got his LCP results and gained insight into how he was showing up as a leader, we invited him do a simple round of face-to-face feedback from his people. We encouraged him to ask these simple questions specifically about his ineffective behaviors:

- What does that behavior look like? How do I do it?
- What is the impact of that behavior on you, on others?
- What should I do differently?
- What should I do more of, less of, keep the same?

We encouraged him to listen nondefensively, make no excuses or arguments, and continue to stay in inquiry. In a follow-up coaching session, we asked him how his feedback meetings went. He said, "I had no idea how I was coming across. I never knew, for example, that a simple look on my face could shut down a conversation."

The CFO began to change. As he dove deeper into the underpinnings of his aggressive leadership, with vulnerably and in deep relationship with his senior team members, he made progress. He eventually became a highly positive influence within the top team and the organization.

The same applies at the team and organizational level. The ELT has the responsibility to create key metrics, and put in place feedback systems to get regular current feedback (current reality) in relationship to intended results. This includes feedback on both team and cultural performance.

People have a lot to tell us, and they want us to succeed. We need to simply ask and listen. It's that simple and not easy. Like transformation, feedback is an acquired taste. But it's probably the single most helpful practice for becoming more effective.

## TRUTH TELLING

Every practice discussed in this chapter depends on each team member's ability to tell the truth to each other in one-on-one conversations, within the team, and to the organization. Teams of leaders that scale leadership get proficient at having difficult conversations, requiring courage to say things that matter in direct, authentic, and compassionate ways. It is a foundational practice. Teams we have worked with for a while often tell us this: "We can now have the conversations we used to avoid—and do them well. This has made *all* the difference."

Scaling Creative leadership requires radical authenticity. If your team does not do this consistently and well, you need to change that.

## LEAD THE CHANGE

The leaders who quickly make the most progress scaling leadership do two additional things that help them change personally while catalyzing systemic transformation: (1) They take a long-term, systemic approach to development, and (2) They lead the change publicly, personally, and vulnerably.

Individual and collective change takes time; it takes a village. Long-term approaches are the only ones that work. Unfortunately, most of our attempts to change are short term, episodic, individual (not collective), exclusively skill-focused (ignoring the deeper internal development required), private (not public/collective), and do not engage the whole system.

Those of us who have scaled leadership, in significant and sustainable ways, have personally led the change. In effect, we became the chief development officer. Recognizing that the organization's development agenda is related to our own development gaps, we take on the personal and team development agenda just as we take on the organization's development.

Leaders learn out loud, and the best leaders do so openly, vulnerably, and in deep relationship. Development gaps do not exist in a vacuum. Our individual and team development gaps are inextricably intertwined and interdependent with the larger system's evolutionary requirement. We are most effective at leading when we understand that:

- Individual, collective, and systemic development is a business imperative.
- Organizations, like people, have an Internal Operating System—culture.
- An organization will never perform at a level higher than the consciousness of its senior leadership.
- The collective consciousness of senior leadership is the primary carrier of the culture.
- Our primary job as leaders is to lead development—that is, to develop other leaders.
- We are not separate from the system.
- We are a microcosm of the whole system.
- Our efforts at personal change, and team effectiveness, are more likely to fail if we do not change the system that supports and sustains the ways of leading that put us at a competitive disadvantage.
- The system's function and dysfunction are in us.

- It will not change unless we do.
- We must do so publicly and vulnerably.
- There is no safe way to be great.

Individual change and system change must happen together. This is what makes leadership a spiritual boot camp and it's why the best leaders make their development gaps public and ask for help. They also implement a change process that encourages the whole system to learn out loud. Specifically, they institutionalize feedback, learning, and ongoing development.

In the deliberately developmental organizations (discussed in Chapters 2 and 8), design determines performance, and these organizations perform—they get remarkable business results. What makes them unique is that they are consciously designed to be developmental—to be a system that naturally and powerfully encourages every member to grow and improve. These organizations are also designed to be vertically developmental, to help each member make the vertical development move *Up*.

These organizations feature several unique design parameters. First, their cultures are led from the top, not in hierarchal way, but rather, the senior leaders have as much to learn as anyone else. They learn out loud together and model the way. Second, feedback is constant. Their cultures are constantly providing feedback and doing it well. As members, we are constantly aware of our strengths and our development gaps. Third, development is an expectation, a job requirement. If we're not improving, it's time to move on. Thus, these organizations set up a feedback-rich, supportive culture that catalyzes development. What follows are business results that are second to none.

Much of the work we do with our clients centers on harvesting the feedback-rich environment using assessments, coaching, and cohort learning groups focused on supportively holding each member accountable to reach his or her development goals. We have them set up accountability circles—groups committed to giving the leaders ongoing feedback. We employ multiple-year, intact team development in which teams of leaders consciously support one another's individual development, as well as their collective effectiveness—how they show up together to lead the organization. All this is done while they have the business conversation, not separate from it.

We help our clients define their leadership agenda and put in place a system for closing individual and collective development gaps. We help then establish the conditions that scale the development of more conscious leadership throughout the organization. In these transformation efforts, development is led from the top, led out loud, vulnerably, and from the inside out (Internal Operating System upgrade). It is systemic, radically human, done in a container of deep relationship, and in service of a higher purpose. The focus is on individual transformation that catalyzes collective leadership effectiveness. These organizations build a crucible of transformation that puts everyone in generative tension and through a spiritual boot camp. The result is a fundamental shift from Reactive leadership to Creative, if not Integral leadership, and culture.

This is how we create more agile, adaptive, resilient, innovative, and engaging organizations. It is how leaders put in place the conditions and practices for scaling leadership. *It is the only way that works.* We cannot cite a single organizational transformation effort that succeeded without senior leadership doing this work. Not one.

## HOMEWORK

- Ongoing supportive feedback is a powerful way to evolve your leadership. The last homework assignment of this book is to set up your accountability circle—a group of people you trust and who know you well. They will provide you with ongoing feedback.

- In the Development Plan that comes with this book, write down a list of people who could serve you in this capacity. Your plan will also suggest how to set up an accountability circle for yourself.

# Chapter 13
# Integral Leadership Informed by Grace
## The Future of Leadership for a World at Stake

It is no secret that our world is facing both a perilous future and one rife with possibilities. Either way, it is an uncertain future. We must wisely lead our way forward, or face dire consequences.

Is the state of leadership in today's world up for the challenges we collectively face? We think not. The current global context puts us in a development gap. We are too often canceling ourselves out. Leadership must evolve.

Geoffrey West recently wrote the book, *Scale: Universal Laws of Growth, Innovation, Sustainability, and the Pace of Life in Organisms, Cities, Economies, and Companies.*[1] West is a physicist who turned to biology to determine if there are any universal laws by which nature scales. What he found is truly amazing.

West discovered what he calls *power laws*. That means nature scales itself with such consistency that it can be mathematically described as a law of nature. This law of nature is *sublinear scaling*, meaning that, as nature scales, it requires less input to sustain its larger size.

For example, a whale eats more than a lion, but a lion eats more in proportion to its weight than a whale. The relationship between mass and energy intake is remarkably predictable across all mammals using a simple formula. So, nature scales sublinearly. On the other hand, human enterprises (e.g., economies, companies) scale *supralinearly,* requiring greater inputs with scale. This sets up the dilemma West presents at the end of his book. There, he examines the global trends of how humans are collectively scaling in relationship to nature and the planet's ecosystem.

West suggests that many of the human trends—growth in population, GDP, pollution, and more—are growing supralinearly and reaching *singularities.* In physics, a singularity is reached when growth becomes infinite within a finite period of time. Since human endeavors are scaling supralinearly, we are fast approaching singularities on multiple fronts in which growth is unsustainable within a finite period. If time could somehow be extended, the growth rate could be sustained for a longer period of time. Innovation has the effect of extending time. Since nature only scales sublinearly, human innovation must intervene to extend the time horizon. In other words, we must innovate our way out of the dilemmas we are creating for ourselves. Humans have done a pretty good job of that so far, although we are now reaching some daunting global limits to scale.

Since innovation is required, West goes on to look at the rate of disruptive innovation—an innovation that is so significant, it changes the foundations of the economy, if not civilization. The computer and the internet are two examples. Innovation has the effect of allowing us to do more with less, and thus, we can have the effect of extending time—continuing to grow without reaching the singularity built into the laws of scale mentioned above. However, the rate of innovation is now reaching its own singularity. The rate of paradigm shifting disruptive innovation has now slipped below 20 to 25 years or so and is decreasing.

We reach a singularity when disruptive innovation becomes so rapid that it tears the fabric of society by overwhelming our ability to adapt.

So, here is the catch-22 West says we are facing: *If we don't innovate disruptively, at an ever-increasing pace, we are in trouble. However, if we do innovate disruptively, we will overwhelm our social fabric.* That's complexity! We are in it, and it will and must accelerate if we continue to pursue the exponential growth of our economies. Of course, we could change our relationship to unbridled growth, and arguably we need to do this. But that choice would usher in a whole new set of complex systemic dilemmas for which we would need to rapidly innovate.

So, no matter how you cut it, we are up against a level of escalating complexity and disruptive change that requires, and will continue to require, an unprecedented level of innovation, adaptability, scalability, sustainability, resilience, collective intelligence, engagement, empowerment, agility, systemic thinking, and global cooperation. Furthermore, we need all this at scale and at every level of scale. Organizations will thrive only if they can do this at scale. Governments are in the same boat (and it's no secret that governments are straining, if not failing, under the weight of such complexity).

What's more, we need all of what's stated above in a global way. Therefore, we need leadership at all levels that is effective enough, mature enough, wise enough, and collectively intelligent enough to see us through. We can make it, but it will take an unparalleled level of collective collaboration, innovation, and mature leadership.

Is the current state of leadership up to the challenge? We don't think so. Furthermore, we think that even Creative leadership is not enough.

This may surprise you as we have spent most of these chapters describing this fundamental shift of mind and heart. It's because, while Creative leadership is much more capable of leading amid complexity than is Reactive leadership—*and* it's a necessary evolutionary step—in our opinion, it is not up to the challenge of the levels of complexity we are moving toward. *Integral leadership is required.* It is the future of leadership.

In *Mastering Leadership*, Integral leadership supported by a Self-Transforming Internal Operating System is described in some depth. Only 5 percent of leaders are operating here. The fact that so few are leading in this way heightens the emphasis on our collective development gap. That said, there is a group of leaders ready to make this move.

In this book, we have proposed that the High-Creative leader group is an upwardly biased sample of Creative and Integral leaders. This suggests there is a substantial number of effective leaders who are poised to move to the next level of leadership effectiveness and maturity. Since most leaders are leading Reactively, or are in transition to Creative leadership, our leadership development efforts must continue to support this developmental imperative. While we do that, however, we must also learn how to support leaders in developing further—that is, into fully mature Integral leaders. This is now a business and global imperative.

The leadership literature is pointing the way. In their book, *Conscious Capitalism*, John Mackey and Rajendra Sisodia describe the kind of organization and leadership that can thrive amid complexity and contributing to our collective welfare.[2] In his book, *Reinventing Organizations*, Frederic Laloux documents the success of organizations that are designed for thriving amid complexity in uniquely innovative ways.[3] These organizations, which he calls Teal organizations, are designed and led Integrally.

In their book, *An Everyone Culture*, Robert Kegan and Lisa Lahey describe successful *deliberately developmental organizations*—organizations that are deliberately and consciously designed to promote the development of everyone in the organization.[4] We also make this argument in *Mastering Leadership*. Each of these books describes a new kind of organization designed to thrive amid complexity.

None of these new types of organizations can advance if they have immature leadership. They require leadership that is Creative at a minimum, and Integral at best. The future of leadership is Integral leadership—creating organizations innovatively designed to scale leadership at every level, to innovate at the pace of change, and to thrive amid complexity.

This puts us right back into our spiritual boot camp. The pressure of the business context relentlessly requires us to develop even further. In the shift from Creative to Integral leadership, we move from being Self-Authored to Authored. That means we are neither authored by others nor exclusively by our own sense of personal purpose. We let go to being authored by something much larger than ourselves—something that seems to want to come through our life and leadership. We let ourselves be used by a great purpose while becoming the servant of our emergent collective future.

In the transition to Integral leadership, arising on a Self-Transforming meaning-making system, the authentic, visionary, purpose-driven self we have worked so hard to refine goes through yet another metamorphosis—disintegration and reintegration. With this transformation, we become more capable of relating to our self as a system— an ecology of different selves.

To go higher, we must go deeper, and so we face yet another level of our "forever unfinished-ness." We can now hold more of our darkness, as well as our light, our masculine and our feminine, our function and dysfunction, our wholeness and brokenness. We do so without harsh judgment and with a newly arising self-compassion.

This new inner capacity transforms our leadership. We now hold more of the function and dysfunction in the world without blaming, taking sides, or championing our own vision. This is because we see ourselves—and we see the world—more systemically. We see that the system's development gap is related to our own development gap. We no longer merely sponsor change in the organization; we radically, humanly, and in deep relationship, *lead* change from the perspective that the system is mirroring the function and dysfunction in us, individually and collectively. We project our shadow less and less, and therefore, we can engage conflict without reactively making the other into an enemy or adversary. We experience others, much like ourselves, as a work in progress, and we engage in dialogue from a place of listening, learning, compassion, and strength. Within our leadership teams and extended leadership teams, and among our stakeholders, we generate the kind of dialogue that's more likely to create innovative, adaptive, breakthrough solutions to complex problems in which all stakeholders win. We learn together and out loud. We let go of our knowing and certainty because the solutions we seek will take a high level of collective intelligence and systemic wisdom. No one person is smart enough.

Together, we innovate new and agile organizational designs that are inclusive, engaging, developmental, and fit for purpose in a VUCA world. As such, we become the servant and system architect of an emergent future that is our collective welfare.

All of this is informed by grace. We trust there is grace enough in the system for us to let go, ask for help, not know, and learn our way forward together. As we progressively let go (let ego) to being used by higher purpose, we are "in-formed" and "in-spired."

We are graced with the wisdom that rides in on intuitive waves of insight when we suddenly know what has to be done, where we need to go, or what/how we need to change, however counterintuitive. We are graced when we break through to deeper levels of self-understanding and find, in that awareness, our deep kinship with humanity. We are blessed and surprised with the synchronicity of events arising at just the right moment to propel us forward.

All this is full of grace!

In the previous chapter, we mentioned the famous speech Steve Jobs gave at Stanford. He said,

> Again, you can't connect the dots looking forward; you can only connect them looking backward. So, you have to trust that the dots will somehow connect in your future. You have to trust in something—your gut, destiny, life, karma, whatever. This approach has never let me down, and it has made all the difference in my life.[5]

As Integral leaders, we learn to count on the unseen forces that move in our favor. As we evolve and step boldly (sometimes blindly) into how life wants to use us, we learn to see how the universe conspires on our behalf, in service of a greater good and a better self. This requires trust and faith. It takes faith to trust that the dots will connect as we stumble courageously forward.

If we have faith in the goodness of humanity and in that which pulls us onward, we trust that we will be informed by grace to navigate, succeed, and thrive in this volatile, chaotic, and uncertain world. Faith will open us up to what is *possible* and turn it into *probable*.

Activating the grace inherent in this providential universe takes a commitment to something higher—to serving the world in which we live and the planet on which all life depends. This commitment connects us to Earth and to the one spirit living within all of us. With commitment and faith, as Goethe[6] said, "Providence moves" and conspires with us for the greater good. Having Providence move on our collective behalf connects the dots moving forward into a bright and hopeful future. Integral leadership evolves and leads best when informed by grace.

Finally, Integral leadership intuits our inherent unity. As we break through to seeing the beauty in the ecology of very different selves within us, we notice that others, including our "enemies," are not so different from us. We are then poised to see through to a deeper unity that we all share—that we all are. *For we are all each other.* This is an essential truth at the core of all spiritual traditions.

We believe the future of leadership is Integral leadership informed by grace and leading from the presumption of our inherent unity. This is how we will create a thriving future for all of Earth's inhabitants. We think our world depends on leaders at every level, but especially those in significant positions of leadership who are evolving toward Integral leadership informed by unity.

By investing in your organization's development agenda, you are contributing to developing the mature and skillful leadership so required by our world's future.

# Appendix A
# Leadership Circle Profile Summary Dimensions

**Relating** summary dimension measures the leader's capability to relate to others in a way that brings out the best in people, groups, and organizations. It is composed of:

- **Caring Connection,** which measures the leader's interest in and ability to form warm, caring relationships.
- **Fosters Team Play,** which measures the leader's ability to foster high-performance teamwork among team members who report to him or her, across the organization, and within teams in which s/he participates.
- **Collaborator,** which measures the extent to which the leader engages others in a manner that allows the parties involved to discover common ground.
- **Mentoring and Developing,** which measures the leader's ability to develop others through mentoring and maintaining growth-enhancing relationships.
- **Interpersonal Intelligence,** which measures the interpersonal effectiveness with which the leader listens, engages in conflict and controversy, deals with the feelings of others, and manages his or her own feelings.

**Self-Awareness** summary dimension measures the leader's orientation to ongoing professional and personal development, as well as the degree to which inner self-awareness is expressed through high integrity leadership. It is composed of:

- **Selfless Leader,** which measures the extent to which the leader pursues service over self-interest, where the need for credit and personal ambition is far less important than creating results that serve a common good.
- **Balance,** which measures the leader's ability to keep a healthy balance between business and family, activity and reflection, work and leisure—the tendency to be self-renewing and handle the stress of life without losing the self.
- **Composure,** which measures the leader's ability, in the midst of conflict and high-tension situations, to remain composed and centered and to maintain a calm, focused perspective.
- **Personal Learner,** which measures the degree to which the leader demonstrates a strong and active interest in learning and personal and professional growth. It measures the extent to which s/he actively and reflectively pursues growing in self-awareness, wisdom, knowledge, and insight.

**Authenticity** summary dimension measures the leader's capability to relate to others in an authentic, courageous, and high-integrity manner. It is composed of:

- **Integrity,** which measures how well the leader adheres to the set of values and principles that s/he espouses; that is, how well s/he can be trusted to "walk the talk."
- **Courageous Authenticity,** which measures the leader's willingness to take tough stands, bring up the "undiscussables" (risky issues the group avoids discussing), and openly deal with difficult relationship problems.

**Systems Awareness** summary dimension measures the degree to which the leader's awareness is focused on whole system improvement, productivity, and community welfare. It is composed of:

- **Community Concern,** which measures the service orientation from which the leader leads. It measures the extent to which s/he links his or her legacy to service of community and global welfare.
- **Sustainable Productivity,** which measures the leader's ability to achieve results in a way that maintains or enhances the overall long-term effectiveness of the organization. It measures how well s/he balances human/technical resources to sustain long-term high performance.
- **Systems Thinker,** which measures the degree to which the leader thinks and acts from a whole system perspective, as well as the extent to which s/he makes decisions in light of the long-term health of the whole system.

**Achieving** summary dimension measures the extent to which the leader offers visionary, authentic, and high achievement leadership. It is composed of:

- **Strategic Focus,** which measures the extent to which the leader thinks and plans rigorously and strategically to ensure that the organization will thrive in the near and long term.
- **Purposeful Visionary,** which measures the extent to which the leader clearly communicates and models commitment to personal purpose and vision.
- **Achieves Results,** which measures the degree to which the leader is goal-directed and has a track record of goal achievement and high performance.
- **Decisiveness,** which measures the leader's ability to make decisions on time and the extent to which s/he is comfortable moving forward in uncertainty.

**Complying** summary dimension measures the extent to which a leader gets a sense of self-worth and security by complying with the expectations of others rather than acting on what s/he intends and wants. It is composed of:

- **Conservative,** which measures the extent to which the leader thinks and acts conservatively, follows procedure, and lives within the prescribed rules of the organization with which s/he is associated.

- **Pleasing,** which measures the leader's need to seek others' support and approval in order to feel secure and worthwhile as a person. People with strong needs for approval tend to base their degree of self-worth on their ability to gain others' favor and confirmation.
- **Belonging,** which measures the leader's need to conform, follow the rules, and meet the expectations of those in authority. It measures the extent to which s/he goes along to get along, thereby compressing the full extent of his or her creative power into culturally acceptable boxes.
- **Passive,** which measures the degree to which the leader gives away his or her power to others and to circumstances outside his or her control. It is a measure of the extent to which s/he believes that s/he is not the creator of his or her life experience, that his or her efforts do not make much difference, and that s/he lacks the power to create the future s/he wants.

**Protecting** summary dimension measures the belief that the leader can protect himself/herself and establish a sense of worth through withdrawal and remaining distant, hidden, aloof, cynical, superior, and/or rational. It is composed of:

- **Arrogance,** which measures the leader's tendency to project a large ego—behavior that is experienced as superior, egotistical, and self-centered.
- **Critical,** which measures the leader's tendency to take a critical, questioning, and somewhat cynical attitude.
- **Distance,** which measures the leader's tendency to establish a sense of personal worth and security through withdrawal, being superior and remaining aloof, emotionally distant, and above it all.

**Controlling** summary dimension measures the extent to which the leader establishes a sense of personal worth through task accomplishment and personal achievement. It is composed of:

- **Perfect,** which measures the leader's need to attain flawless results and perform to extremely high standards in order to feel secure and worthwhile as a person. Worth and security are equated with being perfect, performing constantly at heroic levels, and succeeding beyond all expectations.

- **Driven,** which measures the extent to which the leader is in overdrive. It is a measure of his or her belief that worth and security are tied to accomplishing a great deal through hard work. It measures his or her need to perform at a very high level in order to feel worthwhile as a person. A good work ethic is a strength of this style, provided that the leader keeps things in balance and is able to balance helping others achieve with his or her own achievement.
- **Ambition,** which measures the extent to which the leader needs to get ahead, move up in the organization, and be better than others. Ambition is a powerful motivator. This scale assesses if that motivation is positive, furthering progress—or negative, becoming overly self-centered and competitive.
- **Autocratic,** which measures the leader's tendency to be forceful, aggressive, and controlling. It measures the extent to which s/he equates self-worth and security to being powerful, in control, strong, dominant, invulnerable, or on top. Worth is measured through comparison, that is, having more income, achieving a higher position, being seen as a most/more valuable contributor, gaining credit, or being promoted.

# Appendix B
# Leadership Effectiveness and Business Performance

In *Mastering Leadership*, we reported our research on the relationship between a measure of Leadership Effectiveness on the Leadership Circle Profile (LCP) and a measure of business performance. We created a metric of business performance by asking managers to evaluate the performance of the business on metrics such as market share, profitability, return on assets, and quality of products and services. We then correlated the resulting Index of Business Performance with the Leadership Effectiveness measure on the LCP and confirmed a strong correlation between Leadership Effectiveness and Business Performance of 0.61 (Figure B.1). This figure shows the results from 500 organizations assessed. The study was later expanded to 2,000 organizations and 250,000 surveys with the same result.

We sorted the Business Performance data from highest to lowest. We then looked at the average Leadership Effectiveness scores of the leaders of the organizations whose Business Performance was rated in the in the top and bottom decile. As shown in Figure B.2, the average Leadership Effectiveness score is at the 80th percentile for the leaders in the *highest-performing* organizations and merely at the 30th percentile for the *lowest-performing* organizations. The data speaks for itself. In the highest-performing organizations, Creative leadership predominates while the lowest-performing organizations are led Reactively.

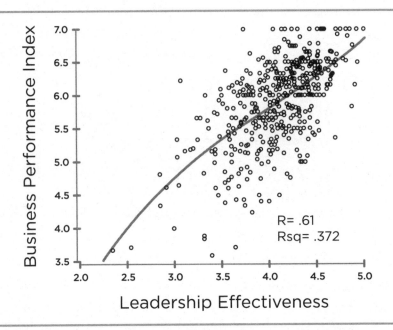

**FIGURE B.1** Leadership Effectiveness and Business Performance

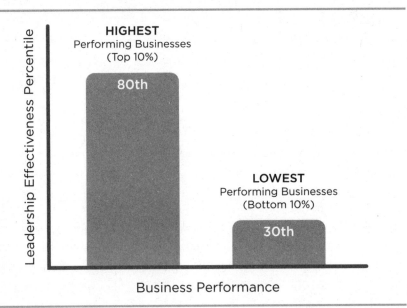

**FIGURE B.2** Leadership Effectiveness Scores for Leaders in the Highest and Lowest Performing Businesses

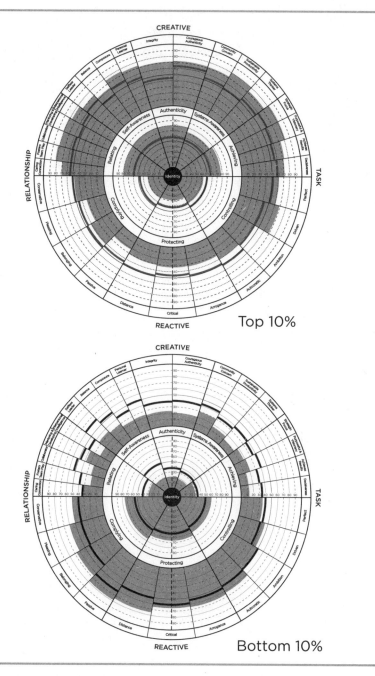

**FIGURE B.3**  Aggregate Profile of the Leaders in the Highest and Lowest Performing Organizations

We also compared the aggregate LCP for businesses rated as *highest performing* with those rated as *underperforming*.(See Figure B.3.)

Businesses evaluated as highest performing have very Creative leadership cultures; in underperforming businesses, Reactive leadership styles abound.

Figure B.4 summarizes this same information differently. In the highest-performing businesses, the average Creative score was measured to be at the 80th percentile, while Reactive scores were low at the 30th percentile. In the lowest-performing businesses, Reactive scores were found to be at the 70th percentile while Creative scores averaged at the 30th percentile. Clearly, Creative leadership greatly outperforms Reactive leadership. Creative leadership is a decided competitive advantage while Reactive leadership is a competitive disadvantage.

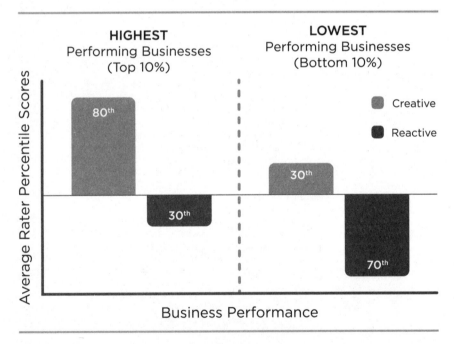

**FIGURE B.4**   Creative versus Reactive Leadership in the Highest and Lowest Performing Organizations

# Appendix C
# Research Methodology

The research for the written comment studies reported in this book was conducted by Worldwide Institute for Research and Evaluation (WIRE), an independent research firm founded in 1978, to provide technical assessment support to individuals and organizations. Lani Van Dusen, Executive Director of WIRE, wrote this appendix on research methodology.

## DESCRIPTION OF LQ INDICATOR AND THE SELECTION
## OF SPECIFIC SAMPLES BASED ON LQ

The Leadership Quotient was used to sort the Leadership Circle database and define the sample groups.

The Leadership Quotient (LQ) is a categorical rating scale based on the progression of leadership development as viewed through the Creative and Reactive lens in comparison to the global database (using standard deviations as the metric for comparison).

There are 16 categorical ratings (scores) possible. (See the matrix in Figure C.1.) They range from .01 to 2.[1] A "tipping point" occurs at 1, indicating when a leader is predominately leading from a Creative stance—that is, an advanced stage of leadership development. Scores less than 1 suggest that leaders are still predominately operating at a level of leadership development in which Reactive tendencies may be overshadowing or canceling out their Creative competencies.

| | | Reactive Scores | | | |
|---|---|---|---|---|---|
| | | Low | Mid-Low | Mid-High | High |
| **Creative Scores** | High | 2 | 1.75 | 1.5 | 1.33 |
| | Mid-High | 1.5 | 1.33 | 1 | .75 |
| | Mid-Low | 1 | .75 | .67 | .50 |
| | Low | .67 | .50 | .33 | .01 |

**FIGURE C.1**   LQ Categorical Scores Based on Comparison with Global Database[3]

The LQ positively correlates with the Leadership Effectiveness scale included with the LCP ($r = .93$). The higher the LQ categorical score, the more likely a leader will be viewed as effective.[2]

For the samples used in this book, we randomly selected leaders with categorical scores that fell in the highlighted cells. We selected these specific leaders because they offered the greatest variance in leadership development and effectiveness, as illustrated in Figure C.2. The

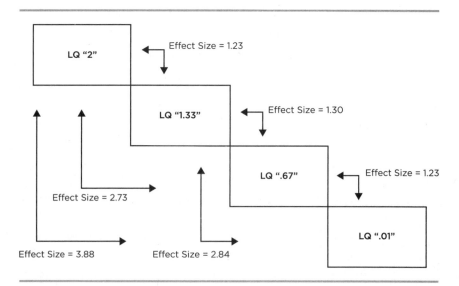

**FIGURE C.2**   Average Leadership Effectiveness Scores and Effect Sizes[4] for the Four LQ Categories Used in This Study

Effect Size scores in Figure C.2 are for Western leaders in our norm base and differ slightly from the sample Effect Size scores reported in the book.

## DESCRIPTION OF QUALITATIVE ANALYSIS OF COMMENT FEEDBACK

We used *Matrix Analysis* to identify common themes within each of the four samples from among the open-ended feedback provided to leaders as part of the LCP assessment. Matrix Analysis[5] is a qualitative technique for coding and interpreting comments using a matrix, or table, of categorical responses by specific groups (e.g., rows reflect general themes and columns reflect the groups of interest—in this study, the specific groups with various Creative-Reactive categories). The themes captured in the rows evolve from the data based on specific catch phrases, concepts, or constructs and their synonyms. If an idea is expressed that is similar in nature to another idea, then it is added as an example of the same theme. The themes themselves reflect shorthand versions of the content as expressed in its overall meaning. This process allows one to capture a number of responses that use different words but are really pointing to the same, common theme. Each time a phrase or sentence within the comment data is related to a theme, a leader code is added to the specific matrix cell associated with that theme (row) and leader group (column).

We have reported only themes that emerged for at least 10 percent of leaders. These can be considered *Core Themes*. Note that core themes reflect the most prevalent and noticeable strengths and challenges that contribute to overall leadership effectiveness from the perspective of raters. It is not meant to be an exhaustive list of strengths and challenges of every leader.

We then calculated an endorsement score for each core theme based on the number of leaders for which that theme was expressed and the strength of endorsement. That is, a core theme might be mentioned by only one or two raters for a leader. In this case, it was deemed a "weak endorsement" and received a half point. However, if the theme were mentioned by more than two raters, it was deemed a "strong endorsement" and received one point. Thus, the endorsement score reflects a percentage of the total points possible. For groups with 100 leaders (High-Creative and High-Reactive), it would be the percentage of 100 points possible, and for groups with 50 leaders (Mid-Creative and Mid-Reactive), it would be the percentage of 50 points possible. A higher endorsement score reflects more prevalence of that trait in those leaders.

# Appendix D
# Definitions of Thematic Strengths and Liabilities

## Thematic Strengths

**Analytical Thinker:** Quickly analyzes situations by sifting through complex information to focus on the main issue.

**Assertive:** Has the courage to speak up and challenge assumptions. Is not afraid to ask the tough questions.

**Balance:** Maintains a healthy work and family life.

**Calm Presence:** Remains calm and present, particularly when under pressure or when dealing with difficult issues. Is level-headed and keeps composure. "Calm, cool, and collected."

**Creative/Innovative:** Thinks outside the box and pushes for change.

**Develops People:** Shares experience and provides mentoring, coaching, career planning, and development experience to ensure the growth and development of others.

**Domain/Technical Knowledge:** Excellent knowledge, technical skills, and experience—particularly related to the organizational culture and market.

**Empowers People:** Shares leadership and encourages people to take ownership, find solutions, make decisions, and learn from mistakes. Trusts people's abilities and their willingness to follow directions.

**Effective Decision Maker:** Uses all available information to make good decisions quickly.

**Fair and Consistent:** Holds everyone to the same standards and does not waver once direction is given.

**Focuses on Continuous Improvement:** Increases efficiency and effectiveness of systems and processes.

**Focuses on Self-Development:** Always trying to learn and grow by soliciting feedback on performance.

**Good Communicator:** In both oral and written communication, clarifies information in a concise and understandable format. Great, articulate speaker.

**Good Listener:** Attentive and present when people are presenting their views.

**Good Negotiator/Mediator:** Gains consensus of opposing views and resolves conflict in the best interest of everyone. Good at finding compromises or win-win solutions.

**Good Problem Solver:** Grasps the root of the problem and comes up with innovative solutions.

**Hard Working:** Good work ethic.

**Intelligent/Brilliant:** Keen mind and sharp thinker.

**Leads by Example:** Is a good role model. "Walks the talk."

**Lives Out Company Values:** Leads in a way that is consistent with company values. Is an example of the values espoused by the company.

**Motivator:** Inspires others to excel. Charismatic.

**Open, Honest, and Forthright in Interactions:** Is transparent, a "straight shooter."

**Open-minded:** Open to new ideas and sees things from multiple perspectives.

**Passion and Drive:** Enthusiastic, driven, and strongly committed to the success of the organization and self.

**Person of Integrity:** Lives out his or her values. Is honest, trustworthy, and honorable.

**Personable and Approachable:** Is friendly, likable, and has a good sense of humor. Maintains an open-door policy. Is accessible and available.

**Positive Attitude:** Optimistic and upbeat with a can-do attitude.

**Provides Good Direction:** Translates the organization's vision into action by laying out a clear and aligned roadmap to achieve goals.

**Provides Feedback:** Gives honest, constructive advice to others.

**Recognizes Contributions:** Openly rewards and praises good effort and performance.

**Responsive to Needs:** Is responsive to others' needs and requests for assistance.

**Results Focused:** Knows what needs to be accomplished and how to get results. Holds people accountable, can be depended on to deliver results. Is reliable and action-oriented.

**Servant Leader:** Puts others' and the organization's needs first. Is humble and selfless.

**Sets High Standards:** Holds him/herself and the organization to high standards.

**Solicits Multiple Views and Stakeholder Perceptions:** Uses them to develop business plans and make decisions.

**Strong Networker:** Builds partnerships with other business leaders. Is good at bringing diverse groups together and provides a strong customer focus.

**Strong People Skills:** Has a high level of interpersonal capability. Is caring, compassionate, big-hearted, and respectful. Connects well with others and makes them feel valuable.

**Team Builder:** Unites, engages, and supports the team's efforts. Gives support to team members and advocates for initiatives.

**Thorough:** Is well organized and attention to detail.

**Visionary:** Communicates a compelling vision of the future that fosters alignment. Knows and sets strategic direction and business plans that allow teams and organizations to thrive.

## Thematic Challenges/Liabilities

**Aloof:** Does not connect with others and can be described as too distant or not approachable.

**Avoids Conflict:** Does not confront issues immediately and waits too long to intervene or solve a problem. Allows situations to linger.

**Places Blame:** Blames others for lack of results or will judge others and finds faults in their work.

**Discussing Personal Issues:** Does not engage in a one-on-one conversation in which issues can be resolved without creating undue stress, biasing others against the individual, or will reprimand in front of others.

**Does Not Admit Mistakes:** Does not take responsibility when things do not turn out well.

**Doesn't Accept Advice or Constructive Criticism:** Tends to take events too personally or becomes defensive.

**Doesn't Connect Well with Others:** Does not empathize with others or appreciate that people bring different strengths to the table.

**Underestimates Resources:** Does not recognize the number of resources needed to meet goals. Risks overburdening others; promises more than can be delivered.

**Exhibits Favoritism:** Inconsistent in behaviors with different team members. Chooses to work with, listen to, rely on, or develop only those s/he likes.

**Hasn't Fully Articulated a Vision:** Hasn't explained vision in terms that others can understand and fails to provide adequate direction, goals, and priorities. Has trouble getting everyone on the same page.

**Impatient:** Becomes easily frustrated when others are too slow to catch on. Tends to rush through things rather than giving them time for understanding and informed decision making.

**Impulsive Reactor:** Passes judgment too quickly and jumps to conclusions without all the facts or without entertaining all views.

**Inattentive/Poor Listener:** Does not listen to others' ideas, especially those ideas that do not match their own. Engages in other tasks while people are speaking or will interrupt them to present his or her own ideas.

**Ineffective Communicator:** Doesn't keep people informed, withholds information, or does not provide information in a timely manner.

**Ineffective Interaction Style:** Off-putting verbal and nonverbal communication style, often described as arrogant, condescending, dictatorial, confrontational, or overly critical.

**Inflexible:** Narrow-minded and controlling by using the same approach for all situations. "My way or the highway."

**Lacks Appreciation:** Doesn't publicly recognize the contributions or share successes with others.

**Lacks Emotional Control:** Has a temper and launches into emotional outbursts and tirades, particularly when things do not go as planned.

**Micromanages:** Does not trust others to get the job done or empower people to make decisions and resolve issues. Tries to do it all by himself/herself.

**No Challenges:** Suggests that a leader had no challenges or that none were noticed or mentioned.

**Not a Team Player:** Operates independently and does not provide enough support for the team, or recognize its needs. Makes decisions in isolation and focuses on only his or her own goals.

**Not Enough Experience:** New to leadership. Has a lack of knowledge, background, and/or experience in the position.

**Not Trustworthy:** Does not do what he or she says; makes promises but does not keep them. Sometimes described as misleading or lacking in integrity.

**Over-Demanding:** Drives others too hard, too fast, and sets unrealistic expectations such that others cannot keep up with their current capability. Is unforgiving and harsh when expectations are not met.

**Overloaded/Overcommitted:** Spread too thin or has too much on his or her plate.

**Poor Decision Making:** Tends to hesitate or postpone the tough decisions. Is said to lack resolve.

**Struggles to Get Others to Embrace Change:** Does not champion change or does not know how to overcome resistance to change.

**Sweats the Small Stuff:** Seems nitpicky on issues or is overly detail oriented.

**Team Not Fully Developed:** Does not provide development opportunities. Does not clearly define roles and responsibilities.

**Team Not Held Accountable:** Teams are not held accountable for quality results and struggle to execute against strategy to meet deadlines. Lacks quality focus by settling for "good enough."

**Too Conventional:** Toes the corporate line or carries on the status quo.

**Too Focused on Details:** Dives too far into the details. Is too tactical.

**Too Focused on Pleasing Others:** Worried about what others will think. Has a high need for acceptance, approval, or being liked.

**Too Negative:** Predominantly negative and is often defeated or negative about team or organization.

**Too Reserved or Passive:** Does not fight for what he or she believes in. Seems too reluctant to change or take on new challenges.

**Too Self-Centric:** Puts personal agenda and gain ahead of the team. Boasts and takes credit for other's work.

**Workaholic:** Puts in too many hours. Does not have time for a personal life.

# Appendix E
# Theorists Integrated into the Leadership Circle Universal Model of Leadership

**Foundational Thought Leaders That Form the Core of the Universal Model of Leadership**

| Thought Leader | Theory/Research | TLC Universal Model of Leadership |
|---|---|---|
| Bill Adams | Whole System Approach | Systems Awareness Dimension; Creative and Integral Level Leadership |
| Peter Block | Authenticity; Caution; Control; Political Scripts | Authenticity Dimension; Reactive Dimension |
| David Burns | Cognitive and Rational Emotive Psychology | All Reactive Dimension; Underlying, Self-limiting Beliefs and Assumptions and associated behavior |
| Robert Fritz | Creative and Reactive Orientations | Two Stages of Development; top half and bottom half of the LCP circle |
| Karen Horney | Character Structure; Three Core Types | Heart, Head, Will Types; Complying Protecting, Controlling; Relating, Awareness, Achieving |

*(continued)*

| Thought Leader | Theory/Research | TLC Universal Model of Leadership |
|---|---|---|
| Robert Kegan | Developmental Psychology; Stages of Adult Development; Immunity to Change | Kegan's Development Model is the vertical axis of the LCP; Immunity to Change describes Reactive Structure's pattern of performance |
| Peter Senge | Systems Thinking and Systems Dynamics; Personal Mastery | Systems Awareness Dimension; Reactive Structure and Creative Structure |
| Ken Wilber | Integral Model | The Universal Model of Leadership is an Integral Model; Ken's seminal work has greatly influenced Its development |

## Stage of Adult Development Thought Leaders

| Thought Leader | Theory/Research | TLC Universal Model of Leadership |
|---|---|---|
| Don Beck | Spiral Dynamics | Stages of Adult Development |
| Susanne Cook-Greuter | Maturity Assessment Profile and Stage Model | Integrated with Kegan's Stage Model, used to research the relationship of the LCP to Stage of Development |
| James Fowler | Stages of Faith | Stages of Spiritual Development |
| Carol Gilligan | In a Different Voice | Stages of Development; Different Types/Voices moving through Structures of Mind |
| Brian Hall | Value Shift | Stages of Adult Development; Stages of Organizational Development, at which stage Vision, Strategy, Intuition, and Systems Thinking typically develop |
| Bill Joiner and Steven Josephs | Leadership Agility | Stages of Adult Development |

| Thought Leader | Theory/Research | TLC Universal Model of Leadership |
|---|---|---|
| Robert Kegan and Lisa Lahey | Developmental Psychology; Stages of Adult Development; Immunity to Change | Kegan's Development Model is the vertical axis of the LCP; Immunity to Change describes Reactive Structure's Pattern of Performance |
| Bill Torbert | Action Logics | Stages of Adult Development |

## Other Integrated Thought Leaders, Framework, and Spiritual Traditions

| Thought Leader | Theory/Research | TLC Universal Model of Leadership |
|---|---|---|
| Wes Agor | Intuitive Management | Intuition Practice |
| Warren Bennis | On Becoming a Leader | Leadership Practices; Creative Level Leadership, Purposeful Visionary Dimension |
| Kevin Cashman | Inside-out Leadership | Inner Game, Leadership Practices |
| CCL, PDI, DDI | 360 Competency Research | Key Creative Leadership Competencies |
| Jim Collins | Level 5 Leadership | The Polarity of Fierce Resolve with Ambition; Hedgehog Concept |
| Stephen Covey | Seven Habits of Successful People | Leadership Practices, Stages of Ego Development—Dependent, Independent, Interdependent |
| Mihaly Csikszentmihalyi | Flow | Creative Level Leadership, Mastery, Intuition |
| Max Dupree | Inclusive Organization | Systems Awareness Dimension, Creative Level Leadership |
| Albert Ellis | Rational Emotive Therapy | Reactive Dimensions, core identity beliefs and assumptions, Leadership Practices |
| Viktor Frankl | Man's Search for Meaning; Logo Therapy | Purposeful Visionary Dimension; Creative Structure of Mind |

*(continued)*

| Thought Leader | Theory/Research | TLC Universal Model of Leadership |
| --- | --- | --- |
| Tim Galway | Inner Game Theory | Inner Game, Operating Systems, Reactive and Creative Structures of Mind |
| Daniel Goleman | Emotional Intelligence | Self-Awareness Dimension |
| Robert Greenleaf | Servant Leadership | Creative to Integral Level Leadership |
| Michael Hammer | Organization Redesign | Systems Awareness Dimension |
| Kathleen Hurley and Theodore Dobson | Enneagram | The Enneagram framework is foundational to the Universal Model; Reactive Structure of Mind, and Pathway of Development |
| William James | As a Man Thinketh | Creative and Integral Structures of Mind |
| Joe Jaworski | Synchronicity | Intuition, Creative Consciousness |
| Barry Johnson | Polarity Theory | Polarities across the LCP Circle; Ability to manage polarities increases with Stage of Development |
| Carl Jung | Ego Shadow Dynamics | Type Shadow Dynamics |
| Robert Kaplan | Beyond Ambition | Controlling Dimension, Sustainable Productivity Dimension |
| James Kouzes and Barry Posner | Integrity | Integrity Dimension |
| Clay Lafferty | Life Styles Instrument | Reactive Dimension and the brilliance of displaying data in a circle |
| Patrick Lencioni | The Five Dysfunctions of a Team | Reactive Structure of Mind played out collectively |
| James MacGregor-Burns | Transactional versus Transformational Leadership | Reactive and Creative Leadership |

| Thought Leader | Theory/Research | TLC Universal Model of Leadership |
| --- | --- | --- |
| Abraham Maslow | Hierarchy of Need, Self Actualization | Hierarchy Model is a Stage Model; Self-Awareness Dimension |
| David McClellend | Achievement Motivation | Achieving Dimension |
| Douglas McGregor | Theory X, Theory Y | Internal Assumptions impact on leadership style and effectiveness; polarity between Relating and Controlling |
| Otto Scharmer | Presence, Theory U | Integral Level Mind, Systems Awareness Dimension, Self Awareness Dimension Intuition Practice |
| Will Schutz | The Truth Option, FIRO-B | Authenticity Dimension, Complying and Controlling Dimensions |
| Lao Tzu | Tao Te Ching | Self-Awareness Dimension |
| Marvin Weisbord | Whole System Redesign | Systems Awareness Dimension |
| Meg Wheatly | Leadership and the New Science | Systems Awareness Dimension, the kind of Systems Thinking that emerges at the Integral Structure of Mind |
| Larry Wilson | Play to Win; Play-Not-to-Lose | Creative and Reactive Structures of Mind |
| Wisdom Traditions | Spiritual Development | Unity Consciousness, Stages of Consciousness Development |
| Zenger-Folkman | Extraordinary Leadership | Leadership Competencies, research on extraordinary leaders |

# About the Authors

**Robert J. Anderson** is the founder and chairman of The Leadership Circle and cofounder and chairman of the Full Circle Group. Bob has dedicated his career to exploring the connections between leadership, mastery, competence, consciousness, spirituality, and business.

Over the past 35 years, he has worked to integrate the best of the leadership theory and research, resulting in a comprehensive framework for developing leaders—the first Universal Model of Leadership to emerge in the field. The Leadership Circle Profile™ (LCP) is a leadership assessment that provides leaders 360-degree feedback through the lens of the Universal Model. The Universal Model and the LCP provide organizations of any size, in any industry, with what they need to measure the effectiveness of leaders (individually and collectively), chart a pathway for their development, and then assess their progress as they develop. Forbes named the LCP one of its top executive development assessments.

Bob is the coauthor (along with Bill Adams) of the book, *Mastering Leadership: An Integrated Framework for Breakthrough Performance and Extraordinary Business Results.* This book is being described as a seminal work in the leadership field. It was a Top Ten Bestseller on 800ceoread and was a Top 10 editorial pick on Amazon.

Bob is a true pioneer in the field of leadership development and research. He spends the majority of his time researching, writing, consulting, and speaking around the world. He is dedicated to impacting the consciousness and effectiveness of leadership globally. Bob's practical wisdom, humility, creativity, humor, and expertise provide a rare and transformative experience for anyone with whom he works.

The Leadership Circle and Full Circle Group earned first place in the Large Leadership Partner and Provider category of the HR.com 2015 Leadership 500 Excellence Awards. Bob serves as adjunct faculty for the Stayer Center of Executive Education at the University of Notre Dame Mendoza College of Business, which awarded him the Partner in Innovation faculty award in 2005. The MEECO Leadership Institute awarded him the International Thought Leader of Distinction in 2018.

Bob holds a bachelor's degree in Economics from John Carroll University and a master's in Organizational Development from Bowling Green State University. Bob and Kim, his wife of 32 years, have three wonderful children and make their home near Toledo, Ohio.

**Bill Adams** is the cofounder and CEO of Full Circle Group and The Leadership Circle. Bill has over 30 years of experience as a trusted advisor to CEOs and their teams around the globe. He partners with leaders to unlock breakthrough performance, develop deep leadership capability/capacity and transformational business results. Bill is known for his practical commonsense approach to sorting through complex and difficult situations and produce exceptional results. Bill works with leaders as a leader himself that is learning and growing. His clients range from Fortune 100 multinational corporations to fast-growth start-ups and include some of the best-known and respected businesses in the world.

Bill coauthored *Mastering Leadership: An Integrated Framework for Breakthrough Performance and Extraordinary Business Results*; *The Whole Systems Approach: Involving Everyone in the Company to Transform and Run Your Business* (with coauthor Cindy Adams); and *The Quest for Quality: Prescriptions for Achieving Service Excellence.* He contributed to *The Change Handbook: Group Methods for Shaping the Future* and *Managing Quality in America's Most Admired Companies.*

Bill holds a master's in Interpersonal Communication from the University of Montana and has over 40 years of hands-on business experience, having started, run, and sold multiple businesses. He is an avid outdoorsman, currently residing in the mountains of Utah and Montana. Bill is married to the love of his life, Cynthia Adams, and together they are actively involved as parents and grandparents to 10 grandchildren.

# Notes

## Chapter 1

1. Bob Johansen, *Leaders Make the Future: Ten New Leadership Skills for an Uncertain World* (San Francisco: Berrett-Koehler, 2009). Latest edition: Bob Johansen, *Leaders Make the Future: Ten New Leadership Skills for an Uncertain World,* 2nd ed. (San Francisco: Berrett-Koehler, 2012).

2. Bob Johansen, The New Leadership Literacies: Thriving in a Future of Extreme Disruption and Distributed Everything (Oakland, CA: Berrett-Koehler, 2017).

## Chapter 2

1. In *Mastering Leadership* (p. 101), we discuss in more detail cultural differences in LCP results. The leadership competencies measured by the LCP are all highly and consistently correlated with Leadership Effectiveness. The Reactive behaviors are all inverse to effectiveness, but there is some variation in the strength of the correlations. What we see is that in some countries, usually developing countries, patriarchal styles of leadership are more highly valued. We also see this in the ideal/optimal profile.

## Chapter 4

1. We make the assumption that most raters are leaders within the organization. Because we selected senior leaders (L1–L3) in large

organizations for this study, most of the raters will also be senior leaders (board members through L4). This, of course, may not be the case of all raters, but we will use the word "rater" and "leader" interchangeably because, for the most part, this study is about is senior leaders providing feedback to other senior leaders.

2. The researchers commented that passion and drive were difficult to pull apart and thus, were kept together. There were other related themes that in some cases helped to distinguish differences in the nature of a leader's drive. Researchers commented in their report that they noticed more of an emphasis on self-centric drive in High-Reactive leaders and more emphasis on service to the mission in the comments about High-Creative leaders. They pulled some of these distinctions out in subthemes, but in many cases, it was not possible to tell what kind of drive was being described, so they kept the two constructs together as passion and drive.

3. https://www.nordea.com/en/press-and-news/news-and-press-releases/news-en/2017/investing-in-female-ceos-pays-off.html.

4. Robert Kegan and Lisa Laskow Lahey, *Immunity to Change: How to Overcome It and Unlock Potential in Yourself and Your Organization* (Boston: Harvard University Press, 2009).

## Chapter 5

1. Robert Kaplan, Beyond Ambition: *How Driven Managers Can Lead Better and Live Better* (San Francisco: Jossey-Bass, 1991).

## Chapter 6

1. https://www.predictiveindex.com/blog/what-a-millennial-learned-from-a-ceo/.

2. https://globalgurus.org/reminder-2014-goals-purpose-success-serve-others-purpose-life-love-loved/.

## Chapter 9

1. An effect size of 0.3 suggests that small but noticeable differences will be seen in the workplace behaviors of two different sample groups. An effect size of 0.8 means large, meaningful differences will be seen. The effect size scores between each of the successive four samples in this study are all beyond 1.2 and as high as 1.7. (See Appendix C.) Effect size scores are as high as 2.8 for between

groups that are separated by another group, for example, High-Reactive and Mid-Creative.

2. In *Mastering Leadership*, we established that the LPC measures well cross-culturally. Therefore, we assume that this Full Spectrum of Leadership applies cross-culturally. Since in this study we chose to sample only English-speaking countries (as we did not want to introduce cultural differences into the written comment study), it remains for future research to see how written comments correlate to the spectrum in different cultures. We expect there will be cultural differences in the verbal descriptions of Creative and Reactive leadership, but that the general conclusions of this study will hold up around the world.

3. Jim Collins, *Good to Great: Why Some Companies Make the Leap ... and Others Don't* (New York City: Harper Business, 2001).

**Chapter 10**

1. We first encountered this three-way character framework in the work of Karen Horney, a psychoanalyst who wrote in the 1940s and 1950s. In her book *Our Inner Conflicts*, she describes each of three Character Structures—Move Toward, Move Against, and Move Away. This three-way description of core personality types or energies shows up in many different systems: Gurdjieff's Enneagram (the Law of Threes), Pathwork (love mask, serenity mask, and power mask), Christian spiritual traditions (the Trinity), Eastern spiritual traditions (Yin, Yang, Neutral), Alchemy, and Science (electron, proton, neutron). It is a universal construct of profound import.

2. In their book *Immunity to Change*, Bob Kegan (one of the foremost researchers on adult development in the world) and Lisa Lahey describe three stages of adult development. Kegan's first stage of adult development is Socialized, in which we define ourselves based on our early life conditioning and the messages and expectations from our past and current surrounding environment. Most adults function from this level of development.

There are many stage-development theories in the field of adult development, and all of them describe the same invariant trajectory of human development (with each drawing the lines between levels at a different point in the spectrum and using different names to label the levels). The same is true in the spiritual traditions, East and West. These frameworks point to the universal process of human development.

3. Self-Authoring is the second adult stage of development in Bob Kegan's model. The shift from Socialized to Self-Authoring is the major developmental transformation in the life of most adults. As this fundamental shift of mind happens, we move from being authored by others—living up to their expectations—to being Self-Authored—living from our own deeply discerned sense of purpose, values, and vision. Self-Authorship is a prerequisite to Creative leadership.

## Chapter 11

1. Ronald Heifetz, *Leadership without Easy Answers* (Boston: Harvard University Press, 1998).

2. In *Mastering Leadership*, we used the Reactive, Creative, and Integral framework as synonymous with Kegan's three-stage model of Adult Development. We have changed our framing a bit since then. We now think of the Stages of Leadership (Reactive, Creative, Integral) as *arising* out of progressively maturing stages of development (Socialized, Self-Authored, and Self-Transforming).

   This diagram is intentionally oversimplified and not intended to represent the statistical and theoretical nuances of how various theories of development relate to one another, to levels of leadership, and to the Leadership Circle Profile normative data. This diagram is intended to be directionally correct. It implies that the progressive stages of leadership are underpinned by progressive stages of adult development. It also suggests there is a relationship between a leader's maturing inner development and how effective they are likely to be (and how they might measure on the LCP) in the complex context of senior leadership in large organizations in today's VUCA environment. The interplay between leaders' current capacity (their current complexity of self) and the environment in which they are trying to be effective (the complexity of context) is the crucible of development. The volatility, complexity, uncertainty, and ambiguity of an operating environment puts a developmental demand on leaders. They respond to that demand with the onboard capacities in their current level of adult development. Others experience this expression of their capacities as leadership—a manifestation of Reactive, Creative, and/or Integral tendencies and behaviors.

We hold that Creative leadership, as described throughout this book, in complex contexts reaches a fuller maturity when a leader's stage of adult development is late Self-Authoring. Creative leadership depends on this shift of mind, heart, and behavior and is thus conveniently drawn across from a late Self-Authoring meaning-making system. Since Kegan's model has three broad adult stages, what we are calling mature Self-Authorship is not inclusive of all those who measure within the Stage 4 bandwidth, but those who are fully configured and maturing beyond Stage 4. We estimate that about 20–25 percent of leaders are in this category.

It is important to note in making this estimate that the stages of development models and measurement are works in progress and that the body of research relating stage measures to leadership measures is in its infancy. So, the estimate of 20–25 percent is based on a pattern we see in the research presented by (1) Bill Torbert's longitudinal study of the relationship between CEO action-logics and organizational transformation efforts, (2) the research Kegan and Lahey reported in their book *Immunity to Change*, on the relationship between Individual mental capacity and business effectiveness, and (3) our own research. This pattern is simple. There is a positive relationship between progressive stages of adult development and measures of leadership effectiveness, but the big jumps in measured performance come at later stages (beyond Stage 4). This pattern is also consistent with the pattern we see in the research we presented in *Mastering Leadership*.

3. For this analysis, we turn to the subthemes identified in the research. While there were 40 thematic strengths culled out of the content analysis, many more subthemes emerged. Because of the way matrix content endorsement scores are calculated, the simple addition of subthemes does not add up to the main theme. This is why some of the subthemes, which have large gaps between High-Reactive and High-Creative leaders, do not end up on the biggest gaps list. The biggest gaps list includes major themes, not subthemes.

4. Robert Kaplan, *Beyond Ambition: How Driven Managers Can Lead Better and Live Better* (San Francisco: Jossey-Bass, 1991).

5. Jack Zenger and Joseph Folkman, *The Extraordinary Leader: Turning Good Managers into Great Leaders*, 2nd ed. (New York: McGraw-Hill, 2009).

## Chapter 12

1. The first two questions come from Patrick Lencioni's book, *The Five Dysfunctions of a Team* (San Francisco: Jossey-Bass, 2002).

2. We are indebted to the work of Robert Fritz (1989) for his work on the creative orientation and for the framework of structural tension.

3. https://news.stanford.edu/2005/06/14/jobs-061505/.

4. https://www.goodreads.com/quotes/1465306-until-one-is-committed-there-is-hesitancy-the-chance-to.

5. Larry Wilson and Hersch Wilson, *Play to Win!: Choosing Growth over Fear in Work and Life* (Austin, TX: Bard Press, 1998). Latest edition: Larry Wilson and Hersch Wilson, *Play to Win!: Choosing Growth Over Fear in Work and Life*, rev. ed. (Austin, TX: Bard Press, 2004).

6. https://ottawa.bibliocommons.com/item/quotation/986822026.

7. https://upliftconnect.com/spiritual-wisdom-of-albert-einstein/.

## Chapter 13

1. Geoffrey West, *Scale: Universal Laws of Growth, Innovation, Sustainability, and the Pace of Life in Organisms, Cities, Economies, and Companies* (New York: Penguin Books, 2018).

2. John Mackey and Raj Sisodia, *Conscious Capitalism* (Boston: Harvard Business School Publishing, 2014).

3. Frederic Laloux, *Reinventing Organizations: A Guide to Creating Organizations Inspired by the Next Stage in Human Consciousness* (Millis, MA: Nelson Parker, 2014).

4. Robert Kegan and Lisa Laskow Lahey, *An Everyone Culture: Becoming a Deliberately Developmental Organization* (Boston: Harvard Business School Publishing, 2016).

5. https://news.stanford.edu/2005/06/14/jobs-061505/.

6. https://www.goodreads.com/quotes/1465306-until-one-is-committed-there-is-hesitancy-the-chance-to.

**Appendix C**

1. Note that the numbers themselves are arbitrary and were selected to maintain the important interpretation of effective leaders as laid out in the *Mastering Leadership* book.

2. Leaders with a categorical score below 0.67 generally score below average (less than the 33rd percentile) on the Leadership Effectiveness scale. This may help explain why they are not seen as more effective. Conversely, leaders with a categorical score above 1.33 typically score above average on the leadership effectiveness scale (more than the 66th percentile).

3. A "Low" score includes scores below the 33rd percentile (one standard deviation below the mean). A "Mid-Low" score includes scores between the 33rd and 49th percentile (within a half-standard deviation of the mean). A "Mid-High" score includes scores between the 40th and 66th percentile (within a half-standard deviation of the mean). A "High" score includes scores above the 66th percentile (one standard deviation above the mean).

4. Effect size is a measure of practical significance—it is not influenced by sample size and thus provides a better indicator of meaningful differences. Effect sizes are calculated based on mean differences divided by the averaged variance within both groups. Cohen has suggested standards for interpretation about the meaningfulness of effect sizes:

   - Effect sizes less than 0.20 have little practical significance.
   - Effect sizes between 0.30 and 0.50 are meaningful but small.
   - Effect sizes between 0.50 and 0.80 can be considered moderate.
   - Effect sizes above 0.80 are large and suggest leaders are showing up quite differently.

5. A more complete understanding of Matrix Analysis can be gleaned from this article by Professor Groenland: A. E. G. Groenland, "Employing the Matrix Method as a Tool for the Analysis of Qualitative Research Data in Business. Center for Marketing and Supply Chain Management, Nyenrode Busines Universiteit, 2014. Available at http://ssrn.com/abstract=2495330.

# References

Abrams, Jeremiah, and Connie Zweig. *Meeting the Shadow: The Hidden Power of the Dark Side of Human Nature*. New York: Penguin Putnam, 1991.

Adams, Cindy, and W. A. Adams. *Collaborating for Change: The Whole Systems Approach*. San Francisco: Berrett-Koehler, 2000.

Adams, W. A., and Michael Bowker. *The Whole Systems Approach Involving Everyone in the Company to Transform and Run Your Business*. Provo, UT: Executive Excellence, 1999.

Agor, Weston H. *Intuitive Management: Integrating Left and Right Brain Management Skills*. Englewood Cliffs, NJ: Prentice-Hall, 1984.

Allen, James. *As a Man Thinketh*. Chicago: Science Press, 1905.

Anderson, Robert. *Leadership: The Uncommon Sense*. Position paper, theleadershipcircle.com, 1990.

Anderson, Robert. *Pathways to Partnership*. Position Paper, theleadershipcircle.com, 1995.

Anderson, Robert. *Mastering Leadership*. Position Paper, theleadershipcircle.com, 1991.

Anderson, Robert J., and William A. Adams. *Mastering Leadership: An Integrated Framework for Breakthrough Performance and Extraordinary Business Results*. Hoboken, NJ: Wiley, 2016.

Autry, James A. *Love and Profit: The Art of Caring Leadership*. New York: Morrow, 1991.

Barks, Coleman. *The Essential Rumi: New Expanded Edition*. New York: Harper Collins, 2004.

Beck, Don, and Christopher C. Cowan. *Spiral Dynamics: Mastering Values, Leadership, and Change: Exploring the New Science of Memetics*. Cambridge, MA.: Blackwell Business, 1996.

Beesing, Maria, and Robert J. Nogosek. *The Enneagram: A Journey of Self Discovery*. Denville, NJ: Dimension Books, 1984.

Belasco, James A., and Ralph C. Stayer. *Flight of the Buffalo: Soaring to Excellence, Learning to Let Employees Lead*. New York: Warner Books, 1993.

Bennis, Warren. *On Becoming a Leader*, 4th ed. New York: Basic Books, 2009.

Bennis, Warren, and Burt Nanus. *Leaders: The Strategies for Taking Charge*. New York: Harper & Row, 1985.

Berger, Jennifer Garvey. *Changing on the Job Developing Leaders for a Complex World*. Stanford, CA: Stanford Business Books, 2012.

Block, Peter. *The Empowered Manager: Positive Political Skills at Work*. San Francisco: Jossey-Bass, 1987.

Block, Peter. *Stewardship: Choosing Service over Self-Interest*. San Francisco: Berrett-Koehler, 1993.

Bly, Robert. *Iron John: A Book about Men*. Reading, MA: Addison-Wesley, 1990.

Bly, Robert. *News of the Universe: Poems of Twofold Consciousness*. San Francisco: Sierra Club Books, 1980.

Bonhoeffer, Dietrich, and Manfred Weber. *Meditations on the Cross*. Louisville, KY: Westminster John Knox Press, 1998.

Burns, D. *Feeling Good: The New Mood Therapy*. New York: Signet, 1980.

Campbell, Joseph. *The Hero with a Thousand Faces*. New York: Pantheon Books, 1949.

Campbell, Joseph. *The Hero with a Thousand Faces: The Collected Works of Joseph Campbell*, 3rd ed. Novato, CA: New World Library, 2008.

Campbell, Joseph, and Bill Moyers. *The Power of Myth*. New York: Anchor, 1991.

Capitalizing on Complexity: Insights from the Global Chief Executive Officer Study. http://www-01.ibm.com/common/ssi/cgi-bin/ssialias?infotype=PM&subtype=XB&htmlfid=GBE03297USEN (accessed June 15, 2015).

Cashman, Kevin. *Leadership from the Inside Out: Seven Pathways to Mastery*. Provo, UT: Executive Excellence, 1998.

Collins, Jim. "Good to Great." *Fast Company*, September 30, 2001.

Collins, Jim. *Good to Great: Why Some Companies Make the Leap ... And Others Don't.* New York: Harper Business, 2001.

Cook-Greuter, Susanne R. "Making the Case for a Developmental Perspective." *Industrial and Commercial Training* 36, no. 7 (2004).

Covey, Stephen. *The 7 Habits of Highly Effective People.* New York: Simon & Schuster, 1989.

Csikszentmihalyi, Mihaly. *Flow: The Psychology of Optimal Experience.* New York: Harper & Row, 1990.

Csikszentmihalyi, Mihaly. *The Evolving Self: A Psychology for the Third Millennium.* New York: HarperCollins, 1993.

Depree, Max. *Leadership Is an Art.* New York: Doubleday, 1989.

Ellis, Albert. *How to Stubbornly Refuse to Make Yourself Miserable about Anything—Yes, Anything.* NY: Carol Publishing, 1988.

—, and Melvin Powers. *A New Guide to Rational Living.* Chatsworth, UK: Wilshire Book Company, 1975.

Emerson, Ralph Waldo. *Nature.* Boston: James Munroe and Company, 1936.

Fowler, James W. *Stages of Faith: The Psychology of Human Development and the Quest for Meaning.* San Francisco: HarperSanFrancisco, 1995.

Fox, Matthew. *Meister Eckhart: A Mystic-Warrior for Our Times.* Novato, CA: New World Library, 2014.

Frankl, Viktor. *Man's Search for Meaning.* New York: Washington Square Press, 1959.

Fritz, Robert. *The Path of Least Resistance.* New York: Fawcett-Columbine Books, 1989.

Gallway, W. Timothy. *The Inner Game of Work: Focus, Learning, Pleasure, and Mobility in the Workplace.* New York: Random House, 2000.

Gilligan, Carol. *In a Different Voice: Psychological Theory and Women's Development.* Cambridge: Harvard University Press, 1982.

Goethe, Johann Wolfgang von. "The Holy Longing." In *News of the Universe.* Trans. Robert Bly. Oakland: University of California Press, 1980.

Goleman, Daniel. *Emotional Intelligence: Why It Can Matter More Than IQ*, 10th anniversary ed. New York City: Bantam, 2005.

Greene, Robert. *Mastery.* New York: Viking, 2012.

Greenleaf, Robert K. *Servant Leadership: A Journey into the Nature of Legitimate Power and Greatness.* New York: Paulist Press, 1977.

Hall, Brian P. *Values Shift: A Guide to Personal and Organizational Transformation*. Eugene, OR: Wipf & Stock, 2006.

Heaney, Seamus, trans. *Beowulf: A New Verse Translation*. New York: Norton, 2000.

Heifetz, Ronald. *Leadership without Easy Answers*. Boston: Harvard University Press, 1998.

Hersey, Paul, and Blanchard, Ken. "Life Cycle Theory of Leadership." *Training and Development Journal* 23 (1969): 26–34.

Hill, Napoleon. *Think and Grow Rich*. Meriden, CT: The Ralston Society, 1937.

Horney, Karen. *Our Inner Conflicts*. New York: W.W. Norton & Company, 1945.

Hudson, Frederic M. *The Adult Years: Mastering the Art of Self-Renewal*. San Francisco: Jossey-Bass, 1991.

Hurley, Kathleen V., and Theodore Elliott Dobson. *What's My Type?: Use the Enneagram System of Nine Personality Types to Discover Your Best Self*. San Francisco: HarperSanFrancisco, 1991.

"Investing in Female CEOs Pays Off." Nordic Financial Services. August 9, 2017. https://www.nordea.com/en/press-and-news/news-and-press-releases/news-en/2017/investing-in-female-ceos-pays-off.html (accessed August 1, 2018).

Isaacson, Walter. *Steve Jobs*. New York: Simon & Schuster, 2011.

Jobs, Steve. *"You've Got to Find What You Love," Jobs Says*. Stanford: Stanford Report, 2005.

Johansen, Bob. *The New Leadership Literacies Thriving in a Future of Extreme Disruption and Distributed Everything*. Oakland, CA: Berrett-Koehler, 2017.

Johansen, Bob. *Leaders Make the Future: Ten New Leadership Skills for an Uncertain World*, 2nd ed. San Francisco: Berrett-Koehler, 2012.

Johanson, Gregory J., and Ron Kurtz. *Grace Unfolding: Psychotherapy in the Spirit of the Tao-te Ching*. New York: Bell Tower, 1991.

Johnson, Barry. *Polarity Management: Identifying and Managing Unsolvable Problems*. Amherst, MA: HRD Press, 2014.

Jung, Carl. *Psychological Types: The Collected Works of C. G. Jung. Vol. 6*. Princeton: Princeton University Press, 1976.

Jaworski, Joseph. *Synchronicity: The Inner Path of Leadership*. San Francisco, CA: Berrett-Koehler, 1996.

Jones, Susan, ed. *The New Jerusalem Bible*. New York: Doubleday, 1985.

Kaplan, Robert. *Beyond Ambition: How Driven Managers Can Lead Better and Live Better*. San Francisco: Jossey-Bass, 1991.

Kauffman, Draper. *Systems One: An Introduction to Systems Thinking.* St. Paul, MN: Future Systems/TLH Associates, 1980.

Kegan, Robert. *The Evolving Self.* Boston: Harvard University Press, 1982.

Kegan, Robert. *In Over Our Heads: The Mental Demands of Modern Life*, 4th edn. Boston: Harvard University Press, 1998.

Kegan, Robert, and Lisa Laskow Lahey. *Immunity to Change: How to Overcome It and Unlock Potential in Yourself and Your Organization.* Boston: Harvard University Press, 2009.

Kegan, Robert, and Lisa Laskow Lahey. *An Everyone Culture: Becoming a Deliberately Developmental Organization.* Boston: Harvard Business School, 2016.

Kelly, Walt. *Pogo: We Have Met the Enemy and He Is Us.* New York: Simon and Schuster, 1972.

Klein, Eric, and John B. Izzo. *Awakening Corporate Soul: Four Paths to Unleash the Power of People at Work.* Lion's Bay, BC: Fairwinds Press, 1998.

Kohlberg, Lawrence. *The Philosophy of Moral Development: Moral Stages and the Idea of Justice.* San Francisco: Harper & Row, 1981.

Kouzes, Jim, and Barry Posner. *The Leadership Challenge: How to Keep Getting Extraordinary Things Done in Organizations.* San Francisco: Jossey-Bass, 1995.

Kouzes, Jim, and Barry Posner. *Leadership Challenge*, 3rd ed. San Francisco: Jossey-Bass, 2002.

Kurtz, Ron. *Body-Centered Psychotherapy: The Hakomi Method: The Integrated Use of Mindfulness, Nonviolence, and the Body.* Mendocino, CA: LifeRhythm, 1990.

Lafferty, J. Clayton, and Robert Cooke. *The Life Styles Inventory and the Guttman Scale: Using the Items to Help the Focal Individual Identify Strategies for Developing Constructive Thinking and Behaviour.* South Melbourne, Australia: Human Synergistics International, 2009.

Laloux, Frederic. *Reinventing Organizations: A Guide to Creating Organizations Inspired by the Next Stage of Human Consciousness.* Millis, MA: Nelson Parker, 2014.

Lao-tzu. *Tao Te Ching.* Trans. S. Mitchell. Radford, VA: Wilder Publications, 2008.

Lencioni, Patrick. *The Five Dysfunctions of a Team: A Leadership Fable.* San Francisco: Jossey-Bass, 2002.

MacGregor Burns, James. *Leadership.* New York: Harper Collins, 1978.

Mackey, John, and Raj Sisodia. *Conscious Capitalism*. Boston: Harvard Business School, 2014.

Marion, Jim. *Putting on the Mind of Christ: The Inner Work of Christian Spirituality*. Charlottesville, VA: Hampton Roads, 2000.

Maslow, Abraham. *Motivation and Personality*. New York: Harper and Row, 1954.

May, Rollo. *The Courage to Create*. New York: Norton, 1975.

McClelland, David. *Human Motivation*. Cambridge, MA: Cambridge University Press, 1988.

McClelland, David. *The Achievement Motive*. New York: Appleton-Century-Crofts, 1953.

McGregor, Douglas. *The Human Side of Enterprise*. New York City: McGraw-Hill, 1960.

Mitchell, Stephen. *Bhagavad Gita: A New Translation*. New York: Harmony Books, 2000.

Mitchell, Stephen. *Tao Te Ching: A New English Version*. New York: Harper & Row, 1988.

Moore, Thomas. *Care of the Soul: A Guide for Cultivating Depth and Sacredness in Everyday Life*. New York: HarperCollins, 1992.

Murray, W. H. *The Scottish Himalayan Expedition*. Denver, CO: J. M. Dent & Company, 1951.

Oliver, Mary. "The Summer Day." *In House of Light*. Boston: Beacon Press, 1990.

Palmer, Helen. *The Enneagram: Understanding Yourself and the Others in Your Life*. San Francisco: Harper & Row, 1988.

Peter, Laurence J., and Raymond. Hull. *The Peter Principle*. Taipei: Imperial Book, Sound & Gift, 1969.

Peters, Thomas J. *Thriving on Chaos: Handbook for a Management Revolution*. New York: Knopf, 1987.

Rilke, Rainer Maria. *Letters to a Young Poet*. Trans. M.D. Herter Norton. New York: W. W. Norton & Company, 1993.

Rilke, Rainer Maria. *The Selected Poetry of Rainer Maria Rilke*. Stephen Mitchell, Trans. New York: Random House, 1982.

Rooke, David, and William R. Torbert. "Organizational Transformation as a Function of CEOs' Developmental Stage." *Organizational Development Journal* 16, no. 1 (1998): 11–28.

Rogers, Carl. *On Becoming a Person: A Therapist's View of Psychotherapy*. Boston: Houghton Mifflin Company, 1962.

Rowan, Roy. *The Intuitive Manager*. New York: Little, Brown and Company, 1986.

Schaef, Anne Wilson, and Diane Fassel. *The Addictive Organization.* San Francisco: Harper & Row, 1988.

Schopenhauer, Arthur. *Parerga and Paralipomena Short Philosophical Essays, Vol. 1*, 1st ed. Oxford: Clarendon Press, 1974.

Schutz, Will. *The Truth Option.* Berkeley, CA: Ten Speed Press, 1984.

Schutz, Will. *Profound Simplicity.* San Diego, CA: Learning Concepts, 1982.

Schweitzer, Albert, in a speech to the students of Silcoates School, Wakefield (along with "a number of boys and girls from Ackworth School"), on "The Meaning of Ideals in Life," at approximately 3:40 p.m. on December 3, 1935. "Visit of Dr. Albert Schweitzer" (as translated from the French of the address by Dr. Schweitzer's interpreter), *The Silcoatian*, New Series No. 25 (December, 1935): 784–785 (781–786 with 771–772 ("Things in General")).

Senge, Peter. *Systems Principles for Leadership.* Cambridge, MA: Massachusetts Institute of Technology, 1985.

Senge, Peter. *The Fifth Discipline: The Art and Practice of The Learning Organization*, Revised ed. New York: Doubleday, 2006.

Senge, Peter M. *Presence: Exploring Profound Change in People, Organizations, and Society.* New York: Doubleday, 2005.

Singh, M. P. *Quote, Unquote: A Handbook of Famous Quotations.* New Delhi: Lotus Press, 2006. 172.

*"Success Is the Enemy" and Other Truths: The CEO Of Johnsonville Foods Inc. Preaches His Management Mistakes and Methods to Those Looking to Improve.* Madison: The Wisconsin State Journal, 1997.

Torbert, William R. *Action Inquiry: The Secret of Timely and Transforming Leadership.* San Francisco, CA: Berrett-Koehler, 2004.

Torbert, W. *The Power of Balance: Transforming Self, Society, and Scientific Inquiry.* Newbury Park: Sage, 1991.

Van Dusen, Lani. "Leadership: The Next Productivity Frontier." Lecture, Leadership and Human Capital Management, 53rd Annual Convention from Equipment Leasing and Finance Association, San Diego, October 21, 2014.

Van Dusen, Lani. "The Importance of Investing in Leadership." *Journal of Equipment Lease Financing*, Spring 2015.

Vries, Manfred F. R., and Danny Miller. *The Neurotic Organization.* San Francisco: Jossey-Bass, 1984.

Wade, Jenny. *Changes of Mind: A Holonomic Theory of the Evolution of Consciousness*. Albany: State University of New York Press, 1996.

Wei, Wu Wei. *Ask the Awakened*. Boulder, CO: Sentient Publications, 2002.

Weisbord, Marvin. *Productive Workplaces Revisited: Dignity, Meaning, and Community in the 21st Century*. San Francisco: Jossey-Bass, 2004.

Wenger, Michael. *Wind Bell: Teachings from the San Francisco Zen Center 1968–2001*. Berkeley, CA: North Atlantic Books, 2002.

West, Geoffrey. *Scale: Universal Laws of Growth, Innovation, Sustainability, and the Pace of Life in Organisms, Cities, Economies, and Companies*. New York: Penguin Books, 2018.

Wheatley, Margaret. *Leadership and the New Science: Discovering Order in a Chaotic World*. San Francisco: Berrett-Koehler, 2006.

Whyte, David. *Songs for Coming Home: Poems*. Revised edn. Langley, WA: Many Rivers Press, 1989.

Whyte, David. *Where Many Rivers Meet: Poems*. Langley, WA: Many Rivers Press, 1990.

Whyte, David. *Fire in the Earth: Poems*. Langley, WA: Many Rivers Press, 1992.

Whyte, David. *The Heart Aroused: Poetry and the Preservation of the Soul in Corporate America*. New York: Currency Doubleday, 1994.

Whyte, David. *Crossing the Unknown Sea: Work as a Pilgrimage of Identity*. New York: Riverhead Books, 2001.

Whyte, David. *River Flow: New and Selected Poems*. Langley, Wash: Many Rivers Press, 2012.

Wilber, Ken. *A Theory of Everything: An Integral Vision for Business, Politics, Science, and Spirituality*. Boston: Shambhala, 2001.

Wilber, Ken. *Integral Psychology: Consciousness, Spirit, Psychology, Therapy*. Boston: Shambhala, 2000.

Wilber, K. *One Taste: Daily Reflections on Integral Spirituality*. Shambhala, Boston, 1999.

Wilson, Larry, and Hersch Wilson. *Play to Win!: Choosing Growth over Fear in Work and Life*, revised ed. Austin, TX: Bard Press, 2004.

Zenger, Jack, and Joseph Folkman. *The Extraordinary Leader: Turning Good Managers into Great Leaders*, 2nd ed. New York: McGraw-Hill Professional, 2009.

# Index

Page references followed by *fig* indicate an illustrated figure; followed by *t* indicate a table.

# M

Have you read *Mastering Leadership*? Take a deeper dive into the theory and framework of The Universal Model of Leadership.

**The Leadership Circle Profile™** is the first 360-assessment connecting leadership competencies with underlying and motivating habits of thought. The profile reveals the relationship between patterns of action and internal assumptions that drive behavior. With this, you can deliver coaching results more quickly and a strong ROI for your clients.

**The Leadership Circle Profile™ Certification** is three days packed with content designed to help you master The Leadership Circle assessment tools. In this session you will gain in-depth knowledge about the framework upon which the Leadership Circle Profile™ 360° is built and much more.

Have an engagement in which you would like Bob Anderson or Bill Adams to speak? Contact us with details at info@theleadershipcircle.com.

For more information about the profile or certification, visit us at www.leadershipcircle.com

The Leadership Circle®